The black presence in English literature

EDITED BY
DAVID DABYDEEN

Manchester University Press

For Dr Walter Rodney (d. 1980)
and Rev. Michael Harding (d. 1980)
and for Yvonne Dabydeen
Stefan, Michael, Angela and Timothy Wheeler

Copyright © Manchester University Press 1985
Whilst copyright in the volume as a whole is vested in Manchester
University Press, copyright in the individual chapters belongs to their
respective authors, and no chapter may be reproduced whole or in part
without the express permission in writing of both author and publisher.
Published by
Manchester University Press
Oxford Road, Manchester M13 9PL, UK
and 27 South Main Street, Wolfeboro, NH 03894-2069, USA
Reprinted with corrections 1986

British Library cataloguing in publication data
The Black presence in English literature.
1. Blacks in literature   2. English literature——History and criticism
I. Dabydeen, David
820.9'3520396   PR151.B5

Library of Congress cataloging in publication data
The Black presence in English literature.
Essays presented at a conference held in Dec. 1982 in Wolverhampton,
U.K.
Bibliography: p. 207
Includes index
1. English literature——History and criticism——Addresses, essays
lectures.   2. Blacks in literature——Addresses, essays, lectures.
3. Race relations in literature——Addresses, essays, lectures.
4. English literature——Black authors——History and criticism——
Addresses, essays, lectures.
I. Dabydeen, David.
PR409.B53B55   1985   820'.9'896   85-5119

ISBN 0 7190 1096 9 *cased*
0 7190 1808 0 *paperback*

Typeset by Pen to Print, Colne
Printed in Great Britain
by the Alden Press, Oxford

Contents

List of illustrations

Contributors

Abena Busia, from Ghana, read English and Social Anthropology at Oxford University, obtaining her doctorate in 1983. She was a visiting lecturer in the Department of Afro-American Studies at Yale University in 1981 and is currently an assistant professor in the English Department at Rutgers University. Her study of the novel on Africa, *Africa in Anglo-American Fiction 1880–1980; an Annotated Bibliography* will be published in 1985.

Ruth Cowhig read English at Cambridge and Manchester Universities, obtaining her doctorate in 1974. She was a tutor at St John's College of Further Education, Manchester, for thirteen years, and is currently a tutor in English Literature for the Workers Educational Association and a part-time lecturer in the Extra-Mural Department of Manchester University.

David Daniell is senior lecturer in English at University College, London University. He is the author of *Coriolanus in Europe* and *The Interpreter's House*, the only book-length study of John Buchan.

Ian Duffield is lecturer in History at Edinburgh University. He has worked in Africa and has published many articles on Pan-Africanism. In 1981 he organised, with Dr Jagdish Gundara, the *International Conference on the History of Blacks in Britain*, and has edited the conference proceedings for publication in 1985.

Paul Edwards is Reader in English Literature at Edinburgh University. After graduating from Durham and Cambridge Universities he taught for nine years in West Africa, six of them at the University of Sierra Leone, Freetown. He has published books and articles on African History and Literature, including modern editions of the writings of Ignatius Sancho and Olaudah Equiano.

John McClure is associate professor of English at Rutgers University. He has published articles on colonial literature and in 1981 published a book on the subject, *Conrad and Kipling – the Colonial Fiction* (Harvard Univ. Press).

Frances Mannsaker was educated at Nottingham University, taught for a year at Bombay University, and wrote her doctoral dissertation on *Literature of Anglo-India 1767–1914*. She is currently senior lecturer in English Studies at Newcastle Polytechnic.

Kenneth Parker, from South Africa, has taught at the Open University and has held visiting professorships at American universities before becoming Principal Lecturer in English at North East London Polytechnic. His book on *The South African Novel in English: Essays in Criticism and Society* was published in 1978.

Brian Street is author of *The Savage in Literature* and *Literacy in Theory and Practice*, as well as several articles on the representation of black peoples in English Literature. He is an anthropology consultant to the BBC and ITV, and is lecturer in Social Anthropology at Sussex University.

David Dabydeen, from Guyana, read English at Cambridge and London Universities, obtaining his doctorate in 1982. His book, *Slave Song*, won the Quiller-Couch Prize at Cambridge and was awarded the Commonwealth Poetry Prize for 1984. He was Resident Fellow at Yale University's Centre for British Art in 1982, and is currently a Junior Research Fellow at Oxford University and Lecturer in Caribbean Studies at Warwick University.

Preface

In December 1982 a conference on the Black Presence in English Literature was held in Wolverhampton, a small West Midlands town which had achieved international attention because of the race-inspired rhetoric of its former member of parliament, John Enoch Powell. From the late 1960s onwards, Powell spoke passionately on the perils of black immigration, warning that Britain was 'heaping up its own funeral pyres' and evoking the calamitous classical image of 'the river Tiber foaming with much blood'. White Britons responded in droves, tramping the streets with proud flags and banners. Skinhead youth – white teenage dropouts, drug addicts and petty criminals – provoked by the literary classicism of Powell, stepped up their campaign of 'Paki-bashing' and burning. In those giddy years Wolverhampton was perceived as the last outpost of the British empire, until the Falkland Islands were rediscovered and the heat and passion transferred there.

By 1982, although Powellism in Wolverhampton was reduced in intensity, there still remained important instances of racial division: the town was still buzzing with news about the Rhoden affair. Mr Ernest Rhoden, a local headmaster and magistrate had allegedly refused to allow a British child of Sikh origin to attend his school because the child wore a turban. Mr N. S. Noor, a Sikh poet, teacher and community leader, publicly described Rhoden as a 'racist' and was promptly sued for libel by the headmaster. The story provoked national and international publicity, the drama heightened by quarrels with the teaching unions, rifts in the local education authority and accusations of conspiracies and betrayals. The poet paid dearly for his courage; he was found guilty of libel and damages of £5,000 with costs in excess of £20,000 were awarded to a triumphant Mr Rhoden. The poet, reduced to a state of classical distress, lodged an ineffectual appeal to the Queen's Bench in 1982, with the massive support of his black community.

It is important to outline this historical context since *any* scholarship relating to black people should not be divorced from consideration of contemporary racist realities, and should not be separated from the struggles engaged in to combat such racism. Moreover I had organised the Conference on behalf of a local black group, Wolverhampton Council for Community Relations, with financial assistance from the Commission for Racial Equality and the local Multi-Cultural Education Service. The Conference, held at the new Afro-Caribbean Cultural Centre, was chaired by Mr N. S. Noor. The 1981 Brixton riots were also a relevant factor in the holding of the Conference: the months following the riots saw the appearance of many official reports recommending revision of the school curriculum to take into account 'the black presence'. Several Local Education Authorities hurried to issue statements about 'multi-cultural' education. Colleges began to examine their curriculum and their institutional practices for evidence of racism, and Centres for Caribbean Studies were planned for London, Nottingham and elsewhere. Typical of this new mood of academic realism was Peter Quartermain's provocative article on Literature Studies in the *Times Higher Educational Supplement* (12 February 82) which attempted to link the riots with ethnocentric scholarship and practices:

The critical complacency with which English literature has been tacitly defined so exclusively is one illustration of that more general complacency which expresses itself as surprise or sadness that the ethnic minorities in English cities should be involved in riots. In these dark days of shrinking budgets and narrowing horizons the absence of undergraduates from ethnic minorities is probably more quickly noticed on courses which focus on Commonwealth topics, but it should provoke concern on any course and especially on those covering English culture in the widest sense, including history, politics and law for example. Until these minorities play a role in English life at every level, and until their own culture which is so intimately entwined with our own recent history receives proper attention, they will remain as remote, in human terms, as Australia is geographically. And this is a situation which no one who professes to work in the humanities should tolerate.

Tolerance, however, being a peculiar British virtue, won the day, so that in 1984, at the time of writing this preface, there has been little significant change to the education system, in spite of the initial flurry of conscience. Indeed it can be argued that there has been a hardening of attitudes to black demands, a regrouping of the forces of security and a resurgence of Imperial emotion. Margaret Thatcher's recent pronouncements on 'Victorian values' and her Falklands victory speech on empire indicate the spirit of the times:

> We have learned something about ourselves, a lesson which we desperately needed to learn. When we started out, there were the waverers and the faint-hearts. The people who thought we could no longer do the great things which we once did . . . that we could never again be what we were. There were those who would not admit it . . . but – in their heart of hearts – they too had their secret fears that it was true: that Britain was no longer the nation that had built an Empire and ruled a quarter of the world. Well, they were wrong.

The immediate aim of the Wolverhampton Conference was to counter the common arguments against a 'multi-cultural' literature curriculum, namely that the curriculum was already too over-crowded for the introduction of African, Asian and Caribbean materials in secondary schools, and that in any case the curriculum was necessarily determined by the syllabi of school examination boards. The counter-argument was that reappraisal of the literature already taught in schools and used as set texts for 'O' and 'A' level examination would reveal its 'multi-cultural' content: it was merely a matter of making the black man visible. The theme of blackness is, not surprisingly, common in English literature since the literature is rooted in a culture characterised by a history of conquest, colonisation and imperialism. The Conference argued an approach to English literature from the standpoint of empire.

The essays in this volume are concerned with locating literary texts within social and historical contexts, and within patterns of popular and scientific ideas. Shakespeare is read against the background of early black settlement in England and the develop-ment of racial hostility which manifested itself in the repatriation edicts of Elizabeth I. Eighteenth century poetry is interpreted in the light of the economics of the slave trade and the moral issues raised by the existence of slavery. The 'ethnographic' novel and boys' adventure stories of the nineteenth century are placed within Darwinian theories of race and Victorian values of racial super-iority. Contemporary novels on Africa are read as post-colonial products which reveal white preoccupations with notions of

Preface

'savagery' and 'civilisation', and which demonstrate enduring capacities for myth-making and fantasy. Inevitably, in such a wide-ranging survey of English literature, authors and genres important to the theme are excluded from proper consideration. Writers like Joyce Cary and Graham Greene for instance are not included, but they have received adequate attention elsewhere, as the bibliography indicates. Anti-slavery literature of the late eighteenth century is not analysed since the earlier surveys of Eva Dykes and Wylie Sypher are commendably comprehensive. Although some of the essays deal briefly with Indian and Australian aboriginal peoples their primary focus is upon the black African. It is hoped, however, that in spite of omissions necessitated by space, the essays collected here will represent a consolidation of, and advance upon, the previous scholarship of Eldred Jones and others, and, in the case of Ian Duffield's essay, a wholly original contribution to the subject.

The Editor wishes to thank the British Academy and the Commission for Racial Equality, especially Mr R. A. German and Ms Ming Tsow, for their assistance in the research and publication of this book. Mr Peter Harris, Director of Wolverhampton Education Authority, and Mr H. K. Rashid, Director of its Multi-Cultural Education Service, are also thanked for additional financial support. Finally, my thanks to the staff of Wolverhampton Council for Community Relations – Chester Morrison, Kofi Boafos, Nimmy Patel, Dorothy Williams, R. K. Bali, Ken Ahmed, David Tonkinson, and others – whose extremely disciplined and professional efforts in dealing with the paperwork and publicity matters, ensured the success of the Conference.

David Dabydeen
Oxford, 1984

1 Blacks in English Renaissance drama and the role of Shakespeare's Othello

RUTH COWHIG

It is difficult to assess the reactions and attitudes of people in sixteenth-century Britain to the relatively few blacks living amongst them. Their feelings would certainly be very mixed: strangeness and mystery producing a certain fascination and fostering a taste for the exotic: on the other hand prejudice and fear, always easily aroused by people different from ourselves, causing distrust and hostility. This hostility would be encouraged by the widespread belief in the legend that blacks were descendants of Ham in the Genesis story, punished for sexual excess by their blackness. Sexual potency was therefore one of the attributes of the prototype black. Other qualities associated with black people were courage, pride, guile-lessness, credulity and easily aroused passions – the list found in John Leo's *The Geographical History of Africa*, a book written in Arabic early in the sixteenth century and translated into English in 1600. Contemporary attitudes may have been more influenced by literary works such as this than by direct experience; but recently the part played by such direct contacts has been rediscovered. The scholarly and original study by Eldred Jones of these contacts and their effects on Renaissance drama has transformed contemporary attitudes.[1]

Black people were introduced into plays and folk dancing in mediaeval England and later, during the sixteenth century, they often appeared in the more sophisticated court masques. In these, the blackness was at first suggested by a very fine lawn covering the faces, necks, arms and hands of the actors. Then black stockings, masks and wigs were used; such items are mentioned in surviving lists of properties. These characters were mainly valued for the exotic aesthetic effects which their contrasting colour provided. The culmination of this tradition can be seen in Ben Jonson's *Masque of Blackness* in 1605, which he produced in answer to Queen Anne's request that the masquers should be 'black-mores at first'. The theme is based upon the longing of the black daughters of Niger to gain whiteness and beauty. This surely contradicts the idea that Elizabethans and Jacobeans were not conscious of colour and had no prejudice: the desirability of whiteness is taken for granted!

Elizabethan drama also used Moorish characters for visual effects and for their association with strange and remote countries. In Marlowe's *Tamburlaine the Great*, for instance, the three Moorish kings play little part in the plot, and have no individual character. Their main contribution to the play is in adding to the impression of power and conquest by emphasising the extent of Tamburlaine's victories. Their blackness also provides a variety of visual effects in the masques. Marlowe's plays reflect the curiosity of his contemporaries about distant countries, and must have whetted the appetites of his audiences for war and conquest; but the black characters are seen from the outside and have no human complexity.

The black villain–hero

At about the same time the tradition of the black villain–hero began to develop. Only a limited number of Elizabethan plays have survived, and the best known black character of this period is Muly Mahamet, the Moorish usurper, in Thomas Peele's play *The Battle of Alcazar*, written probably in 1588. This battle took place in 1578 as a result of the intervention of Sebastian of Portugal, and was glorified as a Christian crusade. It brought European soldiers into direct contact with African armies. Sebastian was defeated and killed, but he and the English adventurer Thomas Stukely, who supported him, were celebrated as heroes. Peele introduces Muly Mahamet as: 'the barbarous Moore/The Negro Muly Mahamet that witholds/The Kingdom from his uncle Abdelmelec' (I.116–18). He is referred to as 'This unbeleeving Moore', and his barbarity is very much emphasised; in one scene, he offers a piece of raw lion's flesh to his wife Calypolis when she is faint with hunger. He is portrayed as cruel and treacherous, and his evil character is directly associated with his blackness. In the final act, the Presenter of the play denounces the 'foule, ambitious Moore', who is thrown from his horse while trying to escape across the river, and drowned. This is the first known Renaissance play in which the central character is a black man, and his villainy has no redeeming qualities.

Shakespeare too followed this tradition in his early melodramatic tragedy *Titus Andronicus*, first performed sometime between 1590 and 1592. This play exploits the contemporary taste for gruesome spectacle and violence on the stage – a taste which we should be well able to understand, though nineteenth and early twentieth century critics found it so offensive that they denied Shakespeare's authorship. Rape, mutilation and death succeed each other with grim monotony, usually as a result of the devilish machinations of the black villain, Aaron. His physical blackness is left in no doubt: he is described at various times as 'raven-coloured', 'a black devil' and a 'coal black Moor' and he himself refers to 'my fleece of woolly hair' (II.ii.34). He takes an active delight in his evil doings:

> O how this villainy
> Doth fat me with the very thought of it.
> Let fools do good and fair men call for grace
> Aaron will have his soul black like his face.
> (III.i.202–5)

There is, however, one memorable scene in which Aaron appears in a more sympathetic light. The Nurse produces Aaron's baby, 'a joyless, dismal, black and sorrowful issue' and Tamora's message is that he should destroy it. Aaron refuses, seizes the child, defies Demetrius and Charon, and stabs the Nurse, carrying off the child, 'this treasure in mine arms'. As he defends his son he momentarily becomes a representative of his race, protesting against prejudice: 'is black so base a hue?', he asks, and turns to Tamora's wretched sons: 'Ye white-lim'd walls! Ye alehouse painted signs!/Coal-black is better than another hue' (IV.ii.99–100). The villain almost becomes hero. Aaron's actions have no adequate motive. He plots the rape of Lavinia by the two dissolute sons of Tamora, Queen of the Goths. He deceives Titus by telling him that his severed hand will secure the release of his two sons: Titus receives instead his sons' heads. Aaron is also the incarnation of lust and a black bastard son is the result. The imagery of the play links him with the old medieval pictures and legends of the black devil, and he is seen as the enemy of religion who invokes devilish powers. Although he is horribly punished at the end, his zest for wickedness remains unabated: 'If one good deed in all my life I did,/I do repent it from my very soul' (V.iii.189–90). Nevertheless, Aaron is the only character in this play of atrocities who attains a certain vitality, and in this sense he belongs to the tradition of the villain–hero.

Another play in this tradition is *Lust's Dominion*, thought to be the same play as *The Spanish Moor's Tragedy* mentioned by Henslowe in 1599, a composite work by Thomas Dekker and others. The black hero, Eleazor, plots a series of violent crimes and has a bastard son after his lustful union with the Queen. Like Aaron, he enjoys evil for its own sake and comes to a violent end, dying with the words, 'Devils, come claim your right!'

This play makes some ironic use of blackness. Eleazor, giving instructions to his two Moorish servants to commit a murder, says to them, 'Your cheeks are black; let not your souls be white'. But on another occasion he expresses the opposite idea, as if in defence of his colour:

> Black faces may have hearts as white as snow;
> And 'tis a general rule in moral roles,
> The whitest faces have the blackest souls. (V.iii.9–11)

Eleazor is also identified with the traditional sexual potency; the Queen is quite besotted, calling him 'the soft-skinn'd negro'. When Eleazor stabs the new king he boasts of his dark skin and proceeds to his revenge with all the panache to be expected of a black villain–hero.

In these three plays, black people are represented as satanic, sexual creatures, a threat to order and decency, and a danger to white womanhood. They are a loud presence, they rant and they curse their way through the plays with obscene antics and treacherous behaviour. Above all, they are cunning creatures, contriving and hatching schemes and plots for the downfall of others. At the same time however there is introduced the tentative notion that their anger and their rage stem at least partly from being victims of race prejudice; that, like Shylock's, their behaviour is a form of retaliation: 'If you prick us, do we not bleed? If you tickle us, do we not laugh? If you poison us, do we not die? And if you wrong us, shall we not revenge?' (*Merchant of Venice*, III, i). The present day reality (as revealed in the Brixton riots) of blacks and whites locked in a pattern of hatred and retaliation is foreshadowed in English drama of the sixteenth century, pointing to a dismal consistency in race relations over four centuries.

Only as we recognise the familiarity of the figure of the black man as villain in Elizabethan drama can we appreciate what must have been the startling impact on Shakespeare's audience of a black hero of outstanding qualities in his play *Othello*. Inevitably we are forced to ask questions which we cannot satisfactorily answer. Why did Shakespeare choose a black man as the hero of one of his great tragedies? What experience led the dramatist who had portrayed the conventional stereotype in Aaron in 1590 to break completely with tradition ten years later? Had Shakespeare any direct contact with black people? Why did he select the tale of Othello from the large number of Italian stories available to him?

Black people in Britain

We cannot answer such questions with certainty, but we may speculate. Until the publication of Eldred Jones' study, *Othello's Countrymen*, in 1965, it was generally assumed that Shakespeare depended only on literary sources for his black characters. Although the presence of black people in England is well documented, it went unrecognised. There are two main sources of information. One is Hakluyt's *Principal Navigations*, the huge collection of narratives of Elizabethan sailors and traders which Hakluyt collected and published in twelve volumes. Volumes VI and XI describe voyages during which black men from West Africa were taken aboard, brought back to England, and afterwards used as interpreters on subsequent voyages. Later, between 1562 and 1568, Hawkins had the unhappy distinction of being the first of the English gentleman slave-traders; as well as bringing 'blackamoores' to England, he sold hundreds of black slaves to Spain.

The other evidence is in the series of royal proclamations and state papers which call attention to the 'great number of Negroes and *blackamoors*' in the realm, 'of which *kinde* of people there are *allready here too manye*'. They were regarded by Queen Elizabeth as a threat to her own subjects 'in these hard times of dearth'. Negotiations were carried on between the Queen and Casper van Senden, merchant of Lubeck, to cancel her debt to him for transporting between two and three hundred English prisoners from Spain and Portugal back to England by allowing him to take up a similar number of unwanted black aliens – presumably to sell them as slaves. Although the correspondence shows that the deal never materialised, since the 'owners' of these 'blackamoors' refused to give them up, it is clear that there were several hundreds of black people living in the households of the aristocracy and landed gentry, or working in London taverns. Elizabeth

5

disapproved officially of slavery, but during her reign, and long afterwards, there were black slaves in England: advertisements in the records of London coffee houses refer to their sales, and quite high rewards were offered for information about any who escaped from their masters.

It is interesting to follow the various acts of Privy Council and the correspondence on this subject between July 1596 and the final edict of 1601. For our purpose it is enough to quote in full the warrant issued on 18 July 1596:

> An open warrant to the Lord Maiour of London and to all Vice-Admyralls, Maiours and other publicke officers whatsoever to whom yt may apertaine. Whereas Casper van Senden, a merchant of Lubeck, did by his labor and travell procure 89 of her Majesty's subjects that were detayned prisoners in Spaine and Portugall to be released, and brought them hither into this realme at his owne cost and charges, for the which his expences and declaration of his honest minde towards those prisoners he only desireth to have lycense to take up so much blackamoores here in this realme and to transport them into Spaine and Portugall. Her Majesty in regard to the charitable affection the suppliant hath showed being a stranger, to worke the delivery of our countrymen that were there in great great misery and thraldom and to bring them home to their native country, and that the same could not be done without great expence, and also considering the reasonableness of his requestes to transport so many blackamoores from hence, doth thincke yt a very good exchange and that those kinde of people may well be spared in this realme, being so populous and numbers of hable persons the subjectes of the land and Christian people that perishe for want of service, whereby through their labor they might be mayntained. They are therefore in their Lordship's name required to aide and assist him to take up suche blackamoores as he shall finde within this realme with the consent of their masters, who we doubt not, considering her Majesty's good pleasure to have those kinde of people sent out of the lande and the good deserving of the stranger towardes her Majesty's subjectes, and that they shalldoe charitably and like Christians rather to be served by their owne contrymen then with those kinde of people, will yielde those in their possession to him.[2]

This mentions a specific number, eighty-nine, which provides us at least with a minimum. We can also see prejudice developing because of growing unemployment ('want of service') against 'those kinde of people', and the age-old remedy, 'to bring them home to their native country'. The tone is so familiar as to be startling, especially since, as so often in modern times, the 'blackamoores' had left their native country under persuasion or duress in the first place.

Thus the sight of black people must have been familiar to Londoners. London was a very busy port, but still a relatively small and overcrowded city, so Shakespeare could hardly have avoided seeing them. What thoughts did he have as he watched their faces, men uprooted from their country, their homes and families? I cannot help thinking of Rembrandt's moving study of *The Two Negroes* painted some sixty years later, which expresses their situation poignantly. The encounter with real blacks on the streets of London would have yielded a sense of their common humanity, which would have conflicted with the myths about their cultural, sexual and religious 'otherness' found in the travel books. The play between reality and myth informs *Titus Andronicus*: Shakespeare presents Aaron as a demon, but at the end of the play suddenly shatters the illusion of myth by showing Aaron to be a black *person* with common feelings of compassion and fatherly care for his child. In *Othello* too there is conscious manipulation of reality and myth: Othello is presented initially (through the eyes of Iago and Roderigo) as a dangerous beast, before he reveals himself to be of noble, human status, only to degenerate later to the condition of bloodthirsty and irrational animalism. It is surely not surprising that Shakespeare, the dramatist whose sympathy for the despised alien upsets the balance of the otherwise 'unrealistic' *The Merchant of Venice* should want to create a play about a kind of black man not yet seen on the English stage; a black man whose humanity is eroded by the cunning and racism of whites.

The importance of Othello's colour

Shakespeare's choice of a black hero for his tragedy must have been deliberate. His direct source was an Italian tale from Cinthio's *Hecatommithi* (1565); he followed this tale in using the love between a Moor and a young Venetian girl of high birth as the basis of his plot, but in little else. The original story is crude and lacking in subtlety. Cinthio, in accordance with the demands of the time, expresses concern that his tale should have a moral purpose. He gives it as recommending that young people should not marry against the family's wishes, and especially not with someone separated from them by nature, heaven and mode of life. Such a moral has nothing to do with Shakespeare's play, except in so far as he uses it ironically, so his choice of the tale remains obscure. Perhaps he regretted his creation of the cruel and malevolent

Aaron, and found himself imagining the feelings of proud men, possibly of royal descent in their own countries, humiliated and degraded as slaves. Whatever his intentions may have been, we have to take seriously the significance of Othello's race in our interpretation of the play. This is all the more important because teachers will find it largely ignored by critical commentaries.

The first effect of Othello's blackness is immediately grasped by the audience, but not always by the reader. It is that he is placed in isolation from the other characters from the very beginning of the play. This isolation is an integral part of Othello's experience constantly operative even if not necessarily at a conscious level; anyone black will readily appreciate that Othello's colour is important for our understanding of his character. Even before his first entry we are forced to focus our attention on his race: the speeches of Iago and Roderigo in the first scene are full of racial antipathy. Othello is 'the thick lips', 'an old black ram', 'a lascivious Moor' and 'a Barbary horse', and 'he is making the beast with two backs' with Desdemona. The language is purposely offensive and sexually coarse, and the animal images convey, as they always do, the idea of someone less than human. Iago calculates on arousing in Brabantio all the latent prejudice of Venetian society, and he succeeds. To Brabantio the union is 'a treason of the blood', and he feels that its acceptance will reduce Venetian statesmen to 'bondslaves and pagans'.

Brabantio occupies a strong position in society. He

> is much beloved
> And hath in his effect a voice potential
> As double as the Duke's (I.ii.11–13)

according to Iago. Although he represents a more liberal attitude than Iago's, at least on the surface, his attitude is equally prejudiced. He makes Othello's meetings with Desdemona possible by entertaining him in his own home, but his reaction to the news of the elopement is predictable. He is outraged that this black man should presume so far, and concludes that he must have used charms and witchcraft since otherwise his daughter could never 'fall in love with what she feared to look on'. To him the match is 'against all rules of nature', and when he confronts Othello his abuse is as bitter as Iago's.

But before this confrontation, the audience has seen Othello and we have been impressed by two characteristics. First his pride:

> I fetch my life and being
> From men of royal siege. (I.ii.21–22)

and secondly, his confidence in his own achievements and position:

> My services which I have done the Signiory
> Shall out-tongue his complaints. (I.ii.95–97)

It is hard to overestimate the reactions of a Renaissance audience to this unfamiliar black man, so noble in bearing and so obviously master of the situation. But however great Othello's confidence, his colour makes his vulnerability plain. If the state had not been in danger, and Othello essential to its defence, Brabantio's expectation of support from the Duke and senate would surely have been realised. He is disappointed; the Duke treats Othello as befits his position as commander-in-chief, addressing him as 'valiant Othello'. The only support Brabantio receives is from the first senator, whose parting words, 'Adieu, brave Moor, Use Desdemona well', while not unfriendly, reveal a superior attitude. Would a senator have so advised a newly-married general if he had been white and equal?

Desdemona's stature in the play springs directly from Othello's colour. Beneath a quiet exterior lay the spirited independence which comes out in her defence of her marriage before the Senate. She has resisted the pressures of society to make an approved marriage, shunning 'The wealthy, curled darlings of our nation' (I.ii.68). Clearly Brabantio had exerted no force: he was no Capulet. But Desdemona was well aware of the seriousness of her decision to marry Othello: 'my downright violence and storm of fortune' she calls it. Finally she says that she 'saw Othello's visage in his mind': obviously the audience, conditioned by prejudice, had to make the effort to overcome, with her, the tendency to associate Othello's black face with evil, or at least with inferiority.

It is made clear that the marriage between Othello and Desdemona is fully consummated: Desdemona is as explicit as decorum allows:

> If I be left behind
> A moth of peace, and he go to the war,
> The rites for why I love him are bereft me. (I.iii.255–7)

Othello, on the other hand, disclaims the heat of physical desire when asking that she should go with him to Cyprus:

> I therefore beg it not
> To please the palate of my appetite,
> Nor to comply with heat – the young affects
> In me defunct. (I.iii.261–4)

These speeches relate directly to Othello's colour. Desdemona has to make it clear that his 'sooty bosom' (her father's phrase) is no obstacle to desire; while Othello must defend himself against the unspoken accusations, of the audience as well as of the senators, because of the association of sexual lust with blackness.

In Act III Scene iii, often referred to as the temptation scene, Othello's faith in Desdemona is gradually undermined by Iago's insinuations, and he is eventually reduced by jealousy to an irrational madness. Iago's cynical cunning plays upon Othello's trustfulness:

> The Moor is of a free and open nature
> That thinks men honest that but seem to be so.
> (I.iii.390–1)

The spectacle of Othello's disintegration is perhaps the most painful in the whole Shakespeare canon: and Iago's destructive cruelty has seemed to many critics to be inadequately motivated. They have spoken of 'motiveless malignity' and 'diabolic intellect', sometimes considering Iago's to be the most interesting character in the play. I think this is an unbalanced view, resulting from the failure to recognise racial issues. Iago's contempt for Othello, despite his grudging recognition of his qualities, his jealousy over Cassio's 'preferment', and the gnawing hatred which drives him on are based upon an arrogant racism. He harps mercilessly upon the unnaturalness of the marriage between Othello and Desdemona:

> Not to affect many proposed matches,
> Of her own clime, complexion and degree,
> Whereto we see in all things nature tends –
> Foh! one may smell in such a will most rank,
> Foul disproportions, thoughts unnatural.
> (III.iii.229–33)

The exclamation of disgust and the words 'smell' and 'foul' reveal a phobia so obvious that it is strange that it is often passed over. The attack demolishes Othello's defences because this kind of racial contempt exposes his basic insecurity as an alien in a white society. His confidence in Desdemona expressed in 'For she had eyes, and chose me', changes to the misery of

Haply for I am black
And have not those soft parts of conversation
That chamberers have . . . (III.iii.262–4)

This is one of the most moving moments in the play. Given Iago's hatred and astuteness in exploiting other people's weaknesses, which we see in the plot he sets for Cassio, the black Othello is easy game. We are watching the baiting of an alien who cannot fight back on equal terms.

Othello's jealous madness is the more terrifying because of the noble figure he presented in the early scenes, when he is addressed as 'brave Othello' and 'our noble and valiant general', and when proud self-control is his essential quality; he refuses to be roused to anger by Brabantio and Roderigo: 'Keep up your bright swords for the dew will rust them' (I.ii.58). After his breakdown we are reminded by Ludovico of his previous moral strengths and self-control: 'Is this the nature/Whom passion could not shake?' (IV.i.265–6). Thus the portrait is of a man who totally contradicts the contemporary conception of the black man as one easily swayed by passion. He is the most attractive of all Shakespeare's soldier heroes: one who has achieved high rank entirely on merit. His early history given in Desdemona's account of his wooing is typical of the bitter experience of an African of his times 'Taken by the insolent foe/And sold to slavery' (I.iii.136–7). Othello's military career is everything to him, and the famous 'farewell' speech of Act IV, with its aura of romatic nostalgia, expresses the despair of a man whose achievements have been reduced to nothing: 'Othello's occupation gone'. Spoken by a black Othello, the words 'The big wars/That make ambition virtue' (III.iii.346–7), have a meaning beyond more rhetoric. Ambition was still reckoned as a sin in Shakespeare's time; but in Othello's case it has been purified by his courage and endurance and by the fact that only ambition could enable him to escape the humiliations of his early life. When he realises that his career is irrevocably over, he looks back at the trappings of war – the 'pride, pomp and circumstance', the 'spirit-stirring drum' and the rest – as a dying man looks back on life.

The sympathies of the audience for Othello are never completely destroyed. The Russian actor, Ostuzhev who set himself to study the character of Othello throughout his career, saw the problem of the final scene as 'acting the part so as to make people love Othello and forget he is a murderer'.[3] When Othello answers Ludovico's rhetorical question 'What shall be said of thee?' with the words, 'An honourable murderer, if you will', we are not outraged by such a statement: instead we see in it a terrible pathos. What we are waiting for is the unmasking of Iago. When this comes, Othello looks down at Iago's feet for the mythical cloven hoofs and demands an explanation from that 'demi-devil', reminding us that blackness of soul in this play belongs to the white villain rather than to his black victim.

The fact that Othello was a baptised Christian had considerable importance for Shakespeare's audience. This is made explicit from the beginning when he quells the drunken broil with the words: 'For Christian shame, put by this barbarous brawl' (II.iii.172). In the war he was seen to be leading the forces of Christendom against the Turks. But once Othello becomes subservient to Iago and vows his terrible revenge he seems to revert to superstitious beliefs. How else can we interpret his behaviour over the handkerchief? He seems under the spell of its long history – woven by an old sibyl out of silkworms strangely 'hallowed', given to his mother by an Egyptian with thought-reading powers, and linked with the dire prophecy of loss of love should it be lost. Yet in the final scene it becomes merely, 'An antique token/My father gave my mother' (V.ii.213–14). This irrational inconsistency is dramatically credible and suggests that when reason is overthrown, Othello's Christian beliefs give way to the superstitions he has rejected. The Christian veneer is thin.

In *Othello* then, Shakespeare presents his Elizabethan audience with a series of propositions which serve to reverse or disturb their settled notions of black people. A Christian African is pitted against a diabolical white, a startling reversal of the norm. An honourable and self-restrained African is also pitted against a sensual, debased white who lusts after his wife, again a reversal of the situation found in plays like *Lust's Dominion*. Finally, a mature, male African of modest sexual inclination and ability is yoked to a youthful, white female who publicly reveals a bold sexual appetite. It is this last contradiction of the norm which lies at the core of the play. Othello, proud of his services to the State, and committed to the State's religion, falsely believes that he is an accepted part of that society, and that marriage into that society would be tolerated. The normally deceitful Iago is unusually truthful when he speaks of Othello's naivety! Othello's 'integration' into white society has involved him in the false conception that white is angelic. At the beginning of the play he lovingly describes Desdemona as his 'fair' wife ('O my fair warrior!') and at the end he is wholly confused by her 'blackness': 'a fine woman, a fair woman!', he mutters to himself, unable to comprehend her supposed evil. He becomes obsessed with the contradiction between whiteness of skin and blackness of deed, and he dwells on her condition of 'fairness':

> O thou black weed, why art thou so lovely fair?
> . . .
> Was this fair paper, this most godly book
> Made to write 'whore' on? (IV.ii.69 f.).

Othello, himself once described as 'far more fair than black' by the Duke (I.iii.290), cannot accept that Desdemona, the 'fair' one, has become as 'black' as the African:

> Her name, that was as fresh
> As Dian's visage, is now begrim'd and black
> As mine own face. (III.iii.392)

Her physical beauty (her 'rose-lipp'd', as opposed to his 'thick lipp'd' features) also conflict with her apparent moral degradation, and he is steeped in sorrowful perplexity:

> Turn thy complexion there,
> Patience, thou young and rose-lipp'd cherubin –
> Ay, here, look grim as hell. (IV.ii.63).

It is not only the audience who associate blackness with ugliness, moral evil and human inferiority: Othello is himself afflicted by the travel-book mythology. Desdemona, in wooing Othello, is also implicated in the mythology. In listening to Othello's stories of the wonders of the African landscape, the vast deserts, the mountains reaching to the heavens, the cannibals, anthropophagi and the rest, is she not more attracted to the exotic myth of 'otherness' than to the real man? Given the enormous popularity of travel books among white women (the Earl of Shaftesbury in 1710 was to lament the fact that 'a thousand Desdemonas' were so obsessed with stories of African men that they would readily abandon husbands, families and country itself, to 'follow the fortunes of a hero of the black tribe'), can we not say that Desdemona was an early travel book 'fanatic'? And, given the long smutty conversation she engages in with Iago on landing at Cyprus, and her previous boldness of sexual confession made openly before the Senators ('my

heart's subdued/Even to the utmost pleasure of my lord' –
I.iii.250), is there not a subtle suggestion that the aspect of the myth
about blacks that she finds attractive in Othello is that relating to
sexual potency?

Shakespeare raises these and other questions about blackness and
whiteness without fully resolving them. It rested upon the Elizabethan audience to consider them, this very act of deliberation
involving a disturbance of racial complacency. If his purpose was to
unsettle or perplex his audience, then he succeeded beyond
expectation, for the question of Othello's blackness, and his
relation with the white Desdemona, is one that provoked contradictory and heated responses in subsequent centuries.

Actors, black and tawny, in the role of Othello

There is no record of any controversy over the type of Moor
intended by Shakespeare until late in the eighteenth century. The
idea that the Elizabethans were confused about the difference
between 'tawny' and 'black' Moors is by now thoroughly exploded.
They were very explicit: and Shakespeare himself makes this clear
enough in *The Merchant of Venice*, where the Prince of Morocco
has a brown skin – 'the shadowed livery of the burnished sun': he is
obviously not a black man. Early actors in the part of Othello
blacked themselves as much as possible.

The part was originally acted by Richard Burbage, and an old
ballad survives as evidence of this:

> Dick Burbage, that most famous man,
>   That actor without peer,
> With this same part his course began,
>   And kept it many a year.
> Shakespeare was fortunate I trow,
>   That such an actor had.

It was the beginning of a long tradition in the production of this
play, which never lost its popularity in the theatre and always
offered a great challenge to the principal actor. Not every famous
actor succeeded in the part. Early in the eighteenth century Thomas
Betterton, the actor-manager, was famous for it; later he was
succeeded by Thomas Quin. But David Garrick, small, volatile and
sensitive, wearing an English military uniform and a large
powdered wig, was a disaster. With blacked face and hands and a
huge turban, it is said that he reminded his audience of the little

black page carrying the tea-kettle in Hogarth's *Harlot's Progress*, plate 2; and when Quin called out, 'Here's Pompey, but where's the tea-kettle?', everyone burst out laughing. Garrick's failure may have had additional causes as there were many other actors who could not realise the part.

Shakespearean acting after Garrick was dominated by the actor-manager, John Kemble. He played the leading tragic roles, including Othello, continuing the tradition of blacking up as much as possible for the part. There is an interesting review of his performance in 1787 which expresses, for the first time, doubts about Othello's colour:

> In his first scenes Kemble was judicious but too studiously so; and though most critically correct in his address to the Senate, evidenced he was more anxious to do justice to the text of his author than the feelings of Othello. But in the subsequent scenes he made ample recompense, and most successfully combined accuracy of expression with spirit of character . . . We must approve his dressing Othello in Moorish habit . . . but is it necessary the Moor should be as *black* as a native of Guiney? [*Public Advertiser*. 29 October 1787]

Since the abolition movement was at its most active at this date, it seems likely that people were becoming reluctant to associate Othello with descriptions of oppressed slaves. Opponents of abolition, on the other hand, built their case increasingly on theories of racial inferiority which were supported by such authorities as David Hume, the philosopher. Both audiences and actors were also becoming more sophisticated and may have been less ready to accept the crudities of the blacking up.

By this time, in fact, the blacking process had become extremely elaborate. Michael Kelly tells us an amusing anecdote of the German actor, Brockman, in Vienna in 1785. He was so successful as Othello that the Emperor commanded a repeat performance, and to the surprise of his friends he appeared at lunch 'with his face made up as black as it had been the night before'! He excused himself by explaining:

> that he had gone through so much fatigue and trouble in blacking his face for the Saturday's performance, that he would not wash it off, as, if he had done so, he should have had to undergo the same painful process on the following evening, rather than which, he had sat up all the preceding night in an armchair.[4]

Ruth Cowhig

Kean, Lamb and Coleridge

It was Edmund Kean who first presented Othello as a 'tawny Moor' or Arab in 1814. He had previously played the part of Kojan, a 'noble savage', in a London pantomime which referred in the playbill to dancing as in 'the Otaheitan method as described by that wonderful navigator, Captain Cook.' Now theatregoers were familiar with *Omiah, or with Captain Cook Around the World*, a musical play which portrayed the South Sea islander, Omai, who had caused a sensation in London society in 1775. Omai was dark, but not black, so perhaps Kean was predisposed to think of Othello in the same way. After the performance, Hazlitt noted in his review that 'Othello was black: but that is nothing': but the critics soon became used to the change. In this they were reinforced by the powerful literary influence of Charles Lamb and especially of S. T. Coleridge, who rationalised their strong racial prejudices and directly attacked the idea that Shakespeare conceived Othello as 'a coal-black Moor'. Lamb even found it 'extremely revolting' to think of the play being so presented on the stage. He did not question that Othello was black, but he reveals an extraordinary degree of physical revulsion, as in this extract from his Shakespearean criticism, written before any black actor had played the part: even assumed blackness was too much for Lamb:

> How many dramatic personages in Shakespeare . . . are improper to be shown to our bodily eye. Othello, for instance. Nothing can be more flattering to the nobler parts of our natures than to read of a young Venetian lady, of highest extraction, through force of love and from a sense of merit in him whom she loved, laying aside every consideration of kindred and country, and colour, and wedding with a *coal black Moor* – (for such is he represented, in the imperfect state of knowledge respecting foreign countries in those days, compared with our own, or in compliance with popular notions, though the Moors are now well enough known to be by many shades less unworthy of a white woman's fancy) – it is the perfect triumph of virtue over accidents, of the imagination over the senses. She sees Othello's colour in his mind. But upon the stage, when the imagination is no longer the ruling faculty, but we are left to our poor unassisted senses, I appeal to everyone that has seen Othello played, whether he did not, on the contrary, sink Othello's mind in his colour; whether he did not find something extremely revolting in the courtship and wedded caresses of Othello and Desdemona; and whether the actual sight of the thing did not overweigh all that beautiful compromise which we make in reading; – and the reason it should do so is obvious, because there is just so much reality presented to our senses as to give a perception of motives – all that

16

which is unseen – to overpower and reconcile the first and obvious prejudices. What we see upon the stage is body and bodily action.[5]

Coleridge took Lamb's line of thought and elaborated it: 'Othello must not be conceived as a negro, but a high and chivalrous Moorish chief. Shakespeare learned the spirit of the character from the Spanish poetry, which was prevalent in England in his time' (*Table Talk*, 1822). In his lectures on Shakespeare his arguments go around in circles:

> Can we imagine him so utterly ignorant as to make a barbarous negro plead royal birth – at a time, too, when negros were not known except as slaves? – As for Iago's language to Brabantio, it implies merely that Othello was a Moor, that is, black . . . It is a common error to mistake the epithets applied by the dramatis personae to each other as truly descriptive of what the audience ought to see or know. No doubt Desdemona saw Othello's visage in his mind; yet, as we are constituted, and most surely as an English audience was disposed at the beginning of the 17th century, it would be something monstrous to conceive this beautiful Venetian girl falling in love with a veritable negro. It would argue a want of balance in Desdemona which Shakespeare does not appear to have in the least contemplated.[6]

Here Coleridge starts, not with an investigation of Shakespeare's intentions, but with his own prejudices, so that his view of Desdemona is Brabantio's rather than Shakespeare's. It inevitably led to underestimation of Desdemona's spirited and independent nature. Such was Coleridge's influence that his view of the matter became the established one for the rest of the century.

Between 1814 and his death in 1833, Edmund Kean, despite his small stature and apparent physical unsuitability for the role, made the part of Othello his own. Many contemporaries paid tribute to the power of his acting; Hazlitt wrote that his 'farewell' speech 'struck on the heart like the sound of years of departed happiness',[7] and Leigh Hunt called his Othello 'the masterpiece of the English stage'[8] It is hardly surprising that between them Coleridge and Kean convinced audiences and critics alike that Othello was a 'tawny Moor'![9]

Ira Aldridge and Paul Robeson

Meanwhile a young black actor who was to challenge these assumptions was serving his apprenticeship in the African Theatre in New York.[10] Ira Aldridge was born in or about 1807 and educated at the African Free School, a remarkable institution established by the Manumission Society to provide free education for black children, most of whom were the families of liberated slaves. The African Theatre was started by a retired steward of a Liverpool liner; it had a great success but a short life, closed down a few years later, mainly because it rivalled the established Park Theatre, and because white prejudice against the blacks was growing. For a year or two Ira Aldridge acted various parts there while James Hewlett, the first black American tragedian, was the star. It is especially interesting that Aldridge would also have had the opportunity to see Edmund Kean in New York when he played in several of Shakespeare's plays, including *Othello*, from 29 November to 28 December 1820. This was at the Park Theatre, where blacks were allowed in the gallery only. Aldridge's interest in acting was furthered by two brothers, Henry and James Wallack, who built and acted in several New York theatres. It soon became obvious that there was no future for a gifted black actor in America, and Aldridge decided, like James Hewlett before him, to emigrate to England. His association with the Wallacks in the Park Theatre as a dresser, and the fact that he embarked for Liverpool with James Wallack, serving his passage as a steward, led to taunts later on that he was 'Mr Wallack's black servant', as we shall see in the review of 1833 in *The Athenaeum*.

Aldridge entered Glasgow University in 1824 and seems to have spent eighteen months there. But clearly his ambitions were for the theatre, and by 1825 he was already playing leading parts in various melodramas at the Coberg Theatre in London. He was not more than twenty, six feet tall, and must have looked impressive. In 1833 he took the part of Othello in the Theatre Royal, Covent Garden. He had immediate success with the audiences but the dramatic critics, accustomed to Kean's tawny Moor played with outstanding success for nearly twenty years, rejected him with contempt. *The Times* was scornful:

> We could not perceive any fitness which Mr Aldridge possessed for the assumption of one of the finest parts that was ever imagined by Shakespeare, except, indeed, that he could play it in his own native hue, without the aid of lampblack or pomatum ... His accent was unpleasantly, and we would say vulgarly, foreign: his manner generally drawling and unimpressive and when, by chance (for chance it is, and not judgement), he rises to a higher strain, we perceive in the transition the elevation of rant, not the fiery dignity of soul-felt passion ... Well might Desdemona's father imagine that sorcery and not nature had

caused his daughter to listen to such a wooer. It is, however, our duty to state that Mr Aldridge was extremely well received. (10 April 1833)

The last grudging admission reveals an important fact. During the following years, Aldridge toured extensively, performing in every sizeable town in Britain, including Ireland, and receiving enthusiastic press notices. Only the London critics were hostile. *The Spectator* is rather more favourable at first, but in due course proceeds to a crushing list of 'glaring defects'. The actor is 'tame and larmoyant' and wholly unsuited to the character. Moreover, his declamation is 'very faulty'.

> It is marked by numerous instances of false emphasis, incorrect readings, and interpolations of the text even, and by a few vulgarisations. It was, however, free from rant. Othello describes himself as being 'unused to the melting mood'. Mr Aldridge's grief is querulous and lachrymose, and his pathos merely whining. (*The Spectator*, 13 April 1833)

These two critics contradict each other over the matter of 'rant', and this leads one to suspect the accusations of false diction. *The Literary Gazette* (13 April 1833) also speaks of 'tameness' – probably because Aldridge did not follow Kean's heightened style of acting. It also refers to 'the question of the inferiority of race', a revealing indication of the underlying prejudice which distorts all these critical reviews. The final example of this distortion is from *The Athenaeum*, which deserves quoting in full:

> On Wednesday, this establishment (one of the two great national theatres, which are constantly complaining of the decline of the drama, and constantly kicking themselves behind, for fear that they should not go down hill fast enough,) aimed another blow at respectability, by the production of Mr Henry Wallack's black servant in the character of Othello – *Othello*, almost the master-work of the master-mind – a part, the study of which occupied, perhaps, years of the life of the elegant and classical Kemble; a part which the fire and genius of Kean have, of late years, made his exclusive property; a part, which it has been considered a sort of theatrical treason for anyone less distinguished than these two variously but highly gifted individuals to attempt; and this is to be personated in an English national theatre, by one whose pretensions rest upon the two grounds of his face being of a natural instead of an acquired tint, and of his having lived as a servant to a low-comedy actor. It is truly monstrous; and if (to quote our own remarks of the week before last), Miss Ellen Tree's beautiful and touching personation of the gentle Desdemona was enough 'to win a nod of approbation from Shakespeare's statue', assuredly, this is sufficient to make his indignant

bones kick the lid from his coffin. We have no ridiculous prejudice against any fellow-creatures, because he chances to be of a different colour from ourselves; and we trust that we have good taste enough to take off our hats to genius wherever we find it: but we are, on the other hand, altogether above the twaddle of helping the drama to bear an indignity of this nature, merely that foreigners may laugh up their sleeves at us, while we quote this silly exhibition as a proof of England's being 'the stranger's home'. Mr Aldridge, formerly calling himself, we believe, Mr Keene, and now distinguished by the appellation of 'The African Roscius', is really an extraordinary person; for it is extraordinary that under all the circumstances, a natural quickness and aptitude for imitation should enable him to get through such a part as Othello with so little of positive offence as he does. But there it ends. Looking up to his birth, parentage, and education, nothing short of inspiration could possibly make him a fit delineator of Shakespeare's Othello; and this is an extent to which it is not very likely that Providence would choose to go, to produce such a result. That Providence has not done so in this instance will be amply evident to those who do not permit their judgement to be run away with by that which we have admitted to be extraordinary, who do not let their hands get the start of their heads, nor suffer a false feeling of compassion for the individual, to supply the place of sound unbiased opinion. It is impossible that Mr Aldridge should fully comprehend the meaning and force of the words he utters, and accordingly, the perpetual recurrence of false emphasis, whenever his memory, as to his original, fails him, shows distinctly that he does not. In the name of common sense, we enter our protest against a repetition of this outrage. In the name of propriety and decency, we protest against an interesting actress and lady-like girl, like Miss Ellen Tree, being subjected by the manager of the theatre to the indignity of being pawed about by Mr Henry Wallack's black servant; and finally, in the name of consistency, if this exhibition is to be continued, we protest against acting being any longer dignified by the name of art. (*The Athenaeum*, 13 April 1833)

This review is unsigned, but I believe it to be by John Hamilton Reynolds, friend of the poet Keats: Reynolds had recently contributed a long obituary on Kean's death on 18 May 1833, after collapsing on the stage while playing Othello. This might account for the jaundiced and venomous tone of his article. It was probably because of influential opposition of this kind that Aldridge did not play again in London for twenty five years. In other British towns and cities and on the continent of Europe, he achieved a series of successes, receiving medals and awards from France, Germany, Russia and many great cities. When he returned to London as Othello in 1865, the theatres were packed and critics were much more polite.

On this occasion, *The Athenaeum* writes with gracious condescension:

> He plays with feeling, intelligence and finish. We were glad that he was
> well received on Monday, and that his merits were acknowledged by a
> numerous audience. We may claim this black, thick lipped player as one
> proof among many that the negro intellect is human, and demands
> respect as such. The tragedy was remarkably well performed. (*The
> Athenaeum*, 26 August 1865)

This kind of praise hardly makes up for the offensive notice of
1833! Its inadequacy is exposed when compared with the enthusiasm with which Aldridge had been received in Europe. Theophile
Gautier, for instance, describes the impression made on him by a
performance in St Petersburg.[11] He felt that he was watching
Othello himself, as Shakespeare had created him, and this is all the
more remarkable since Aldridge was speaking the English words of
the play while the rest of the company, a German one, used
Schlegel's translation. Gautier understood neither language, but
found Aldridge's style of acting controlled, classical and majestic,
producing a tremendous effect and endless applause.

No late nineteenth century English actor was successful as
Othello. In 1861 Charles Fachter, who was half French and half
German, caused a sensation by the exaggerated style of his acting,
but the critic G. H. Lewes thought 'his Othello one of the very
worst I have ever seen'.[12] Then in 1875 the Italian actor, Tommaso
Salvini, interpreted the part in such a way that the violence was
terrifying and Othello's barbarism was uppermost. Many who saw
him were greatly impressed, but he suppressed large parts of the
text and departed a long way from Shakespeare's conception.[13]
Even the great Henry Irving failed. In 1876 he played the part
'slightly tinged with brown, according to the Edmund Kean
precedent, so much applauded by Coleridge'. He was given a
scathing press notice, not because of his unusual appearance ('no
turban, no white burnouse, no sooty face, no "thick lips", and no
curled hair'), but for his hysteria and lack of dignity. In 1881 he
played Othello as 'practically black' but to no better effect. He is
reported by Ellen Terry to have rolled up the clothes of his costume
one by one after the last performance 'and then, half humorously
and very deliberately said, "Never again!"'.

It is surely significant that it was another black man who made
the biggest impact of this century. Paul Robeson played Othello at

the Savoy Theatre in London in 1930, and many who saw this production felt that the part took on a new significance when played by a black man. Robeson himself said that 'this play is about the problem of minority groups – a blackamoor who tried to find equality among the whites'. This production did much to change the establishment view. Herbert Farjeon wrote an article in 1933 entitled *Othello was a Black Man*, and after the prestigious production of the play in New York in 1943, John Dover Wilson recorded, in his introduction to the New Cambridge edition of *Othello*, the lasting impression which Robeson made on him:

> For me, however, the crowning proof of Othello's race is that I once had the good fortune to see him played by a Negro – that great gentleman with the golden voice, Paul Robeson: and I felt I was seeing the tragedy for the first time, not merely because of Robeson's acting, which despite a few petty faults of technique was magnificent, but because the fact that he was a true Negro seemed to floodlight the drama. Everything was slightly different from what I had previously imagined; new points, fresh nuances, were constantly emerging and all had, I felt, been clearly intended by the author. The performance convinced me, in short, that a Negro Othello is essential to the full understanding of the play.

Coming from a Shakespearean scholar of his distinction, Dover Wilson's categorical assertion that Robeson was in tune with Shakespeare's original intentions is impressive.

This New York production was by Margaret Webster, and the play ran for seven weeks, longer than any previous production. The matter of Othello's colour was naturally a sensitive and controversial one since the racial issue was more obvious than in London. The producer herself wrote:

> There is no mistaking it, Othello is a black man. That being so all the elements of the action fall automatically into place, as they do not when he's merely played in blackface. Iago becomes a credible villain. The simplicity of the noble Moor, caught in the toils of that villainy, no longer strains belief when Paul Robeson gives it the very image of nature ... In this performance, the basis of conflict upon which all that happens rests – is self-evident. (*New York Times Magazine*. 30 January 1944)

Ira Aldridge's youngest daughter, Amanda, who was only an infant when her father died in 1867, became a talented singer and musician and lived in London until her death in 1956. When Paul Robeson came to London he studied voice and diction with her while preparing to play *Othello*. It is thus more than likely that some of the tradition of the first great black actor was passed on to the next, since Amanda would have known many people who had seen her father act. Both these black actors played Othello over a very long period: Ira Aldridge was probably only nineteen when he first performed in London in 1826, and he last appeared there thirty-nine years later, in 1865. Paul Robeson was thirty-two at the time of the Savoy production in 1930, and last played in Stratford in 1959. This provides an interesting example of the potential timespan of theatrical tradition.

Those who are interested in Ira Aldridge may like to know that I have identified a painting in the Manchester Art Gallery, until recently only entitled *Portrait of a Moor*, as almost certainly the earliest known portrait of Aldridge (Fig. 1).[14] It was painted by James Northcote in 1826, and bought by the Manchester Royal Institution during their first exhibition in 1827. Northcote was then aged eighty, and was a very well-known artist who had studied under Sir Joshua Reynolds. But the sitter for this portrait has never been identified. When it was re-labelled at the recent reorganisation of the Manchester Collection, the original reference to the sitter as Othello was restored: I then realised that Aldridge was acting the part of Othello in London when Northcote painted the picture. It was previously thought by some to be of Francis Barber, Dr Johnson's black servant: but as Barber died in 1801 and Northcote always painted from life, this is impossible. Aldridge also played Othello in Manchester in February 1827, which would create local interest which might have supported the decision to purchase the painting, 'the best executed painting in the exhibition'.

It seems strange that, even today, there is a resistance to a black Othello. We have had a white actor, Laurence Olivier, trying to make himself walk and speak like a black man: he lowered his normal voice by an octave in order to play Othello. We continue to be offered white Othellos in our National Theatre, in Stratford, and on television. Why is this? Are people in the twentieth century England, like Lamb and Coleridge and many after them, closer to Brabantio in their reactions than to Desdemona? And what *were* Shakespeare's intentions? Isn't it possible that he wrote a play about a white girl who defied social pressures and married the black man she desired, meeting a tragic fate because they were both infected by the false values of Venetian society? There can still be an

James Northcote: *Head of a Negro in the character of Othello*, 1827.
The earliest known portrait of Ira Aldridge

infinite set of variations in the interpretation of *Othello*; but for myself, I only want to see black actors in the part.

Notes

1. Eldred Jones: *Othello's Countrymen; the African in English Renaissance Drama* (Oxford 1965); see too my unpublished PhD diss., *Haply for I am Black; A Study of Othello's Race, of Changing Racial Attitudes, and of the Implications of such Changes for the Production and Interpretation of the Play* (Manchester Univ., 1974).
2. *Acts of the Privy Council* (ed. J. Dasent), Vol. XXVI, pp. 16–17, 20–1.
3. R. Samarin and A. Nikolyukin: *Shakespeare in the Soviet Union* (Moscow, 1966), pp. 150–64, provides a most interesting study of the play from the actor's point of view. It shows how Ostuzhev's ideas developed from his basic conviction that the play should evoke deep sympathy for Othello.
4. M. Kelly: *Reminiscences*, ed. Theodore Hook (London, 1826), Vol. I, pp. 210–11. Kelly was a very successful musical director and opera singer who was Director of music at Drury Lane for several years. Kelly also recalls an occasion when Kean was invited to visit the Sheridans at home. He read *Othello* to them, and Sheridan was much pleased and told Kelly that 'he had once studied the part of Othello himself, to act at Sir Watkin Williams Wynn's private theatre in Wales; and that Kean's conception of Othello was the precise counterpart of his own.' (Vol. II, p. 285)
5. C. Lamb: *Works* (London, 1818), Vol. 2, pp. 1–36.
6 Nichol Smith (ed.): *Shakespeare Criticism* (Oxford, 1916), pp. 301–2.
7. W. Hazlitt: *The Examiner*, 7 January 1816.
8. Leigh Hunt: *The Theatrical Examiner*, 8 October 1818.
9. For an indication of the strength of the Coleridge tradition regarding Othello's colour see Joseph Hunter: *New Illustrations of the Life, Studies and Writings of Shakespeare* (London, 1845), pp. 280–1; Henry Reed: *Lectures on English History and Tragic Poetry as Illustrated by Shakespeare* (London, 1856), pp. 268–9.
10. H. Marshall and M. Stock: *Ira Aldridge, the Negro Tragedian* (London, 1958).
11. T. Gautier: *Voyage en Russie* (Paris, 1895 ed.). For an indication of the acting genius of Aldridge, see P. Fryer: *Staying Power: The History of Black People in Britain* (London, 1984), pp. 252–6.
12. G. H. Lewes: *On Actors and the Art of Acting* (London, 1875), p. 31.
13. Lewes: *On Actors*, p. 134.
14. See my article in *Burlington Magazine*, December 1983.

The paragraph beginning 'These three plays' on p. 4 and the two paragraphs beginning 'In *Othello* then' on pp. 12–14 were contributed by David Dabydeen.

2   Eighteenth-century English literature on commerce and slavery

DAVID DABYDEEN

Eighteenth-century Britain experienced a rapid expansion of commerce, with the growth of colonies, the spread of empire and British domination of the trade in African slaves. 'There was never from the earliest ages', Samuel Johnson wrote, 'a time in which trade so much engaged the attention of mankind, or commercial gain was sought with such general emulation'. One writer in the *Craftsman* of 1735 described the 'Torrent of Riches, which has been breaking in upon us, for an Age or two past'. John Brown wrote of 'The Spirit of Commerce, now predominant', and Revd. Catcott preached breathlessly on the commercial supremacy of Britain:

> In a word, the whole earth is the market of Britain; and while we remain at home safe and undisturbed, have all the products and commodities of *the eastern* and *western Indies* brought to us in our ships and delivered into our hands . . . Our island has put on quite a different face, since the increase of commerce among us . . . In a word, commerce is the first mover, the main spring in the political machine, and that which gives life and motion to the whole, and sets all the inferior wheels to work.[1]

Addison some three decades earlier had described London as 'a kind of *Emporium* for the whole Earth' (*Spectator*, 69), a view echoed, on a national level, in Defoe's *A Tour Thro' the whole Island of Great Britain* (1724–6) with its sense of unbounded progress, agricultural, commercial and industrial.

The age therefore, whilst being one of 'high culture' (the rise of British art, the establishment of tastes for Italianate music and architecture, and a general cultivation of 'civilised' values) was to a greater extent an age of commercial achievements. As J. A. Doyle puts it, 'if the eighteenth century was the age of Addison and Horace Walpole, it was in a far more abiding sense the age of Chatham and Wolfe and Clive'.[2] The great trading companies established in the previous century flourished and there was a general sense of the manifold possibilities of money-making, of financial development through international trade and commerce with the colonies. Schemes for making money by taking out patents on new inventions abounded, as did speculation in the stock of all kinds of companies, the mood of financial adventurism reaching a giddy height in the South Sea period of 1720, the South Sea disaster being the first great crisis in British capitalism.

'It is money that sells all, money buys all, money pays all, money makes all, money mends all, and money mars all'; "'tis Money makes the Man'; 'All Things are to be had for Money'; 'Money, th' only Pow'r . . . the last Reason of all Things'; 'Money answers all Things': these are the often repeated maxims of the age.[3] The greater proportion of this money was derived from the traffic in human beings, the buying and selling of African peoples and the enforced labour of these peoples. The slave trade was of vast economic importance to the financial existence of Britain. It was the revenue derived from slavery and the slave trade which greatly helped to finance the industrial revolution.[4] In seventeenth and eighteenth century opinion blacks were 'the strength and sinews of this western world', the slave trade 'the spring and parent whence the others flow', 'the first principle and foundation of all the rest, the mainspring of the machine which sets every wheel in motion', 'the Hinge on which all the Trade of this Globe moves on' and 'the best traffick the kingdom hath'.[5] The profits from the slave trade were seen as benefiting the whole British nation without exception: as one writer in 1730 stated, *there is not a Man in this Kingdom, from the highest to the lowest, who does not more or less partake of the Benefits and Advantages of the* Royal African Company's *FORTS and CASTLES* in Africa.' Other writers told of the 'immensely great' profits made by sugar planters who have 'remitted over their Effects, and purchas'd large Estates in England', of the 'many private Persons in England [who] daily gain great Estates in every Branch of the Trade' and of investors in the African Company who have 'for Sixty Years past, got great Estates out of the Subscriptions'.[6] West Indian merchants and planters educated their children in Britain and supported them in a state of opulence; thousands of black slaves were also brought to Britain by returning merchants and planters.[7]

The trade in black people was at the time justified on economic and moral grounds. Slavery was right and allowable, the argument ran, because it was profitable and therefore 'necessary'. According to Defoe '[It is] an Advantage to our Manufacturers, an encreasing the Employment of the Poor, a Support to our General Commerce, and an Addition to the General Stock of the Nation'. Grosvenor in parliament admitted euphemistically that the slave trade 'was an unamiable one' but added with no recognition of the callousness of his comparison that 'So also were many others: the trade of a butcher was an unamiable trade, but it was a very necessary one, not withstanding'.[8] The term 'necessity' appears again and again in works excusing the slave trade. William Bosman for instance, writing in 1705, admits that 'I doubt not but this Trade seems very barbarous to you, but since it is followed by meer necessity it must go on'. William Snelgrave some thirty years afterwards echoed Bosman's sentiments:

> Tho' to traffic in human Creatures, may at first sight appear barbarous, inhuman and unnatural; yet the Traders herein have as much to plead in their own Excuse, as can be said for some other Branches of Trade, namely, the *Advantage* of it.[9]

Such a brutal economic rationale was indicative of the materialist mood of the age, one which saw profit as the main criterion of behaviour, and morality only as a secondary consideration.

The moral justification of the slave trade ranged from the argument that the trade was 'benevolent' in that it provided poor white people with employment, to the argument that the slave trade saved Africans from the bloody tyranny of their own countrymen and from being eaten by their fellow cannibals. As John Dunton put it, 'they must either be *killed* or *eaten*, or both, by their barbarous conquering enemy'. James Grainger, James Boswell, Edward Long and others were all agreed on the compassionate nature of slavery, using exact arguments as Dunton's.[10] One writer in 1740 spoke not of 'enslaving' blacks but of 'rather ransoming the Negroes from their national Tyrants' by transplanting them to the colonies where 'under the benign Influences of the Law, and Gospel, they are advanced to much greater Degrees of Felicity, tho' not to absolute Liberty'.[11]

Viewing the African as a primitive, sub-human creature was necessary to the whole business of slavery since it avoided or made easy any problems of morality: Christians were not enslaving human beings, for blacks were not fully human. Africans embodied all the qualities that Lord Chesterfield, a self-conscious gentleman of taste and culture, abhorred. According to Chesterfield Africans were 'the most ignorant and unpolished people in the world, little better than lions, tigers, leopards, and other wild beasts, which that country produces in great numbers.' It was thus morally acceptable 'to buy a great many of them to sell again to advantage in the West Indies'.[12] An indication of the primitivism of the African was the supposed absence of manufactures, sciences, arts, and systems of commerce within African society. It was repeatedly asserted that blacks were ignorant, unskilled and undeveloped creatures, their lack of scientific, industrial and commercial knowledge accounting for their savage morality.[13]

The literary response: commerce and civilisation
Many eighteenth century men of letters were directly involved in the business world, holding prominent government posts, holding investments in financial schemes and companies, or writing on money matters. Addison, Defoe, Cleland, Steele, Swift, Pope, Prior and Smollett, among others, were in one way or another connected with the world of commerce. Addison for instance was a commissioner of trade and plantations; Cleland, a commissioner of land tax and house duties; Smollett, once a surgeon on a slave-ship, married a colonial, slave-owning heiress. Inevitably, perhaps, a great deal of eighteenth century literature concerned itself with financial matters. As T. K. Meier has written,

> literary men of the seventeenth and eighteenth centuries, including Dryden, Pope, Steele, Thomson, most of the georgic poets, and a number of lesser dramatists, essayists, and poets did heap high praise upon both the concept of capitalistic business enterprise and upon businessmen who practiced it . . . Commerce and industry had caught the literary imagination of the period and represented for a time at least, the progressive hope of the future.

Bonamy Dobrée in discussing eighteenth century poetry has described commerce as 'the great theme that calls forth the deepest notes from poets of the period'. No other theme, Dobrée writes, 'can compare in volume, in depth, in vigour of expression, in width of imagination, with the full diaspon of commerce'.[14]

Poets like James Thomson, Richard Glover, Edward Young, James Gaugh, George Cockings and John Dyer celebrated

29

David Dabydeen

commerce as the catalyst of social, cultural and economic progress. Thomson's *The Castle of Indolence* (1748) views urban development, the establishment of empire and the expansion of markets as laudable ideals; his 'Knight of Industry' is an imperialist and property developer, creating a city out of undeveloped land, just as Defoe's Crusoe transforms his desert island into a flourishing town:

> Then towns he quickened by mechanic arts,
> And bade the fervent city flow with toil;
> Bade social commerce raise renownèd marts,
> Join land to land, and marry soil to soil,
> Unite the poles, and without bloody spoil
> Bring home of either Ind the gorgeous stores.
> (Canto II, 20)

In *The Seasons – Autumn* (1730; ll. 22–150) Thomson traces approvingly the long historical process whereby the city rises out of the wilderness, with the evolution of man from the horrors of a primitive existence into a blissful state of commercial and scientific activity. Glover's *London: Or, the Progress of Commerce* (4th ed., 1739) celebrates, in a similar vein, the development of nature and the growth of the city through commerce:

> . . . She in lonely sands
> Shall bid the tow'r-encircled city rise,
> The barren sea shall people, and the wilds
> Of dreary nature shall with plenty cloath. (ll. 127–30)

It is commerce that has awakened the whole world from its primitive slumber, bringing development, progress and civilisation:

> thou beganst
> Thy all-enlivening progress o'er the globe
> Then rude and joyless . . . (l. 173f.)

Urban development is the theme too in poems like Cockings' *Arts, Manufacture, And Commerce* (c. 1769), Gaugh's *Britannia* (1767) and Young's *The Merchant* (1741). The sense of the limitless possibilities of expansion and gain is given perfect expression by Young as he urges Englishmen to seize the present opportunities of commerce:

> Rich *Commerce* ply with Warmth divine
> By *Day*, by *Night*; the *Stars* are Thine
> Wear out the Stars in *Trade*! Eternal run
> From Age to Age, the noble Glow,

A Rage to gain, and to *bestow*,
Whilst Ages last! In *Trade* burn out the Sun! (Strain IV, 19)

In this poem Young's model of the world is a purely economic one, the relationship between earth, sea and air seen as a series of commercial transactions:

Earth's Odours *pay* soft *Airs* above,
That o'er the teeming Field *prolific* range;
Planets are Merchants, take, return
Lustre and Heat; by Traffic burn;
The whole *Creation* is one vast *Exchange*. (Strain III, 26)

The kindling of commercial activity is compared to natural awakenings, to the rain from heaven which cheers the glebe, activates the bees and rouses the flowers. Blake may have seen 'a Heaven in a Wild Flower' (*Auguries of Innocence*, l. 2), but Young is more down-to-earth. Such a commercial response to nature is a distinguishing feature of much of eighteenth century literature. Trees existed to be cut down and fashioned into merchant ships. When one writer described 'beautiful forests', he meant not their aesthetic qualities but their commercial potential: 'The farther one advances into the country, the more beautiful Forests are found, full of Gummy Trees, fit to make Pitch for Ships; as also infinite Store of Trees fit for Masts.'[15]

The consensus of opinion in many pieces of eighteenth century literature is that commerce is a wonderful activity, creative of progress, culture and civilisation. Glover writes of the mathematics, philosophy, poetry and laws that result from commerce:

Barbarity is polish'd, infant arts
Bloom in the desart, and benignant peace
With hospitality, begin to soothe
Unsocial rapine, and the thirst of blood.
(*London*, ll. 209–12)

Young makes similar claims for the civilising power of commerce:

Commerce gives Arts, as well as *Gain*;
By Commerce wafted o'er the Main,
They barbarous Climes enlighten as they run;
Arts the rich Traffic of the Soul!
May travel *thus*, from Pole to Pole,
And gild the World with Learning's *brighter* Sun.
(*Merchant*, Strain II, 1)

31

The contact between men as a result of mutual trade is seen as conducive to tolerance, morality and culture. The merchant, the agent of commerce, was also celebrated as the agent of progress and civilisation, the embodiment of civilised standards derived from his commercial experience. No praise was great enough to lavish upon him, all poetic eulogies fell short of their mark:

> Is *Merchant* an inglorious Name?
> No; fit for *Pindar* such a Theme,
> Too great for Me; I pant beneath the Weight!
> If loud, as *Ocean's* were my Voice,
> If Words and Thoughts to court my Choice
> Out-number'd *Sands*, I could not reach its Height.
> (*Merchant*, Strain III, 24)

The merchant was also seen as a force for liberty, 'liberty' being a key word in literature celebrating commerce. Commerce meant the rise of the middle class which, as it gained political influence, sought protection from the tyranny and arbitrary laws of the aristocratic class, its main ambition being the legal protection of property. Hence Young's verse:

> *Trade*, gives fair *Virtue* fairer still to shine;
> Enacts those Guards of Gain, the *Laws*;
> *Exalts* even *Freedom's* glorious Cause. (*Merchant*, Strain IV, 14)

There was, as C. A. Moore has said, 'one dark blot' in this bright picture of progress, civilisation and liberty through commerce: 'The one detail out of moral keeping was the slave traffic'.[16] Slavery was such an undeniably crucial aspect of colonial and international commerce that the men of letters could not avoid touching on the subject. Their problem was how to reconcile their belief in the civilising effects of commerce to the barbaric realities of the slave trade. Cornelius Arnold and John Dyer provided one way out of the dilemma. Arnold interrupts briefly his eulogy on commerce to express perfunctory regret at the fact of African slavery, but he blames the Africans for the existence of the slave trade, the argument being that Africans, in their civil wars, capture their fellow countrymen and sell them into slavery:

> . . . Onward they [i.e. British merchants] steer their Course,
> To *Afric's* parched Clime, whose sooty Sons,
> Thro' Rage of civil Broils . . . hard Destiny!
> Forc'd from their native Home to *Western Ind*,
> In Slavery drag the galling Chain of Life.[17]

Dyer's *Fleece* (1757) contains a similar perfunctory pity for the condition of the black, Dyer not wishing to appear inhumane and uncivilised; nevertheless the black is shouldered with the blame for slavery:

> On Guinea's sultry strand, the drap'ry light
> Of Manchester or Norwich is bestow'd
> For clear transparent gums, and ductile wax,
> And snow-white iv'ry; yet the valued trade,
> Along this barb'rous coast, in telling, wounds
> The gen'rous heart, the sale of wretched slaves;
> Slaves, by their tribes condemn'd, exchanging death
> For life-long servitude; severe exchange!
> (Book IV, l. 189 f)

Young and Glover deal with the problem of slavery in different ways. There is in Young's poem a brief, scornful reference to blacks, describing, of all things, their laziness:

> *Afric's* black, lascivious, slothful Breed,
> To clasp their *Ruin*, fly from *Toil* . . .
> (*Merchant*, Strain V, 20)

Africa is attacked because it does not practise the principles of capitalist development which Young celebrates, the African is seen as being ignorant of the principles of science and commerce:

> Of *Nature's* Wealth from *Commerce* rent,
> *Afric's* a glaring Monument:
> Mid *Citron* Forests and *Pomgranate* Groves
> (Curs'd in a Paradise!) she pines;
> O'er *generous* Glebe, o'er *golden* Mines
> Her *begger'd*, *famish'd*, Tradeless Natives roves.
> (*Merchant*, Strain V, 21)

Young, in an indirect way, is saying that slavery is a benevolent institution, since it teaches the African the virtues of labour. Glover, though equally deceitful, is not so breathtakingly perverse; his poem (*London, op. cit.*) attacks the Spanish for enslaving and destroying the Indian natives but he makes no reference to the British participation in slavery and British treatment of the Africans – his poem was written in 1739 when anti-Spanish sentiment was running high in Britain, British traders angry at the liberties taken by Spanish merchants and jealous of Spanish commercial rivalry, a rivalry that erupted into war in 1739 (the 'War of Jenkins' Ear'). Glover's reference to slavery, and Indian slavery at that, is merely political therefore.

Another way of reckoning with slavery whilst being faithful to the ethic of commerce was to minimise the brutality of the trade through careful choice of diction. James Grainger for example, in his poem *The Sugar-Cane* (1764) strives to reduce the horror of slavery by 'wrapping it up in a napkin of poetic diction'. *The Sugar-Cane* is as good an example as any of the way in which 'the raw materials of human experience were habitually transmuted in eighteenth-century poetry'.[18] Instead of 'slave-owner', Grainger prefers to use the term 'Master-Swain'; he prefers 'Assistant Planter' to the term 'slave'. The use of poetical phrases such as 'Afric's sable progeny' to describe the black slaves further softens the stark realities of their actual condition. It is such callous abstractions that provoked Samuel Johnson's attack on Grainger's acceptance of slavery.

Picturesque descriptions of slave labour and the slave environment was another feature of pro-commerce literature. Grainger's *The Sugar-Cane* contained idyllic descriptions of the golden canefields with their contentedly laborious black swains,

> Well-fed, well-cloath'd, all emulous to gain
> Their master's smile, who treated them like men.
>
> (Book I, ll. 611–12)

The author of *The Pleasures of Jamaica* written some three decades before, presented a view of slave plantations that was similarly picturesque:

> Hither retiring, to avoid the heat,
> We find refreshment in a cool retreat;
> Each rural object gratifies the sight,
> And yields the mind an innocent delight;
> Greens of all shades the diff'rent plats adorn,
> Here the young cane, and there the growing corn;
> In verdant pastures interspers'd between,
> The lowing herds, and bleating flocks are seen:
> With joy his lord the faithful Negro sees,
> And in his way endeavours how to please;
> Greets his return with his best country song,
> The lively dance, and tuneful merry-wang.
> When nature by the cane has done her part,
> Which ripen'd now demands the help of art,
> How pleasant are the labours of the mill,
> While the rich streams the boiling coppers fill.

As one of the characters in La Valée's anti-slavery novel explains to the African, avarice 'borrows the voice and colours of fiction.

34

Fiction gilds your chains ...'.[19] The same 'fiction' was being employed to describe the condition of England's peasants and workers – hence the masses of eighteenth century pastoral verse which romanticised agricultural labour, erasing from it any notion of toil and exploitation. And if, as in *The Pleasures of Jamaica*, the African slaves trip over each other in their joyful haste to greet their returning master, so in Addison's version of country life are the English peasants gladdened by the approach of their squire Sir Roger:

> I could not but observe with a great deal of Pleasure the Joy that appeared in the Countenances of these ancient Domesticks upon my Friend's Arrival at his Country-Seat. Some of them could not refrain from tears at the Sight of their old Master; every one of them press'd forward to do something for him, and seemed *discouraged if they were not employed*. (*Spectator* 106; my italics)

It is no wonder that abolition pamphleteers made frequent appeals to English workers, urging them to recognise in the servitude and distress of blacks the conditions of their own existence.

The fact is that many of the pro-commerce writers who either justified slavery or minimised its inhumanity were in one way or another involved in the profits to be made from slavery. Glover, for instance, was the son of a merchant, and also a member of parliament, noted for his defence of West India merchants before parliament. In 1742 a petition drawn up by Glover and signed by 300 merchants complaining of the inadequate protection of English trade, was presented to parliament. Glover afterwards attended to sum up their evidence before the house of commons. In 1775 he received a plate worth £300 from West India merchants in acknowledgement of his services to them. His will mentions property in the City of London and in South Carolina. Cornelius Arnold was in later life beadle to the Distillers Company with its interests in West India sugar. Grainger, who died in St Christopher in 1766 was married to the daughter of a Nevis planter, and took charge of his wife's uncle's plantations; he invested his savings in the purchase of slaves.[20]

The involvement in the economic benefits of slavery meant a warped ethical response to it. We catch the sense of wealth beyond the dreams of avarice in William Goldwin's poem *Great Britain: Or, The Happy Isle* (1705), specifically in the compounded descriptive phrases like 'Massy heaps of shining Treasure':

> See! How the Busie Merchant Ploughs the Main
> In Vessels big with weighty Heaps of Gain; . . .
> Huge Loads of Wealth, the distant World's Encrease (p. 5)

The feeling of great wealth is carried over in Goldwin's *Poetical Description of Bristol* (1712) in which the sole reference to slavery is an indirect one – 'Jamaica's Growth, or Guinea's Golden-dust'; also in R. J. Thorn's *Bristolia* (1794)

> Around the quays, in countless heaps appear,
> Bales pil'd on bales, and loads of foreign ware.

The alternative response to commerce

The alternative response to the wealth pouring into society took many forms. To begin with there was a sense of the physical ugliness and the despoilation of the landscape resulting from commercial and industrial activity. Goldwin's response to the growing signs of industrialisation, for example, is more ambivalent than Dyer's or Thorn's. In Dyer's *Fleece*, the smoke rising over Leeds was described as 'incense' and praised as a sign of industrial activity. Thorn's poem on Bristol was also optimistic about industrial fumes – standing upon Brandon Hill like a latterday Moses upon Pisgah, he surveyed the promised land of money and machinery:

> Here, whilst I stand, what clouds of smoke appear
> From different work-shops, and dissolve in air!

Goldwin, in his *Poetical Description of Bristol*, whilst celebrating the city's commercial and manufacturing wealth, rejects the accompanying destruction of nature, the uprooting of Kingswood Forest and the rape of the earth as miners tear 'Magazines of Coals from Nature's Bowel'. The mine and miners present a 'horrid' sight to the eye. He launches into an attack on the ugliness and pollution of a glass manufacturing works:

> Thick dark'ning Clouds in curling smoky Wreaths
> Whose sooty Stench the Earth and Sky annoys,
> And Nature's blooming Verdure half destroys.

The sulphur emitted from the factory's chimney 'blasts the Fruit of fair Sicilia's Fields'. Goldwin's poem ends with a paeon on natural beauty, the 'Grotesque' rocks and cliffs along the river which 'afright the climbing Eye' in a different way from the 'horrid' sight of the coalmine. Goldwin's anxieties about progress accumulate throughout the eighteenth century, culminating in the next in Mrs Gaskell's polluted Milton in *North and South* and Dickens' Coketown in *Hard Times*, a pessimism about progress perfectly expressed in Hopkins' *God's Grandeur*.

Bound up with the disgust at the physical pollution created by 'progress' was a sense of the city as a hideous, dirty, chaotic phenomenon. The pro-commerce writers may have celebrated the evolution of the city from the barren wilderness as a sign of civilisation, but others – Pope, Swift, Gay, Smollett – depicted the city as corrupt, putrid and anarchic to the point of insanity. London is depicted as a gigantic Bedlam riddled with crime and disease, as Max Byrd in his recent study of the image of the city in eighteenth century literature has shown.[21]

If the spirit of commerce was seen as having stimulated crime it was also seen as having created inhumane attitudes in people, a selfishness and hardness of heart. R. Lovell, in *Bristol. A Satire* (1794), described the soullessness of Bristolians who are motivated only by 'sordid wealth':

> Foul as their streets, triumphant meanness sways,
> And groveling as their mud-compelling drays.

Bristolians have become mere emblems of money, devoid of 'the nobler cares of mind', 'soft humanities', 'mild urbanity' and 'sympathetic feeling':

> In all his sons the mystic signs we trace;
> Pounds, shillings, pence, appear in every face.

Another eighteenth-century observer of Bristolians described how 'Their Souls are engrossed by lucre', with the more gentle qualities of mind 'banished from their republic as a contagious disease'. Samuel Johnson noted the same quality in Bristolians: according to Johnson, Richard Savage's rejection at Bristol was because his wit, culture and conversation were not valued in this 'place of commerce', the traders more conscious of 'solid gain'.[22]

Both Dyer and Thomson in their eulogies on commerce had asserted its benevolent effect upon the labouring classes in raising their standard of living to glorious levels. According to Thomson, commerce fuelled by the spirit of liberty has enriched the whole nation – 'The poor man's lot with milk and honey flows' (*Liberty*, V, l. 6). Although the principle of subordination still holds sway in

David Dabydeen

society, the wealth derived from commerce is equally enjoyed,
Thomson claimed. Dyer similarly described the national benefits of
industry which 'lifts the swain,/And the straw cottage to a palace
turns' (*Fleece*, book III, l. 332). Other writers were more realistic
than Thomson and Dyer, recognising an unequal distribution of
wealth and a stark division in society between the haves and have-
nots. 'Under the present Stage of Trade', John Brown wrote,

> the Increase of Wealth is by no means equally or proportionally
> diffused: The Trader reaps the main Profit: after him, the Landlord, in a
> lower Degree: But the common Artificer, and still more the common
> Labourer, gain little by the exorbitant Advance of Trade.
> (*Estimate, op. cit.*, p. 192)

Thomas Bedford, in a sermon bitterly attacking commerce,
colonisation and slavery, observed that because trade and commerce had introduced inflation in Britain and a more expensive
manner of living, 'the bulk of its people may still continue poor, in
the midst of a thousand like advantages'.[23]

Those who attacked commerce as a force for squalor and
degradation focused increasingly on slavery for the substance of
their views. The bulk of British anti-slavery literature was written in
the latter part of the century, spurred on by the propaganda of the
abolition movement, but by 1750 there was already considerable
public awareness of the brutality of the slave trade. Hence
Postlethwayt in 1746 produced a tract in defence of slavery, to
counter the 'Many [who] are prepossessed against this Trade,
thinking it *a barbarous, inhuman, and unlawful Traffic for a
Christian Country to Trade in Blacks*'. The 'many' in the first half
of the century included the Quakers, John Dunton, Ralph
Sandiford, Jonathan Swift, Samuel Johnson, Charles Gildon,
Joseph Warton, Richard Savage, and others. Even Defoe had at one
time written anti-slavery verse, denouncing the slavetraders and
their brand of Christianity.[24] Major poets like Wordsworth, Blake,
Southey and Cowper were later to make similar protests against
slavery. William Blake, in addition to poems like *The Little Black
Boy*, created some powerful engravings of slave abuses as illustrations for John Stedman's 1796 *Narrative of a five year's
expedition against the revolted Negroes of Surinam* (Figs. 3 and 4).
The production of poetry was spurred on by the formation of the
Abolition Society in 1787, and the relationships that leading social
crusaders sought to forge with eminent writers. The Revd. John

38   I. Cruikshank: *The Abolition of the Slave Trade*, 1792 →

W. Blake: 'A Negro hung alive by the Ribs to a Gallows', 1796

W. Blake: 'Flagellation of a Female Samboe Slave', 1796

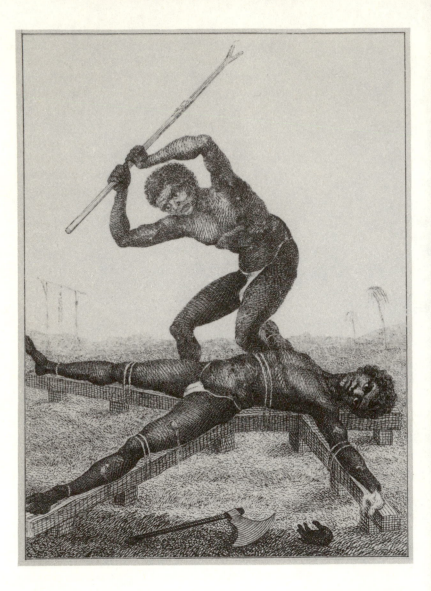

Anon.: 'The Execution of Breaking on the Rack', 1796

Newton for instance, an ex-Guinea merchant turned penitent, urged Cowper to put his pen to the service of black humanity. Cowper responded with some anti-slavery ballads which were instantly popular and distributed in their thousands throughout the country. Wordsworth's contact with William Wilberforce and Thomas Clarkson (the former a close acquaintance of his uncle, the latter a fellow resident in the Lake District) led to verse supportive of their campaigns, such as the 1807 sonnet on Clarkson's Abolition Bill. Such poets, however, were merely being perfunctory in their anti-slavery productions – the triteness and laboured sentiments of their expressions betray an absence of deep, personal involvement or vision.[25] Indeed Cowper in a letter of 1788 admitted that 'the subject, as a subject for song, did not strike me much' and Wordsworth in a passage in the *Prelude* dealing with abolition agitation confessed that

> For me that strife had ne'er
> Fasten'd on my affections, nor did now
> Its unsuccessful issue much excite
> My sorrow . . . (A-version, Book. X, ll. 202 ff.)

The French revolution, being a white affair and closer to home, excited more profound and lasting interest than the Haitian revolution of the identical period. There were indeed a scattering of verse and pamphlets singing the courage and genius of Toussaint L'Ouverture, but it took nearly one hundred and fifty years, with the appearance of C. L. R. James' *The Black Jacobins*, before a full assessment of the profundity of the Haitian revolution was made. James is, significantly, a black West Indian: given the established and enduring European belief that black people have no history to speak of,[26] the burden of revelation has fallen on black scholars and slave-descendants like James.

The lack of integrity on the part of English eighteenth-century writers can be startlingly glimpsed in Coleridge's attitude to blacks. His first major poem was a Greek ode against the slave trade which earned him the Browne Gold Medal at Cambridge University.[27] He was to write that 'my Greek ode is, I think, my *chef d'oeuvre* in poetical composition'. Coleridge's interest however lay more in the exercise of scholarship than in the plight of blacks: slaves were mere fodder for conceptualisation and poetical practice conducted in Greek with the aim of winning a coveted prize. His real attitude to blacks is revealed in his nausea at Othello's embrace of

Desdemona. It was one thing to sympathise spaciously and within the elegant, classical boundaries of a Greek ode with blacks, but quite another thing to have them marrying into the family. Similar hypocrisy can be imputed to other English writers. From the 1770s onwards England was deluged with anti-slavery verse, the sheer bulk of it, and the bewildering variety of poetical expression (odes, pastorals, eclogues, sonnets, doggerel, even creole jingles) being an overwhelming aspect of the literary history of the period. There is little evidence though to suggest that any of these poets devoted any personal time or effort, or dug deep into their pockets, to support the abolition cause. Indeed, it is more probable that the theme of slavery fed them, providing an opportunity for grubs and hacks to indulge in sentiment, to try out verse techniques, and to make some money by either capitalising on popular feeling or else by cashing in on the latest sensational revelation in the newspapers of West Indian brutalities.

Unlike the black writers of the eighteenth century (Equiano for instance, who trudged all over England organising anti-slavery rallies and publicising his slave autobiography) whose finances and very lives were bound up with their literary productions, English writers merely exploited the slave theme for their own gain and recognition. For Swift, the theme provided an opportunity for the exercise of wit and display of satirical prowess. He thunders against the brutishness and hypocrisy of the business of colonisation:

> Ships are sent out with the first opportunity, the natives driven out or destroyed, their princes tortured to discover their gold, a free licence given to all acts of inhumanity and lust, the earth reeking with the blood of its inhabitants: and this execrable crew of butchers employed in so pious an expedition, is a *modern colony* sent to convert and civilise an idolatrous and barbarous people. (Bk. 4, Ch. 12)

Yet Swift was quite happy to invest hundreds of pounds, in 1720, in the South Sea Company whose sole business at the time was to ferry African slaves to the Spanish colonies. In 1713, by the Treaty of Utrecht, Britain had gained the 'Asiento' privelege of supplying the Spanish colonies with slaves, and this monopoly was granted to the South Sea Company. The 'Asiento' privelege was considered at the time to be the 'jewel' clause of the Treaty. Alexander Pope published his *Windsor Forest* in 1713 to celebrate the Treaty, a poem in praise of the values of liberty and civilisation: English liberty and civilisation that is, for apart from the odd jejeune pastoral expression of hope that the 'freed Indians' would eventually be able to 'woo their sable loves' in the liberty and civilisation of 'their native groves', there is no hint of the real barbarity of the 'Asiento' monopoly. In 1720, Pope, like Swift, was busily investing capital in the South Sea Company in the hope of a quick killing.[28]

The profits to be made from slavery, then, conditioned or compromised the literary expressions of both pro-commerce and anti-slavery writers. As C. A. Moore puts it, 'the conscience of the public was so blinded to the moral issue by the widespread participation in dividends that it was very difficult to bring independent judgement or sentiment to bear upon the subject'.[29] The dilemma over the slave trade – the recognition of its immorality, and yet at the same time its profitability – was one aspect of the general dilemma of the age in its attempt to reconcile the moral with the economic. 'Religion is one thing, trade is another' – it is this separation between the two, or, as Anderson puts it, 'the withdrawal of economic affairs from the jurisdiction of morality', which posed crucial, central problems at the time to many writers on economic matters. These problems lay at the very core of Britain's commercial existence; indeed they provoked questions about the country's very survival as a world power. Davenant for instance recognised the evils resulting from trade but also its 'necessity' in terms of Britain's continued supremacy over its rivals and competitors:

> Trade, without doubt, is in its nature a pernicious thing: it brings in that Wealth which introduces Luxury; it gives a rise to Fraud and Avarice, and extinguishes Virtue and Simplicity of Manners; it depraves a People and makes for that Corruption which never fails to end in Slavery, Foreign or Domestick. *Licurgus*, in the most perfect Model of Government that was ever fram'd, did banish it from his Commonwealth. But, the Posture and Condition of other Countries consider'd, 'tis become with us a necessary Evil.

Some fifty years later John Brown came up against the same hurdle – he rails against the luxury and immorality created by the wealth from commerce, but realises that to discourage or curtail such commerce would lead to national decline with rival countries overtaking Britain in economic and military might. 'Thus are we fallen into a kind of Dilemma', Brown muses, uncertain of the solution.[30] The dilemma was also faced by some pro-slavery writers, particularly on the issue of baptising and christianising blacks. Slave-owners, one apologist pointed out in 1730,[31] were reluctant to educate their slaves to the christian gospel because of the economic costs. The slaves would have to be given time off work to attend Bible classes which would mean a loss in production. This would be 'too great an Invasion on the property of the Masters'. If for instance, the writer calculates, a planter were to allow one-fifth of his total collection of one hundred slaves to be educated once a fortnight in the gospel, and estimating that each slave made six pence profit per day for his owner, then the owner would lose a whole £13 *per annum*, and £65 *per annum* if he let all his blacks be educated; to educate all the hundred thousand blacks in the West Indies would cost a massive sum of £65,000. As to the morality of the slave trade itself the writer does not deny that 'Millions of Lives it destroys', but stresses that it is still 'absolutely necessary' for reasons of national supremacy – Britain, France, Spain, Holland and Portugal are all involved in the slave trade and

> were any of them to break it off on the Topick of Unlawfulness, they would soon lose their Share in the Profits arising from it, which is hardly to be expected from them unless their Neighbours could be prevail'd to drop theirs too.

Because of this international competition, the writer concludes, it is unlikely that the slave trade will decline, unless God personally intervenes! God of course did not intervene, but the black slaves themselves did. Whenever opportunity presented itself they revolted – in the slave factories on the West African coast, on board the slaveships taking them to the colonies, and on the plantations. These revolts, and the bloodletting and barbarities they unleashed, made more impact on the dismantling of slavery than the poems issued by English writers. The sword was mightier than the pen: the irrationality of whites, their refusal to be persuaded by reasoned and moral arguments, forced blacks into violent behaviour. This legacy of the 'criminalisation' of blacks is, according to contemporary opinion, still a distinguishing feature of the racial encounter between blacks and whites. As Joe Harte, a black British political campaigner put it, in writing about the Brixton riots of 1981, 'our community the world over resents the burden imposed on us by white society to dramatize our grievances before they are met'.[32]

Notes

1. Samuel Johnson, cited by L. Whitney: *Primitivism And The Idea Of Progress* (Baltimore, 1934), p. xviii; *Craftsman* of 1735 reproduced in *The Gentleman's Magazine*, Vol. 5, 1735, pp. 717–18; John Brown: *An Estimate Of The Manners And Principles Of the Times* (2nd ed., London, 1757), p. 22; A. S. Catcott: *The Antiquity and Honourableness of the Practice of Merchandize. A Sermon* (Bristol, 1744), pp. 13, 14, 15.
2. J. A. Doyle cited by A. A. Ettinger: *James Edward Oglethorpe. Imperial Idealist* (Oxford, 1936), p. 110; T. Seymour: *Literature And The South Sea Bubble* (unpublished PhD diss., Chapel Hill, 1955), p. 12.
3. *Maxims of Wisdom for Gaining Wealth* (London, 1788), p. 20; *Put Money in your Purse* (London, 1754), p. 321; *The Universal Merchant: Containing The Rationale of Commerce, in Theory and Practice* (London, 1753), p. 6; *A Trip To Leverpoole By Two of Fate's Children In Search of Fortunatus's Purse. A Satyr* (London, 1706), title-page quoting from Butler's *Hudibras*; J. Vanderlint: *Money answers all Things* (London, 1734).
4. Eric Williams in *Capitalism & Slavery* (Chapel Hill, 1944), p. 52, has written that 'the profits obtained provided one of the main streams of that accumulation of capital in England which financed the Industrial Revolution'. James Walvin in *The Black Presence: A Documentary History of the Negro in England, 1555–1860* (London, 1971), p. 8, states that such commerce 'underpinned Britain's transition towards an industrial society'.
5. Williams, *Capitalism and Slavery*, pp. 30, 51; J. Houstoun: *Some New and Accurate Observations . . . Of the Coast of Guinea* (London, 1725), p. 43; Peter Hogg: *Slavery: The Afro-American Experience* (British Library Publication, London, 1979), p. 3.
6. *The Case Of The Royal African Company of England* (London, 1730), p. 31; *The Dispute between the Northern Colonies and the Sugar Islands, set in a Clear View* (1731 broadside, in *The Goldsmiths Library's Collection of Broadsides IV*, no. 343.3, Senate House Library, London University); *A Letter To The Right Reverend The Lord Bishop of London From An Inhabitant Of His Majesty's Leeward-Caribbee-Islands* (London, 1730), p. 14; *Some Matters of Fact Relating to the Present State of the African Trade* (n.p., 1720), p. 1.
7. By 1768 the estimate of the number of blacks in Britain was 20,000 (F. Shyllon: *Black People in Britain 1555–1833*, Oxford, 1977, p. 102). The figure may have been higher – the *London Chronicle* of 1756 gave a number of 30,000 (D. A. Lorimer: *Colour, Class and the Victorians*, London, 1978, p. 25). The *Daily Journal* of 5 April 1723 reported that 'Tis said there is a great Number of Blacks come daily into this City, so that 'tis thought in a short Time, if they be not suppress'd, the City will swarm with them'.
8. Daniel Defoe: *A Brief Account Of The Present State Of The African Trade* (London, 1713), p. 55; *Review* (ed. A. W. Secord. New York, 1938), IX, p. 82. Defoe also declares that the British plantations 'can no more subsist without Negroes, than *England* could without Horses' – see R. P. Kaplan: *Daniel Defoe's Views on Slavery And Racial Prejudice* (unpublished PhD diss., New York Univ., 1970), p. 120. For Grosvenor statement, see *Report of the Debate on a Motion For the Abolition of the Slave Trade in the House of Commons on Monday and Tuesday, April 18th and 19th, 1791* (London, 1791), p. 47.
9. *A New and Accurate Description of Guinea . . .* (London, 1705), cited by M. Craton, J. Walvin and D. Wright: *Slavery, Abolition and Emancipation* (London, 1976), p. 220; William Snelgrave: *A New Account of some Parts of Guinea, And the Slave-Trade* (London, 1734), p. 160.

10. *The Athenian Mercury*, VIII, no. 30 (1691). See C. A. Moore's *Backgrounds of English Literature* (Minneapolis, 1953), p. 153. Edward Long's views are cited by O. Wali: *The Negro in English Literature* (unpublished PhD diss., North Western Univ., 1967), pp. 391–2. For Grainger's and Boswell's views see Wylie Sypher: *Guinea's Captive Kings* (Chapel Hill, 1944), pp. 169f.; p. 59.

11. 'The African Slave Trade defended', in *The London Magazine*, IX, 1740, pp. 493–4; cited by E. Donnan: *Documents Illustrative Of The History Of The Slave Trade To America* (4 vols, Washington, 1930–5), II, p. 470.

12. *The Letters Of The Earl of Chesterfield To His Son* (ed. C. Strachey, with notes by A. Calthrop, 3rd ed., London, 1932), p. 116.

13. For a sample of such opinions see *A Brief Discovery . . . of . . . The Island of Madagascar*, in *A Collection of Voyages and Travels* (London, 1745), II, p. 633; *A True Relation Of The Inhuman and Unparalleled Actions And Barbarous Murders, Of Negroes or Moors ibid.*, II, p. 515. The first writes that there are 'no ingenious manufactures . . . no arts, no sciences' among the Negroes, that they show no 'symptoms of ingenuity'; the second and third writers describe blacks as 'idle, sluggish, . . . free from having any tillage whatsoever'; 'they make little use of labour or manufactures'.

14. Tom K. Meier: *Defoe And The Defense of Commerce* (unpublished PhD diss., Columbia Univ., 1971), pp. 1, 18. Bonamy Dobrée: 'The theme of patriotism in the poetry of the early eighteenth century', in *Proceedings Of The British Academy* XXXV, 1949, p. 60.

15. *The Four Kings of Canada* (London, 1710), p. 46.

16. Moore, *Backgrounds*, p. 133.

17. Cornelius Arnold: *Commerce* (1751), in *Poems On Several Occasions* (London, 1757), p. 129. The truth was that the European actively encouraged Africans to fight against and enslave each other by the bribery of tribal leaders – see W. Rodney: *A History Of The Upper Guinea Coast 1545–1800* (Oxford, 1970), pp. 102–6, 113, etc.

18. I borrow James Sutherland's words from a different context: *A Preface To Eighteenth Century Poetry* (Oxford, 1948), p. 89.

19. Poem in *The Gentleman's Magazine* VIII, 1738, p. 158. Joseph La Valée: *The Negro Equalled By Few Europeans* (Dublin, 1791), I, pp. 81–2.

20. Details from *The Dictionary of National Biography*.

21. Max Byrd: *London Transformed. Images of the City in the Eighteenth Century* (New Haven and London, 1978).

22. P. T. Marcy: *Eighteenth Century Views Of Bristol And Bristolians* (Bristol, 1966), p. 13; S. Johnson: *Lives of the Poets* (2 vols., Oxford, 1975), II, p. 168.

23. Thomas Bedford: *The Origin Of our Grievances: A sermon* (London, 1770), p. 14.

24. M. Postlethwayt: *The National and Private Advantages Of The African Trade Considered* (London, 1746), p. 4. The Quakers declared against slavery in 1727 – see T. Clarkson: *An Essay On The Slavery And Commerce Of The Human Species, Particularly The African* (London, 1786), p. viii; for Dunton's change of heart about slavery see Moore, *Backgrounds*, p. 135; R. Sandiford: *The Mystery of Iniquity* (2nd ed., London, 1730); J. Swift: *Gulliver's Travels* (Oxford, 1956), pp. 293, 352; *Boswell's Life of Johnson* (ed. G. B. Hill, 6 vols., Oxford, 1934), II, pp. 476–7; Charles Gildon: *The Life And Strange Surprizing Adventures of Mr. D------- De F----- * (2nd ed., London, 1719), p. 14; J. Warton: 'Ode to Liberty', in *The Works Of The British Poets* (ed. Thomas Park, London, 1808, XXXVII, p. 15); R. Savage: *Of Public Spirit in Regard To Public Works*, l. 301f., in *Poetical Works* (ed. C. Tracy, Cambridge, 1962), p. 233; D. Defoe: *Reformation of Manners, A Satire* (n.p.; 1702), p. 17.

25. See Sypher: *Guinea's Captive Kings*, pp. 186–9; 215–17.
26. See Peter Fraser's 'Introduction' to the *Africa Beyond Africa* catalogue, published by the Commonwealth Institute (London, 1984).
27. E. B. Dykes: *The Negro in English Romantic Thought* (Washington, 1942), p. 75.
28. The names of Pope and Swift are to be found in the company's subscription books which are now kept in the House of Lords Records Office.
29. Moore, *Backgrounds*, p. 133.
30. Hans H. Anderson: *Daniel Defoe: A Study of The Conflict Between Commercialism And Morality In The Early Eighteenth Century* (unpublished PhD diss., Univ. of Chicago, 1930), p. 107; Charles Davenant: *An Essay Upon The Probable Methods Of making a People Gainers In The Ballance of Trade* (London, 1699), pp. 154–5; John Brown, *op. cit.*, p. 217.
31. *A Letter To The Right Reverend The Lord Bishop Of London*, p. 15.
32. *Team Work* (Journal of the West Indian Standing Conference), I, October 1984.

3 Black writers of the eighteenth and nineteenth centuries

PAUL EDWARDS

This paper will not be concerned to any great extent with black people as characters in the literature of the period: the subject is amply treated in books listed in the bibliography, and in other papers in this volume. My purpose is to draw attention to black authors writing between the late eighteenth and the early twentieth centuries – about whom pupils ought for obvious reasons to be informed, but many teachers remain unaware – if only to dispel the idea that black people have in the past simply been written about, and have not spoken for themselves.

A body of black writing with an important bearing on the recent as well as the past experience of black people in Britain, is to be found as early as the eighteenth century. In fact, black people have been resident in Britain far longer than is generally realised. Shortly after 200 AD, a unit of African troops which would have numbered at least two or three hundred men was stationed on Hadrian's Wall a few miles outside Carlisle. It included one African daring enough to poke fun at the visiting Emperor Septimius Severus, and the comic encounter found its way into Roman historical records.[1] There is some evidence that black troops such as these may have settled in Britain when their period of service was over: a community of black people and their descendants lived in York, for example, several centuries before the English themselves began to settle in celtic Britain.[2] Occasional contacts continued by way of British vikings, and crusaders, and by 1500 AD a number of Africans were living as free men and women in the Scottish royal households at Edinburgh, Dunfermline and Linlithgow. King James IV of Scotland (1488–1513) had a black drummer ('the moor taubronar') who accompanied him along with four Italian minstrels on his travels, and devised entertainments at court. The accounts record payments not only to the drummer, but to his wife and child, the latter probably the 'blak barn' born in Scotland and brought before the king in 1505–6. The Bishop of Moray had a black servant, and also resident in Edinburgh at that time were two African friars. Queen Margaret had two personal black maid-servants, Ellen and Margaret, who received many presents of money and clothing from the crown including, along with other New Year gifts for the servants of the royal household on New Year's day 1513, 'to the twa blak ledeis, x Franche crounis'.[3]

One of these ladies, Ellen Moir, was the subject of a ribald poem, 'Ane Blak Moir', by William Dunbar.[4] Some commentators have seen it as racist, though it might better be understood as illustrating the raw humour of the period, since Dunbar wrote some brutally uncomplimentary poems even about his best friends. Dunbar's poem gives us the first literary description in English of an African.

Apart from the questions of interpretation raised by this poem, there are many signs by the sixteenth century that the seeds of racial intolerance lay in fertile soil. Black men had long been identified with the devil, and as familiars of witches; it was commonly believed that blackness was a curse laid by God upon Noah's son Ham by way of his offspring; Queen Elizabeth was, by the end of the century, to issue proclamations and deportation orders against the 'divers blackamores brought into this realm'; and there were many travellers ready to witness that Africans were irredeemably ugly in their appearance, tastes and desires.[5]

English involvement with the slave trade was to expand considerably in the 1670s after the Restoration, coinciding with an expansion of the trade in West Indian sugar and a decline in the legal status of black people, as the expression 'negro slave' began to replace 'negro servant'. By 1701, an Englishman making his will could write of his black servant, 'I take him to be in the nature of my goods and chattels'.[6] There were critical voices to be heard, but no serious focus of protest until the 1760s when Granville Sharp won a series of cases against slave-owners in Britain, culminating in Lord Chief Justice Mansfield's ruling of 1772 in the Somerset case that black servants in Britain had the right to refuse to return to service – that is, to slavery – in the Americas. Mansfield was ambiguous about the exact status of such servants, but the question was resolved unambiguously by Scottish law in a series of cases leading in 1778 to the declaration, in *Knight* v. *Wedderburn*, that there could be no slaves in Scotland. A bill abolishing the slave trade was passed in parliament in 1807. It was during this half-century that black writing in English was first to appear.

Of the books published by black people in the latter half of the eighteenth century, two in particular stand out: the *Letters* of Ignatius Sancho, and the autobiography of *Olaudah Equiano, or Gustavus Vassa, the African.*[7] The two men's lives present something of a contrast, though both were enslaved in childhood. Sancho would have remembered little or nothing of his African origins, having been born aboard a slave ship and sold from the Americas to an English household in the early 1730s at the age of two or three. As a teenager, he was taken up by the abolitionist and humanitarian Duke of Montagu, on whom his character and intelligence had made an impression. The Duke loaned him books, encouraged his ambitions, and took him into service. After a career in which he ended up as the family butler, Sancho was laid low by corpulence and gout, but set up in business as a grocer and chandler in Mayfair with his West Indian wife and growing family, the six 'Sanchonets' as he called them. He was on familiar terms with a number of literary celebrities, Sterne, Garrick and Samuel Johnson being among them. When he died in 1780, some of Sancho's letters were assembled by a family friend (including his best known letter, written to Sterne on the subject of slavery), and published in 1782. His letters reveal a man largely assimilated to English middle-class society, good-natured, easy-going, patriotic, liberal and devout. His literary style is modelled on Sterne's – 'If I am an enthusiast in anything', he writes, 'it is in favour of my Sterne'. Much of his correspondence is devoted to his domestic life: the ups and downs of the children's health, the trade at his shop, the war with 'Washintub's army' in America. There are several letters describing London life, notably those on the Gordon riots – 'I am not sorry I was born in Afric' he remarks, observing the excesses of the mob – and a good many letters in the Shandean manner about nothing in particular:

> Lord! what is man? – and what business have such lazy, lousy, paltry beings of a day to form friendships, or to make connexions? Man is an absurd animal – yea, I will ever maintain it – in his vices, dreadful – in his few virtues, silly – religious without devotion – philosoph[ic] without wisdom – the divine passion (as it is called) love too oft without affection – and anger without cause – friendship without reason – hate without reflection – knowledge (like Ashley's punch in small quantities) without judgment – and wit without discretion. Look into old age, you

will see avarice joined to poverty – lechery, gout, impotency, like three monkeys or London bucks, in a one-horse whisky, driving to the Devil … (p. 6)

But at times he shows his unease to go deeper than pseudo-melancholy antics, particularly when some flying fragment of racial abuse strikes home, when good manners or common sense compel him to conceal or suppress his rage, when he glimpses with discomfort the ugly sources on which even his own comparative prosperity depends:

> Look around upon the miserable fate of almost all of our unfortunate colour – superadded to ignorance – see slavery, and the contempt of those very wretches who roll in affluence from our labours. Superadded to this woeful catalogue – hear the ill-bred and heart-racking abuse of the foolish vulgar … (pp. 31–2)

Sancho's letters show him both attached to, and detached from, the English values of his time. A good example of this detachment expressed in the very process of lamenting the decline of those values occurs in this letter on the recent defeats of the Navy:

> L[or]d S[andwic]h has gone to Portsmouth, to be a witness of England's disgrace – and his own shame. – In faith, my friend, the present time is rather *comique* – Ireland almost in as true a state of rebellion as America – Admirals quarrelling in the West-Indies – and at home Admirals that do not chuse to fight – The British Empire mouldering away in the West, annihilated in the North – Gibraltar going – and England fast asleep. What says Mr. B— to all this? – he is a ministerialist – for my part, it's nothing to me, as I am only a lodger, and hardly that. (p. 213)

Reading letters such as this, one wonders just how much Sancho had been assimilated into the life of eighteenth-century England, for as the final phrase here shows, he is well aware of himself as an alien of a kind, for all the pleasure he feels at the very considerable degree to which friends and colleagues make him feel a part of white society. While he can make cheerful play with his colour – with a touch of popular sentimentality of feeling – 'blessed times for a poor Blacky grocer to hang or drown in'!' (p. 30) or 'Figure to yourself, my dear Sir, a man of convexity of belly exceeding Falstaff – and a black face into the bargain' (p. 238) – the sentimental and the jocular can at times have a sharp edge to them: '… my hearty wishes … to all who have charity enough to admit dark faces into the fellowship of Christians' (p. 143); '… our best respects to Miss

A—s, and to every one who delighteth in Blackamoor greetings' (p. 155). And though his experience generally, living as he did principally in middle-class white society, was of kindness and genuine affection, life was not always so easy: as he tells us of one journey, 'we went by water – had a coach home – were gazed at etc. etc. – but not much abused', but on another occasion 'they stopped us in the town and most generously insulted us' (pp. 101, 209–10).

Equiano, on the other hand, after spending the first ten or eleven years of his life in the seeming stability and security of his native Ibo home, had from the time of his capture and enslavement to face all the cruelties and indignities that the slave trade could impose upon him. Unlike Sancho, Equiano remembered always the early years of his life, described in the opening chapters of his book, and justified in this significant apology:

> I hope the reader will not think I have trespassed on his patience in introducing myself to him with some account of the manners and customs of my country. They had been implanted in me with great care, and made an impression on my mind, which time could not erase, and which all the adversity and variety of fortune I have since experienced served only to rivet and record; for, whether the love of one's country be real or imaginary, or a lesson of reason, or an instinct of nature, I still look back with pleasure on the first scenes of my life, though that pleasure has been for the most part mingled with sorrow. (I.45–6)

Equiano employs his memories of Africa from time to time in his book as a critical strategy, in contrast with his treatment in 'civilised' countries, and also, specifically, with the way he was treated in Islamic society during his visits to Smyrna, and later by the Central American Indians, the Miskito, with whom he spent several months in 1776 as servant to a Dr Irving. The story of Equiano's life makes excellent reading: he begins with a description of Ibo society in the mid-eighteenth century, tells of his capture, his journey to the coast, and his first acquaintance with slave traders, 'white men with horrible looks, red faces, and loose hair' whom he feared were about to eat him. He describes the middle passage, his sale in the West Indies, his purchase by a British naval officer, and his subsequent years as a boy servant in the British Navy. He was re-sold to America but managed to save enough to buy his freedom, and travelled widely in the Americas and Europe as a merchant seaman, a gentleman's valet, and in 1772, as the surgeon's assistant on the Phipps expedition to the Arctic. By the time he published his book in 1789, he had become a leading spokesman for black people in Britain, a regular contributor to the press on the subject of the abolition of the slave trade, and a vigorous propagandist travelling throughout British selling his book, though he did take a little time off to get married to a Cambridgeshire girl, as he tells a friend in a letter:

> Sir, I went to Ireland and was there 8½ months – & sold 1900 copies of my narrative. I came here on the 10th inst. – & I now mean as it seem pleasing to my Good God! – to leave London in about 8 – or 10 days more, and take me a Wife – one Miss Cullen – of Soham in Cambridge shire – & when I have given her about 8 or 10 Days of Comfort, I mean Directly to go to Scotland – and sell my 5th. Editions – I trust that my going about has been of much use to the Cause of Abolition of the accursed Slave Trade . . . (I. xiv–xv)

A contemporary reviewer wrote of the narrative as 'a "round unvarnished tale" . . . written with much truth and simplicity', and particularly in its avoidance of extravagance and sentimentality it convinces the reader of its honesty and authenticity. Apart from its revelation of the horrors of slavery, the narrative is full of lively observation, and Equiano is capable of seeing the absurd aspects of some of his predicaments, and of indulging, tongue-in-cheek, a tendency to feel pretty pleased with himself when his skill, his nerve or his good luck bring him out on top in a tricky situation, as in his account of how he dealt with a drunken Amerindian governor who had stolen the chief's hat, and whose riotous conduct had sent Equiano's white companions running for cover (II.184–7).

Like Sancho, Equiano exhibits a sense of humour, sometimes against himself, as in this splendid passage:

> While we were here an odd circumstance happened to the captain and me, which disappointed us both a great deal. A silversmith, whom we had brought to this place some voyages before, agreed with the captain to return with us to the West Indies and promised at the same time to give the captain a great deal of money, having pretended to take a liking to him, and being, as we thought, very rich. But while we stayed to load our vessel this man was taken ill in a house where he worked, and in a week's time became very bad. The worse he grew the more he used to speak of giving the captain what he had promised him, so that he expected something considerable from the death of this man, who had no wife or child, and he attended him day and night. I used also to go with the captain at his own desire, to attend him, especially when we saw there was no appearance of his recovery: and in order to recompense me for my trouble, the Captain promised me ten pounds

when he should get the man's property. I thought this would be of great service to me, although I had nearly money enough to purchase my freedom if I should get safe this voyage to Montserrat. In this expectation I laid out above eight pounds of my money for a suit of superfine clothes to dance with at my freedom, which I hoped was then at hand. We still continued to attend this man and were with him even on the last day he lived till very late at night, when we went on board. After we were got to bed, about one or two o'clock in the morning, the captain was sent for and informed the man was dead. On this he came to my bed, and waking me, informed me of it, and desired me to get up and procure a light, and immediately go to him. I told him I was very sleepy and wished he would take somebody else with him; or else, as the man was dead and could want no further attendance, to let all things remain as they were till the next morning. 'No, no,' said he, 'we will have the money tonight, I cannot wait till tomorrow, so let us go.' Accordingly I got up and struck a light, and away we both went and saw the man as dead as we could wish. The captain said he would give him a grand burial in gratitude for the promised treasure, and desired that all the things belonging to the deceased might be brought forth. Amongst others, there was a nest of trunks of which he had kept the keys whilst the man was ill, and when they were produced we opened them with no small eagerness and expectation; and as there were a great number within one another, with much impatience we took them out one of the other. At last, when we came to the smallest and had opened it, we saw it was full of papers, which we took to be notes, at the sight of which our hearts leapt for joy, and that instant the captain, clapping his hands, cried out, 'Thank God, here it is.' But when we took up the trunk and began to examine the supposed treasure and long-looked-for bounty, (alas! alas! how uncertain and deceitful are all human affairs!) what had we found! While we thought we were embracing a substance we grasped an empty nothing. The whole amount that was in the nest of trunks was only one dollar and a half, and all that the man possessed would not pay for his coffin. Our sudden and exquisite joy was now succeeded by as sudden and exquisite pain, and my captain and I exhibited for some time most ridiculous figures – pictures of chagrin and disappointment! We went away greatly mortified and left the deceased to do as well as he could for himself as we had taken so good care of him when alive for nothing. (II, pp. 7–11)

He can refer to blackness in comic terms:

A black cook, in melting some fat, overset the pan into the fire under the deck, which immediately began to blaze, and the flame went up very high under the foretop. With the fright, the poor cook became almost white, and altogether speechless. (II, p. 95)

But this is placed in a context of the cruel and vicious exploitation of black people, presented sometimes with devastating bluntness, sometimes with the kind of ironic edge noticed in Sancho, but a deeper ferocity:

> I have often seen slaves, particularly those who were meagre, in different islands, put into scales and weighed, and then sold from three pence to six pence or nine pence a pound. My master, however, whose humanity was shocked at this mode, used to sell such by the lump. (I, 220)

And besides the more obvious barbarities of the slave trade, Equiano constantly describes the lesser, but profoundly painful humiliations suffered by the slaves, and, indeed, the free black people too, the theft by white men of the few possessions they had struggled to acquire, the demands for service on those few days set aside for the black people to relax, the little, nagging, needless cruelties.

Equiano emerges above all as a survivor, though he was still only in his early 50s when he died in 1797. However, he left enough to provide a decent upbringing for his surviving daughter, Johanna, and a legacy of £950 which was paid to her on her twenty-first birthday in 1816.[8]

Several other books of the period by black writers deserve attention. Ottobah Cugoano, a Fanti, formerly a West Indian slave but later personal servant to the court painter, Cosway, published his attack on the slave trade in 1787.[9] The book presents a problem, however, in that a holograph letter written about four years after Cugoano's polemic shows that his English was not good enough for the book to be, like those of Sancho and Equiano, an authentic product of his own hand, and that it must have been at the very least extensively revised. There is some evidence that the reviser might have been Equiano, who was collaborating with Cugoano at the time in representing the cause of the black poor. The book contains plenty of vigorous rhetoric, some interesting comments on the fears of the black people going out on the 1787 settlement to Sierra Leone, and an authentic-sounding account of the author's capture and enslavement. Most other books by black authors of this period are acknowledgedly 'ghosted': readers may find the pieties of the *Narrative* of James Albert Ukawsaw Gronniosaw or John Jea rather hard to take, but there are some sharp observations and powerful feelings expressed, particularly in Gronniosaw's book.[10] There is also the very competent poetry of Phyllis Wheatley, again perhaps too bland and conventionally of its time to impress all readers, though recent commentators have argued the case for deeper commitments.[11] And there is the striking account of slave life by Venture Smith,[12] another great survivor; no Uncle Tom he:

> I earnestly requested my wife to beg pardon of her mistress for the sake of peace, even if she had given no just occasion for offence. But whilst I was thus saying, my mistress turned the blows which she was repeating on my wife to me. She took down her horse whip, and while she was glutting her frenzy with it, I reached out my great black hand, raised it up and received the blows of the whip on it which were designed for my head. Then I immediately committed the whip to the devouring fire. (pp. 17–18)

Venture earned enough money on his own account to buy freedom for himself and his family: 'In the space of six months I cut and corded upwards of four hundred cords of wood. Many other singular and wonderful labours I performed in cutting wood there, which would not be inferior to the one just recited, but for brevity's sake I must omit them' (p. 23). Understandably, Venture is cash-orientated:

> About this time I chartered a sloop of about thirty tons burthen, and hired men to assist me in navigating her. I employed her mostly in the wood trade to Rhode Island, and made clear of all expenses about one hundred dollars with heir in better than one year. I had then become something forehanded and being in my forty-fourth year, purchased my wife Meg, and thereby prevented having another child to buy, as she was then pregnant. I gave forty pounds for her. (pp. 24–5)

Meg, 'whom I married for love and bought with my money', was still alive when Venture was sixty-nine. In his last days, Venture stood six feet one-and-a-half inches, weighed 300 lbs and measured six feet round the waist. His prodigious feats of strength became a legend and were recorded in the 1897 edition of his narrative.

Equiano's autobiography achieved great success: it went into nine editions in his lifetime, was translated into Dutch and German, and appeared in many posthumous editions, the last (apart from modern editions) published in America in 1837. In the early nineteenth century, interest in the slave narrative tended to shift towards the States, where the debate on abolition was more immediate and vital. As a result, we might trace one line of continuity from Equiano through the narratives of Frederick Douglass (1845), William Wells Brown (1847), Henry Bibb (1849) and Solomon Northrup (1854), and on to writers of the twentieth century from Booker T. Washington and W. E. B. Du Bois to Richard Wright, James Baldwin and Ralph Ellison. This is outside the province of the present essay, but the reader might follow it up by way of the work of such critics and scholars as John W. Blassingame, Robert B. Stepto and others referred to in the bibliography. The flow of this literature has been towards the correction of black stereotypes and white attitudes, the creation of a black self-image no longer merely the passive subject of white mythmaking.

It has also had as a recurrent theme the rediscovery and payment of honour to the ancestors. This suggests another line of continuity from Equiano: we saw that a vital measure of conduct and values throughout Equiano's narrative was the memory of his African childhood in Ibo. Much the same might be said of Chinua Achebe's *Things Fall Apart* (1958), the first internationally recognised work of African fiction in English. Achebe has said about this novel: 'Although I did not set about it consciously in that solemn way, I now know that my first book, *Things Fall Apart*, was an act of atonement with my past, the ritual return and homage of a prodigal son'.[13] And at a date almost exactly between Equiano and Achebe appeared a remarkable book by yet another writer of Ibo origins, *West African Countries and Peoples*[14] (1868), by James Africanus Beale Horton, born in Sierra Leone in 1835, the son of an Ibo couple released from slavery and re-settled in Freetown. Horton graduated in medicine from London and Edinburgh Universities, and was appointed an army medical officer, achieving the rank of major. His many books and articles were published in the fields of medicine, ethnology and politics, and the declared aim of his most important book was to examine 'the requirements necessary for establishing . . . self-government'. Its sub-title was *A Vindication of the African Race.*

This is not to say that the three writers see their Ibo origins in the same way. Each of them offers the perspective of his own age and experience. As a Victorian, and very much a man of his time, Horton saw the future of West Africa in terms of the growth of independent states, founded on the best of British religious and political values. But unlike many commentators he had no time for the influential racist theorists of the period, such as Robert Knox, Arthur de Gobineau, Richard Burton and James Hunt. Although

Horton disliked much of what he saw in native African institutions, his 'Vindication' is founded on the human spirit and potential of African peoples, as in his remarks on the Ibo:

> Stout-hearted, or, to use the more common phraseology, big-hearted, they always possess a desire of superiority, and make attempts to attain it, or excel in what is praiseworthy, without a desire of depressing others. To them we may well apply the language of Dryden – 'A noble emulation beats their breasts.' Place an Egboe man in a comfortable position, and he will never rest satisfied until he sees others occupying the same or a similar position. (pp. 157–8)

Along with his 'Vindication' of the African nations of West Africa, Horton has specific recommendations to make of a practical kind, 'in the hope that in process of time their turn will come, when they will occupy a prominent position in the world's history and when they will command a voice in the council of nations'. His proposals for his native Sierra Leone, for instance, include the establishment of 'the University of Western Africa' in Freetown, including in its curriculum 'the study of the physical sciences, which are closely connected with our daily wants and conveniences'; there should be free grammar schools in each of the educational districts, a national bank, a dry dock, an experimental programme of agriculture sustained by local research, a medical school, and so on. Many of his proposals were to be realised, but not until a hundred years later, when the issues facing Africa had cast doubt on what in Horton's day had seemed self-evident. As Christopher Fyfe has said:

> It is no wonder that Horton attracted attention in the early 1960s, the bright confident morning of African independence. In that honeymoon era of euphoric optimism, when Africans and Europeans laid aside old animosities, and a golden future seemed to await the newly independent African states, his visions appeared to have come true. Colonial rule was vanishing. Everywhere African governments were investing massively in the policies he had advocated – economic development, education, medical and sanitary reform. Horton could be unhesitatingly acclaimed as the prophet of the new Africa . . . Now, in the 1970s, his optimism seems perhaps less well grounded.[15]

It is to be hoped, too, that Horton helped to alter British attitudes to Africa, though again many of the prejudices he tried to dispel are still with us. An interesting footnote on these attitudes is to be found in the account of a 'typical' Freetowner, in that adventure story for imperial boyhood, G. H. Henty's *By Sheer Pluck: A Tale of the Ashanti War* (1883):

> 'They are just like children,' Mr. Goodenough said. 'They are always laughing or quarrelling. They are good-natured and passionate, indolent, but will work hard for a time; clever up to a certain point, densely stupid beyond. The intelligence of an average negro is about equal to that of a European child of ten years old. A few, a very few, go beyond this, but these are exceptions, just as Shakespeare was an exception to the ordinary intellect of an Englishman. They are fluent talkers, but their ideas are borrowed. They are absolutely without originality, absolutely without inventive power. Living among white men, their imitative faculties enable them to attain a considerable amount of civilisation. Left alone to their own devices, they retrograde into a state little above their native savagery.' (p. 118)

When they had reached their destination of the Ashanti war, Mr Goodenough and his young friend would have found themselves, were they to be wounded or fall sick, in the medical care of one of these backward citizens of Freetown, Major Africanus Horton.

Along with Horton, one other black writer of the period stands out, Edward Wilmot Blyden, whose best-known book, *Christianity, Islam and the Negro Race*[16] was published in 1887. Blyden's outstanding qualities are marked by his many achievements: he was a scholar in Arabic, Hebrew and the European classics, and fluent in several modern European languages; he was editor of a number of important early West African journals, including *The Liberia Herald* and *The Negro*, the latter founded by himself; he held the chair of classics at Liberia College, and was later President of the College; and his public service to Liberia included appointments as Secretary of State, Minister of the Interior, and ambassador to the Court of St James; he worked in Sierra Leone as director of Mohammedan education, and published many volumes of essays. All this was something of an achievement for a man born in 1832 of humble parents on the small Caribbean island of St Thomas, schoolboy in the mornings, apprentice tailor in the afternoon who, travelling to the United States in his teens, was denied the education for which his talents and his scholastic efforts had clearly fitted him. A man of wit and presence, he could also go for the opposition with the blunt end of a rapier. Here he is, describing his conversations with a disgruntled missionary on the mail-boat to Britain:

He had a great deal to say of the 'hopeless inferiority' of the negro, and was particularly vehement in his denunciations of the Africans of Sierra Leone. He failed, however, to impress me with his own superiority, which I did not recognise half so distinctly as I did his absolute want of good-breeding, his immense vanity and self-conceit, and his marvellous unsuitableness for the work to which he had been appointed on the coast, and in which he had made no movement so important, prudent, and beneficial as when he removed his baggage and his person from the mission premises to the steamer homeward bound, with the resolution never to return.[17]

Like Horton, Blyden was very much a man of his age: but there is also a striking difference. Horton saw the future of Africa in terms of its potential for the growth of a western-style society. Blyden, for all his western Christian background, insisted on the need for Africa to retain its Africanness.

Christianity, Islam and the Negro Race takes up the debate on the future of black people central to Horton's 'Vindication' chapters, but gives it a different direction. A view such as Horton's, says Blyden,

proceeds on the assumption that the two races are called to the same work and are alike in potentiality and ultimate development, the Negro only needing the element of time, under certain circumstances, to become European. But to my mind . . . the two races are not moving in the same groove, with an immeasurable distance between them, but on parallel lines . . . They are not *identical*, as some think, but unequal: they are *distinct* but equal. (p. 277)

And with this assertion of a distinct, shared Negro destiny, Blyden establishes what was to become one of the underlying principles of *nègritude*, a line of racial and political thought that was to be a potent force in the coming century. Also central to the argument of the book is the idea, uneasily assimilated to his own Christian beliefs, that Islam rather than the missionary Christianity he disliked so much, ought to be the unifying religious faith of Africa, another of the major consolidating ideas of black thought in the twentieth century. Blyden was a man of ideas: readers have disagreed with him often enough, but he is not a man to dismiss, and the force of what in his own time sometimes appeared eccentricity has been acknowledged:

During the colonial era in Africa, Blyden's voice sounded an uncertain note – verging on the tragic or ridiculous, according to the reader's own background. Today he speaks to the world of independent Africa in clear tones . . . as the seminal, original, prescient philosopher that a few years ago only a few recognised.[18]

Christopher Fyfe's words are as applicable to black readers in Britain and America as they are to those in Africa, which brings me back to the argument from which I began: the need to find a place for books such as these in British programmes of education.

Equiano's autobiography, because of its interest and its easy availability in paperback, is the only one which could be suggested seriously for school reading. Studies in modern American black fiction and autobiography might, as I suggested earlier, be related both to Equiano and eighteenth-century slave narratives, and to the writings of Frederick Douglass and others in the nineteenth century. Again, if pupils in British schools were to be reading Achebe's *Things Fall Apart*, in many respects a very suitable work of fiction, reference to Equiano, Horton and Blyden could be made to deepen its perspective. But it would be too much to ask pupils to look into the intimidating volumes of Sancho, Horton and Blyden for themselves, even if such works were easily available, which they are not. It was to overcome such a problem in African schools that Lalage Bown prepared her anthology *Two Centuries of African English* (1973) for the Heinemann African Writers Series, and it might well be worthwhile for teachers in British schools to have a look at this anthology as a source of teaching material. I had the same sort of idea in mind when preparing the anthologies *West African Narrative* (1963) and *Through African Eyes* (two vols., 1966). Both of them are now out of print and out of date, but their contents might still be found useful by teachers looking for extracts from African writing, from the eighteenth century to the mid-twentieth, of one to six pages roughly, and selected for classroom use. One of the aims was to offer, for a change, a black writer's view of things usually presented, if at all, through the eyes of white observers: one passage chosen came from C. C. Reindorf's *History of the Gold Coast and Asante* (1895), not the most readable of volumes though of great importance to the West African historian. Reindorf was a Fanti on his mother's side, and had learned his earliest lessons in the history of Ghana from his grandmother, Okako Asase, as oral tales. One such tale, satiric in purpose, embedded in Reindorf's history, was about the reaction of a Fanti king, Firempong, to his first sight of white men:

All the trade with the Danish merchants was placed in his hands. But he had never seen a white man; the reports he used to hear from traders, especially the Akwamus, were that the Europeans were a kind of sea-creature. He therefore expressed his desire of seeing a European, and Mr. Nicolas Kamp, the book-keeper, was commissioned to Da, the capital of Kotokus, to be seen by the king. A grand meeting was held for his reception. In saluting the assembly, Mr. Kamp approached the king, took off his hat, and when he was bowing to salute him, Firempong thought he was an animal who would jump upon him. The king fell down flat from his stool and cried loudly for his wives to assist him. The drummer Adam Malm, whose native name was Kwabena Nyamkum, and Noi Adafi, the government interpreter, did their utmost to convince the poor king that Mr. Kamp was a human being, and that his movements were the mode of Europeans in paying their respect to superiors. The king got up from the ground and sat on the stool, ordered his wives to sit between him and the European and his men. By this he could cool down his fears. Upon seeing the cue, i.e. a tail-like twist of hair hanging down the back of Mr. Kamp (as people were then in the habit of wearing, as the Chinese do nowadays), he said, 'Dear me, all animals have their tails at the extremity of the trunk, but Europeans have theirs at the back of their heads!' The interpreters explained to him that it was no tail, but hairs so twisted. All this while, the king's wives were watching every movement of Mr. Kamp to know whether he was a man or an animal. Not being satisfied yet with all he had seen, the king requested Mr. Kamp to take off his clothes, which he declined to do, saying he might do so at home, when no lady was present. The meeting retired and Mr. Kamp went to his quarters, where a table was prepared for him. During his repast, the king's wives stood by, peeping at him; some said, 'He eats like a man, really he is a human being!' After all, Mr. Kamp took his clothes off before old Firempong, who now could touch him, when he said, 'Ah, you are really a human being, but only too white, like a devil!'

The story may be no masterpiece of English literature, but it makes its point entertainingly and served certain classroom purposes very well. In comic terms, it reverses both the stereotype of the African as 'animal', and as devil, and in mocking simultaneously the assumptions of white superiority, and the dignity of chieftainship, it raises questions about conventional 'authority'. Other extracts included Sancho's description of the Gordon riots of 1780 in London; Blyden's visit to the Pyramids in 1866; an account of a business trip to England made in 1880 by John E. Ocansey of Accra; a story of a South African mixed marriage of 1782 told by the traveller and adventurer Harry Dean (born 1864, the grandson of the famous American black sea-captain, Paul Cuffee).[19] Quite apart from the fact that they are interesting, amusing, or exciting in themselves, as well as being as 'complete' as an extract from a book can be, they raise lively questions: about the social status of the assimilated black man in eighteenth-century London, who can be shocked by the anti-royal, anti-establishment behaviour of the London mob, but censure it with the words 'I am not sorry I was born in Afric'; about the perplexity of the great Pan-African patriot Blyden, rejoicing in his race at the heart of one of the ancient African monuments, the Pyramids, but finding that his guides will not show him the way out until he gives them a 'dash'; or the way in which John Ocansey, who surely could not have read Blake, recreates the effect of Blake's 'Holy Thursday' (*Songs of Innocence*) when describing his visit to a Liverpool school for orphans.

From the West Indies, a spirited local reply to the imperialist historian J. A. Froude's influential *The English in the West Indies*, J. J. Thomas's *Froudacity* (1889); or the Jamaican Mary Seacole's *Wonderful adventures in many lands* (1858), recently reissued as a result of the efforts of Ziggi Alexander and Audrey Dewjee who have drawn attention to the part Mary Seacole played in nursing the Crimean wounded, comparable with the work of Florence Nightingale.[20] The work of Alexander and Dewjee, in fact, is only one striking example of the recent unearthing of forgotten black writing, now starting to gather impetus, a process which, it is to be hoped, publishers will encourage, and which will be reinforced by the appointment of lecturers to university and higher education posts specifically to teach courses on the history of blacks in Britain (as has recently happened at Warwick University). Travellers in Africa were not all of them white: the accounts given by Thomas Birch Freeman, Samuel Adjei Crowther and Benjamin Anderson, along with those of Horton and Blyden, indicate a considerable field of black travel literature in the nineteenth century. Independence movements in mid-twentieth century West Africa had their antecedents in the writings, at the turn of the century, of Solomon Attoh Ahuma, J. E. Casely Hayford and Henry Carr.[21] In the present economic climate it seems unlikely that teaching materials will be available in the form of textbooks, or even xeroxes and stencils. The responsibility for gathering and presenting them is bound to fall on the teacher, and if pupils are to be made aware of the long history of black writing in Britain, a great deal will depend on the teachers' own flexibility, imagination, and knowledge of the field. However a new attitude is called for, not only in the schools,

Paul Edwards

but from academics, who need to be urged and encouraged to set up courses and carry out research in those fields, not simply in the form of special 'black' programmes, but by integrating black history and writing more closely into the traditional syllabus, and from publishers, who, while they are prepared to publish from time to time relevant works in expensive, hardback, library editions, might more generously consider the marketing of these and other books in less expensive, paperback copies.[22]

Notes

1. *Scriptores Historiae Augustae*, ed. David Magie (Loeb Library, London, 1922), I.424–7; Anthony R. Birley: *Septimus Severus: The African Emperor* (London, 1971), pp. 265–6.
2. Roger Warwick: '*The skeletal remains*' in L. P. Wenham: *The Romano-British Cemetery at Trentholme* (London, 1968), pp. 111–76; Paul Edwards and James Walvin: *Black Personalities in the Era of the Slave Trade* (London, 1983), pp. 3–4.
3. Recorded in the *Accounts of the Lord High Treasurer of Scotland*, ed. Sir James Balfour Paul (Edinburgh, 1902), II.465–77; III.148, 182; IV.51, 61, 62, 64, 82, 100, 116, 119, 129, 401; V.328; *The Historie and Cronicles of Scotland by Robert Lindesay of Pitscottie*, ed. E. G. Mackay (Edinburgh, 1899), I.242–4.
4. *The Poems of William Dunbar*, ed. James Kinsey (Oxford, 1979), p. 106.
5. Edwards and Walvin: *Black Personalities*, pp. 5–13.
6. *The Will of Thomas Papillon, 1700–1*, Kent Archives, V.1015.T.44.
7. *Letters of the late Ignatius Sancho [with] Memoirs of His Life by Joseph Jekyll* (London, 1782); reprinted with an introduction by Paul Edwards in the Dawson Colonial History Series (London, 1968).
   The Interesting Narrative of the Life of Olaudah Equiano, or Gustavus Vassa, the African, written by himself (2 vols., London 1789); reprinted in the Dawson Colonial History Series with an introduction and notes by Paul Edwards (London, 1969); selections in the Heinemann African Writers Series, *Equiano's Travels*, ed. Paul Edwards (London, 1969).
   There is a general discussion of African writing in the eighteenth century in Edwards and Walvin, *Black Personalities*, chapter 4, and selections from five writers appear in chapter 5. Equiano, Sancho and Cugoano are discussed by Paul Edwards, 'Three West African writers of the 1780s', in *The Slave's Narrative: Texts and Contexts* eds. Charles T. Davis and Henry L. Gates (Oxford, New York, 1985), pp. 175–198.
8. *Papers of John Audley*, Cambridgeshire Record Office, R. 63. 12.
9. *Thoughts and Sentiments on the Evil and Wicked Traffic of the Slavery and Commerce of the Human Species . . . by Ottobah Cugoano, a Native of Africa* (London, 1787): reprinted in the Dawson Colonial History Series with an introduction and notes by Paul Edwards (London, 1969).
10. *A Narrative of the Most Remarkable Particulars in the Life of James Albert Ukawsaw Gronniosaw . . . as related by Himself* (Bath, n.d., c. 1770); *The Life, History and Unparallel Sufferings of John Jea, the African Preacher, compiled and written by himself* (Portsea, n.d., c. 1815). Gronniosaw's book was reprinted, along with several others, in a Kraus Reprint (Nendeln, 1972). The other books in this volume are as follows: *Narrative of the Lord's Wonderful Dealings with John Marrant* (1785); *Narrative of the Uncommon Sufferings*

and Surprizing Deliverance of Briton Hammon (1760); Jupiter Hammon: *Winter Piece* (1782), *An Address to the Negroes in the State of New York* (1787), and *An Evening's Improvement* (n.d.); and *A Narrative of the Proceedings of the Black People during the Late Awful Calamity by A.J. and R.A.* [Absalom Jones and Richard Allon] (1794). The volume also includes a reprint of the poems of Phillis Wheatley.

11. Phillis Wheatley: *Poems on Various Subjects, Religious and Moral* (London, 1773); *The Poems of Phillis Wheatley*, ed. Julian D. Mason (Chapel Hill, 1966); William H. Robinson: *Phillis Wheatley: A Bio-Bibliography* (Boston, 1981).

12. Venture Smith: *A Narrative of the Life and Adventures of Venture* (1798); the same, ed. H. M. Selden (Middletown, Conn., 1897) with the addition of further information about Venture supplied by his family and friends.

13. Chinua Achebe: *Morning Yet on Creation Day* (London, 1975), 70.

14. Horton's book was republished by Edinburgh University Press in the African Heritage Series in 1969, with an introduction by Professor George Shepperson. Horton's *Letters on the Political Condition of the Gold Coast* (1870) has also been reissued in an edition by E. A. Ayandele (London, 1970), and there is also a volume of selections from Horton's work, *Africanus Horton: The Dawn of Nationalism in Modern Africa* ed. Davidson Nicol (London, 1969). There is an excellent short biography by Christopher Fyfe: *Africanus Horton: West African Scientist and Patriot* (Oxford, 1972).

15. Fyfe, *Africanus Horton*, p. 158.

16. Blyden's book was republished by Edinburgh University Press in the African Heritage Series in 1967, with an introduction by Christopher Fyfe. For a good biography, see Hollis R. Lynch: *Edward Wilmot Blyden: Pan-Negro Patriot 1832–1912* (Oxford, 1967); very informative but rather loosely organised is Edith Holden: *Blyden of Liberia* (New York, 1966). *The Selected Letters*, ed. Hollis R. Lynch are also available (New York, 1978).

17. Edward W. Blyden: *From West Africa to Palestine* (Freetown, 1873), p. 27.

18. Introduction to *Christianity, Islam and the Negro Race*, xvi.

19. *Through African Eyes*, ed. Paul Edwards (Cambridge, 1966), I.51; II.82; II.37; II.11.

20. Mary Seacole's autobiography was reissued by the Falling Wall Press in 1984. There is a short article on Mary Seacole by Ziggi Alexander and Audrey Dewjee in *History Today* XXXI, September 1981, p. 45.

21. A useful survey of African political writers, including these three, is to be found in Robert W. July: *The Origins of Modern African Thought* (London, 1968).

22. The author gratefully acknowledges the assistance of a research grant from the British Academy which enabled the production of this essay.

4 Alexander Harris's *The Emigrant Family* and afro-black people in colonial Australia

IAN DUFFIELD

Outside Australia, where his works have been in vogue in certain circles since their rediscovery from 1953 onwards by the distinguished historian Manning Clark and others, the mid-nineteenth-century writings of Alexander Harris are little known, except perhaps among those interested in the study of early colonial Australian life. Indeed, between 1953, when Manning Clark published the first modern edition of Harris's autobiographical work *Settlers and Convicts, or Recollections of Sixteen Years' Labour in the Australian Backwoods*,[1] and 1961, when the later autobiographical work, *Religio Christi*, was republished under the title *The Secrets of Alexander Harris*,[2] his very identity was the subject of lively speculation in Australia. In fact he was that classic export from nineteenth-century Britain to the Australian colonies, the ne'er-do-well son of a respectable English family. His father was a prosperous, sober nonconformist clergyman, and the young Harris was well-educated. However, as such young men will, he developed a taste for fast women, strong drink and adventure. He apparently thought that enlistment in the army as a trooper in the Life Guards would aid the indulgence of these pleasures, but soon found the discipline of army life distasteful, and so deserted. Far from disowning him, his obliging family petitioned the army for his discharge – which very naturally was refused *prior* to his surrender. Rather than face a court martial, young Harris and his family decided on his rapid and clandestine departure for New South Wales. This was in 1825, and he was to remain in the colony for sixteen years, roaming about, undertaking a variety of occupations, keenly and sympathetically observing the formative years of a new nation. Thus a rogue went voluntarily to a colony of rogues, to which, ironically, he might well have been transported as a convict had the military authorities been able to lay their hands on him.

Perhaps it was this mode of emigration that made Harris sympathetic to the convicts, ex-convicts and their descendants who, in the period before cheap assisted emigration and the lure of gold, formed the mass of New South Wales white society. In his writings, all of which drew heavily on his Australian experience, he is frequently critical of those with wealth and those in authority in the colony. This coincides with a point of view still strongly held by many Australians; that the convicts were victims of oppression and resisters of tyranny; and that colonial officials were arbitrary and corrupt, and the overlapping class of rich squatters, the main employers of convict labour, were tyrannical and greedy. Although modern scholarship has questioned these romantic certitudes, it is equally true that for thirty years Australian social historians have drawn deeply on Harris's writings for information about life, especially in the bush, in the period 1825–40. They have been encouraged to do so by his commendable ability not to let what he observed be coloured by his preconceptions. Nor does he draw a veil over the typical vices (as he saw them) of the convicts, such as drunkenness, sexual promiscuity when the opportunity arose, and thievishness, notably in the acute form of bushranging or outlawry. However, as he himself freely admits, he was for long not merely a drinker but a drunk, and although not admitting to having had sexual relations with prostitutes and loose women, freely admits to having sought the company of such. These he met in the long notorious Sydney district of The Rocks (now safely sanitised as a picturesque tourist attraction, complete with wine bars and duty free shops, but not a place a modern scapegrace would think to go whoring, nor a place where unwary seamen would be likely to be knocked over the head and robbed). However, his great Australian romance was with the bush rather than Sydney whores. He admired the comradeship, fortitude and skills of the bush men who worked the great sheep and cattle properties in the interior. These men were, of course, almost entirely convicts, ex-convicts or the children of convicts, the very stuff of 'The Australian Legend'.

One of the constant complaints of high-minded persons in Britain who concerned themselves with such matters was that the tone of the Australian convict colonies, far from reforming the convicts, made them morally worse. Be that as it may, for Harris life in Australia was ultimately a reforming experience, and when he returned to England it was with something like the acute religious mania of the reformed drunkard and rake. As the years went by, this trend became more pronounced, and unfitted him for normal human companionship. He departed for the United States in 1851, and died in Canada in 1874, but during these years his second wife Ursula and three children drifted apart from him, and ultimately separated from him permanently. He died a solitary death.

If the author of *The Emigrant Family* was something of an oddity, so is this work itself, his sole novel. It was published in London, in 1849, and sold sufficiently well for there to be a second edition, significantly retitled *Martin Beck: or, The Story of an Australian Settler*, in 1852. Indeed, there is almost a catalogue of oddities about this work. To begin with – although commentators on the novel have made surprisingly little of this – its central character is, in the terminology of the book, a 'negro' (lower case 'n'), born in Australia of 'negro' convict parents. I have chosen to use the rather cumbersome phrase 'Afro-Black', as 'Negro' (even capitalised) is now considered offensive by many black people, while in the Australian context 'black' would normally be taken to refer to Aborigines, a quite distinct group. Harris's views on *them* will be discussed later. These terminological problems apart, the oddity here is that an Afro-Black central figure should be considered remotely plausible in a novel set in the New South Wales of, one presumes, the 1830s. No country has been less suspected of having an Afro-Black presence than Australia. Search the many excellent works on early colonial Australian social history, and specifically on transportation, at leisure. You will either find no reference whatsoever to such people or at most a fleeting reference to an odd individual. And this, after all, is what everyone would expect.

In the introduction to his novel, Harris does give an explanation of sorts about this apparently fundamental oddity:

> Of course, all must not expect to meet with a Martin Beck for an overseer; but with the single exception of the introduction of a character necessary to furnish the tale with sufficient plot to interest the lovers of romance, everything exhibited is a simple copy from actual everyday life.
>
> The use, moreover, which I have made of the character of Beck will be found a most legitimate and important one: that of exhibiting to the new settler the various great errors which may be fallen into and must be guarded against. For, in fact, I have merely concentrated in him

singly, but what the settler may easily enough meet in a more dissipated form at the hands of several.[3]

This explanation has satisfied, at any rate, the novel's modern editor, the critic and philologist, W. S. Ramson. Ramson appears to accept that Beck is merely, as it were, a chocolate flavouring to allure readers who might choke on 'interesting and useful information about life in the colony'. This is art and part with the novel's rather creaking love sub-plots, in forming a general device; 'using a romantically contrived plot to display a full and fair conspectus of Australian society'.[4] All this has something to recommend it beyond Harris's own explanation, for the series of non-fiction works which preceded the novel included, as Ramson has pointed out, one out-and-out 'handbook for emigrants'.[5] *Settlers and Convicts* too is, to some extent, a work of this sort. In *The Emigrant Family* there are passages that could be read virtually as handbook instructions for the would-be emigrant, detailing, for instance, the stores, utensils and equipment that must be purchased in Sydney before proceeding on a journey to a distant up-country station.

However, Harris's 'explanation' and Ramson's interpretation are unsatisfactory. Now consider a second oddity; the portrayal of Martin Beck is highly unusual, possibly unique, among fictional portrayals of Afro-Blacks by white English-speaking authors in the nineteenth century. Martin Beck is emphatically not a forerunner of Uncle Tom, nor is he the faithful 'darky' of the type that surfaces later in the century in the boys' adventure stories of G. A. Henty. He is not a bloodthirsty savage, although he eventually turns to violence. He is emphatically not idle, simple or childlike. And he is not a slave to his sexual passions. Harris does not achieve the impossible, and provide the reader with an authentic, broad and deep psychological study of an Afro-Black man in New South Wales in the age of squattocracy. Yet, after a remarkably cursory introduction of his emigrant family, the Bractons, and a little more care over the delineation of Reuben Kable, the Australian-born hero of the book (and the only man in it to be a match for Beck), Harris takes immense pains, even perhaps labours, to establish an Afro-Black remarkably different in almost all respects from any of the stereotypes I have just discarded.

There is only one trait attributable to Beck which smacks of the kind of racial stereotyping that had long been established in English writing about Afro-Blacks. Beck is described as growing up in Australia 'with all the fire of Africa in his veins', this being specifically a sexual reference, linked with his rejection by young Australian white women. There was 'none among them for him'. However, it is made quite clear at the same time, and repeated as the novel proceeds, that Beck is not the 'lustful blackamoor' of the type that can be found in English literature at least from the renaissance onwards. On the contrary, Harris endows his creation with 'a fine and, even in some degree, noble person', whose countenance lacked 'the expression that low vices imprint' or traces of 'habitual debauchery of any kind'. Given Harris's own growing religious obsessions, and not least obsessions about purity at the time the novel was written, Beck's chastity, when linked with his 'fire', suggests exceptional virtue, or at least sexual self-control. With his wide experience of New South Wales, Harris would have been well aware that his kind of virtue was a comparative rarity in the colony. In Sydney, and wherever white women of the lower classes are available, prostitution, casual sex and cohabitation were rife. In the bush, where few white women were to be found, buggery was common enough, as rape of Aboriginal women. Beck's vices are quite other; 'a continuous and vigilant endeavour to conceal', 'unbounded avidity' and 'selfishness'. All this hints at a man whose response to social, and specifically sexual isolation, is indifference or even contempt for others; the manipulation of those less intelligent or self-controlled; and the burning desire to achieve power through wealth. In the latter, on an individual basis, Beck actually anticipates a whole school of thought and action within the Pan-African Movement![6]

A few other points are worth extrapolating from Harris's initial delineation of Beck. Beck is a 'native', that is to say born in Australia, as opposed to an immigrant. This generally goes a good way in anyone's favour with Harris, sympathetic as he was to distinctively Australian virtues. Beck speaks English as well as an Englishman, though using Australian idioms; in fact, he speaks better than 'our mechanics at home'. He dresses exceptionally well and neatly for one of his class. From the very beginning Beck dominates Lieutenant Bracton and his son Willoughby. A master of bush skills as well as of most men, Beck is hired not only as the carpenter but also the overseer for their newly acquired station, on terms effectively dictated by himself. He chooses the hands, and arranges the purchase of those indispensable items for a settler departing from Sydney into the bush, a bullock cart, a bullock team and stores and utensils. Without his energy and expertise, the Bractons would be lost – the typical fate of a 'new chum' in New South Wales without the guidance of a 'native'.

This is a very unusual portrayal of a 'negro' for a British writer in the year 1849. Despite his growing yen for evangelical christianity and its good works, Harris is evidently unaffected by the standard British abolitionist picture of Afro-Black people as supplicants, helpless, humble and grateful.[7] He is even further removed from that vitriolic portrayal of idle, undisciplined 'niggers', subversive of all moral or civilised order unless under drastic white control, that came from the pen of Thomas Carlyle in his notorious tract *An Occasional Discourse on the Nigger Question* (1849). Indeed, from a Carlylian viewpoint, apart from his colour, as initially presented Beck is almost an ideal type! If one is to look for parallels in fiction writing, John Buchan's Rev. Laputa in *Prester John* – a work written with the ideology and sensibility of a later and different age – would seem closer. Admittedly Beck's aspirations are almost purely and selfishly individual, and never reach the grandeur of Laputa's plan for the restoration of a great African ruled empire. However, even Beck does on one occasion muse: 'Why should I not go back amongst the men and women of my own kind? They would know I was one of themselves: they would not eat *me*. But it won't do yet; I must have more money'. (p. 158) Again Harris seems to display an uncanny prescience here of Pan-African yearnings among the Africans of the Diaspora for a return to their motherland. What he knew (if anything) about 'Back to Africa' movements up to 1849, or what he may later have learned about such movements while living in North America, remains conjectural. However, by the end of the novel Beck's last bold if despairing plan is to seize a small vessel and escape by sea, having wreaked revenge on Kable and the Bractons.

In plot, *The Emigrant Family* is over-complicated and exceeds Harris's narrative skills in many places, competent though he is at straightforward descriptions of bush scenes and life. Within a complicated mishmash of events, Beck is almost invariably the prime mover; others react, for good or ill, to his initiatives. He not only dominates men of his own class, manipulating them to his purposes through ruthless exploitation of their drunkenness, fecklessness, greed or stupidity, but, as we have seen, is more than a match for the Bracton men. Only the women see through him from the beginning, but for Harris women, though delightful if young and respectable, are irrational, intuitive creatures, who swoon their way through the novel, either in ecstasy or terror. *The Emigrant Family* would provide much more conventional illustration of sexism than of racism in fiction, though it has plenty of the crudest racism in its portrayal of Aborigines.

Beck's grand plan is to become rich, understandably enough in a colony where wealth and power were related with crude directness. Free of the vices of drunkenness and whoring by which the colonial lower orders commonly dissipated their often quite substantial earnings, he is not content with gradual accumulation. In the key passage on Beck's character and motivation, in which it is also claimed that 'the character of Martin Beck is not a fictitious one; but one which the writer had long and ample opportunities of studying', contradicting the introduction to the novel, Harris writes:

> Beck was a man whose abilities compelled homage; but the contempt of society had repelled him – insulated him; first made him selfish and then rendered him cunning. And that cunning, isolation and selfishness, is at this period a complete definition of his character. He was no drunkard, no petty thief, no libertine; on the contrary he delighted in labour, in economy, and – but for the vice that was so singularly swallowing up his whole nature – in manliness. But man was his enemy. Then what faith had he to keep? None, except to himself. How was he to keep that? He thought, by getting power. What was power as he had the opportunity of discerning? Wealth. (p. 69)

Without exonerating Beck, this appears to be as much an attack on society as on Beck himself. Within the novel there are examples of the worst kind of colonial big-wig; Dr Mercer, and the wealthy landowner and magistrate Major Jennings, a high-handed, mean-minded and ignorant local tyrant of the type that Harris also pilloried in *Settlers and Convicts*. But Jennings and Mercer have wealth, status and power, although none of Beck's talents and virtues. Even before the action of the novel starts, Beck, 'along with his mechanical work in the bush', has also 'pursued the system of cattle stealing, till he had possessed himself of several hundred head.' As overseer of the Bractons' Rocky Springs cattle and sheep station, Beck soon makes himself indispensable, but his energies are directed to enriching himself at the expense of his employer by stealing cattle and secreting them in the nearby mountains. At the same time he sets about the ensnarement and ruination of an honest but cantankerous Welsh convict station hand, John Thomas, who is all the more the object of Beck's venom for having a sweetheart and being a general favourite with the Bracton ladies. Beyond this, Beck is soon aiming at the ruination of his employer, thus to acquire Rocky Springs cheaply, completing a transformation from covert cattle thief to wealthy landowner.

Harris cannot allow Beck to succeed in this grand design. Gradually circumstances turn against him, driving him to more and more desperate and reckless expedients, including violence. He incites 'myalls' or 'wild' Aborigines to attack Rocky Springs when the men are absent, and incidentally turns out to have a wide knowledge of Aboriginal speech and custom. By this time the 'decent' English local magistrate, Mr Hurley, has already penetrated his plot against Thomas and his depredations on Bracton's cattle. But although ruthless, he is not yet a man of blood; 'Beck, however reckless in matters of ordinary honesty, felt shocked at the anticipation of bloodshed', and attempts to restrain the myalls 'within due bounds'. Nevertheless, in the attack, the Aborigines find a keg of rum, get drunk, and a bloody massacre is imminent.[8] The Bracton womenfolk are saved in the nick of time, above all through the Australian pluck and daring of Reuben Kable. Then Kable, by confronting Beck with his earlier life of crime, and promising to inform Lieutenant Bracton of it, drives Beck into the life of a hunted outlaw bushranger.

Even as a bushranger, Beck easily dominates, and is far above in human stature, his little band of associates. They are of the type that modern Australians would refer to as 'ratbags'. They are feckless, drunken and stupid; one informs, and is ruthlessly executed by Beck, his first and only murder. At last, seeing nothing left but revenge and escape, with unquenchable spirit Beck leads his gang to Kable's property on the coast, pursued by Kable and the military. Haunted by the murder he has committed, his personality now begins to disintegrate. He begins to drink, and on the eve of his death he has lost all his old coolness and judgement; 'now he neither told his comrades, nor comprehended himself what he meant to do; his wrath refused to be limited to a form, – his only feeling was a maddening desire to reach the field for setting it loose'. Above all, he seems to wish to humiliate the womenfolk of his enemies. Earlier he has planned, unsuccessfully, to descend on Rocky Springs, and shave the heads of Lieutenant Bracton's daughter Marianna and niece Katherine (an indignity inflicted on convict women at the Parramatta penitentiary). Now it is Kable's sister Mary who is to be terrified, though there is no hint of intended rape. But even at the moment before attempting this final outrage, Beck, biding his time in the bush, momentarily recalls his earlier vision, which turns out to include the equality and greatness of his race:

> There, within little more than a gun-shot, lay one whom he remembered a magnate in the land, sleeping proudly in his own mausoleum. *Who had destined him to any meaner grave? Was he not a man? Who could prove that white in colour was greater than black?* (p. 401)

The last three sentences (emphasised by the author of this essay) could serve as Martin Beck's epitaph. They seem to indicate that, at the end of his life, he acknowledges a wider purpose than self-advancement. But the mood soon changes as he recalls 'the true stress of the case'. All that is left is 'true African hate'. If assertion through worldly elevation is not possible, then he will assert himself through revenge. Shortly afterwards, mere melodrama overtakes this heroic and tragic moment. Beck is shot by Willoughby Bracton while in the act of twisting Mary Kable's arm. Mary and Willoughby are, it will be no surprise to learn, in love. The novel then peters out, with all the leading young men and women marrying each other and anticipating a future of prosperity and happiness.

So much for Martin Beck, a fictional Afro-Black in early colonial Australia. Yet the puzzle remains as to why Harris, who was at pains to give his novel Australian authenticity, should invent such a central figure. Despite Harris's claims that Beck was based on an actual individual, nothing could seem more fanciful, or even fantastical. However, recent and previously unpublished research[9] reveals that, far from being fanciful, Harris is displaying a hitherto unsuspected level of observation and knowledge about the society of early colonial New South Wales. This is that from the First Fleet in 1787/8, up to the end of transportation of convicts to the colony in 1842, Afro-Blacks were scattered among the much larger numbers of white convicts. It will be interesting to see if the Black First Fleet convicts are remembered in Australia's bicentennial celebrations in 1988.

Within the period 1788–1842, I have been able to identify, mainly from *Indents of Convict Ships* in the archives office of New South Wales, 390 convicts who were without question Afro-Blacks; 373 males and 17 females. This is, I am certain, substantially less than the total. To begin with, I have excluded all doubtful cases. Many convicts are physically described in the indents as dark-haired, dark-eyed and dark complexioned. Such people, although no doubt predominantly 'white' (many Irish are given such descriptions), could easily include some people of partially African descent. Before 1812, indents give no physical descriptions, and few other details such as place of birth. Thus, until the second decade of the nineteenth century for males, and the third decade for females, there are only random rather than systematic sources for identifying Afro-Black transportees, many of whom also have typical British names. (None have the name Beck.) Given all this, it is safe to say that the actual input of Afro-Black convicts into New South Wales was substantially higher than my figure of 390. 500 would be conservative, 600 possible. Preliminary evidence suggests that hundreds may also have been sent to Van Diemen's Land.[10] Whatever the total, they seem to have been overlooked because not supposed to have been an element among Australia's convict transportees. For example, the Chartist William Cuffay is the only Afro-Black mentioned in George Rudé's *Protest and Punishment* (1978). Rudé's remit was to identify social and political protesters among a mass of criminal convicts. Yet the New South Wales Afro-Black convicts included two other Black Chartists; John Tharpe, one of the leaders of the Montego Bay rebellion in Jamaica (1831–2) as well as several others involved in that event; David Stuurman, the last independant Khoikhoi chieftain from the Cape Colony; arsonists from the West Indies and Mauritius and mutinous black soldiers from the West Indies and the Cape Colony.[11] I would also maintain that even what look like commonplace criminal offences may not be so, when committed by people living under the shadow of black slavery. To such people, theft from the masters was a justified act of resistance rather than a crime. Such is the implication of the Jamaican proverb, 'massa's horse, massa's grass'.

So in New South Wales, hundreds of Afro-Black convicts took their place alongside roughly 68,000 white males and 12,000 white females. If invisible to twentieth century historians, they were

surely noticeable enough to contemporaries, even though there is
no evidence to suggest that they were kept in segregated groups
within the convict system, nor that they formed separate communities after completing their sentences.

All this puts Martin Beck, and Harris's novel generally, in a new
and more realistic light. Yet, in relation to the historical evidence,
Beck does pose problems. For instance Harris makes Beck the child
of Afro-Black convict parents, not a transportee himself. With so
few Afro-Black women being transported, the chances of an Afro-
Black man finding an Afro-Black wife were, to say the least,
remote. There are unlikely to be many Afro-Black female transportees concealed by gaps in the historical evidence, for among the
New South Wales convicts in general there was a ratio of over five
males to every female. Partial deprivation of the company of
women was the experience of *all* male convict transportees, not
only of the Martin Becks of the colony. Among the Afro-Black
convicts identified, there is only one married couple.[12] So there is
something very unconvincing in Beck having an Afro-Black mother,
and if Harris is right in his assumption that a black male would be
cold-shouldered by white females, then Beck remains a very
unlikely native-born Australian. Furthermore, Harris describes
Beck's parents as 'from different parts of the British Islands: both
blacks of American birth'. These ambiguous words could either
mean they were convicted in the West Indies, and born either there
or elsewhere in the Americas (e.g. in the USA); or that they were
convicted in Britain, but born in the Americas. For early transportees, the latter case would be more apt. All the identified Afro-
Black transportees to New South Wales up to 1819 were convicted
in Britain, but most were born in the West Indies or North America.
Indeed, the same could be said, as far as natal place goes, of many
in the large black population of late eighteenth and early nineteenth
century Britain. However, in Harris's day in New South Wales, and
especially in the 1830s and early 1840s, almost all the Afro-Black
transportees were natives of and transported from the West Indies,
the Cape Colony or Mauritius, with West Indians predominating.
The practice in these territories of transporting black convicts to
Australia was prohibited by a Colonial Office circular in 1837.[13]
(However, this prohibition seems to have been widely ignored.) So
Harris may have assumed that, as was the case in the 1830s, most
Afro-Black transportees were West Indians.

None of Harris's other writings show more than a passing interest in Afro-Black people, either in Britain or in New South Wales. Yet his few references seem to suggest that he saw them as a normal part of the social scene, whether in London,[14] Sydney or the New South Wales bush. He never expresses surprise at their presence. As a young man in London, aged eighteen, he had noted 'the swart giant African with the cymbals' in the band of the Horse Guards.[15] His wonder at this was no more than his general wonder at life in the London streets, and not surprisingly. Black musicians had long been in vogue in smart regiments in the British army.[16] Recalling in 1858 his early days in Sydney, boozing in a sly grog shop in The Rocks called 'The Sheer Hulk', he described with appalled fascination the following scene:

> In the mid-area danced bearded men, many of them with their shirt sleeves rolled up to their very shoulders, amidst women the unseemliest in nature, haggard and hollow-eyed and sallow, their hair dishevelled, capless or with their caps awry, smoking their pipes as they vaulted crazily and awkwardly hither and thither; and mingling with them gentle young girls, with beauty still in their features and grace in their forms; if not even lingering tokens of bashfulness and reclaimability. The huge malformed negro who fiddled was capering with the rest.[17]

Harris's retrospective horror of this scene, in which the black fiddler seems to be the ultimate image of depravity, seems to stem not least from the intimate proximity of the fiddler to white women. Perhaps this could be the very fiddler (called Francis), who according to the newspaper *The Australian* of 2 March 1838 had cohabitated with a white woman who had died and been the subject of an inquest.[18]

Settlers and Convicts provides two further references to Afro-Blacks in New South Wales. One, of 'American negro descent', was also like Beck in being a highly skilled bush sawyer, earning high wages by his industry. His partner was an Irishman, the two engaging in friendly rivalry in feats of skill and strength.[19] So in the world of work, as well as of leisure, black and white New South Walians might associate on terms of easy equality (although undoubtedly such comradeship did not commonly extend to Aborigines). Secondly, and even more significant is the reference in *Settlers and Convicts* to Billy Blue, the Sydney ferryman. Blue arrived in Sydney as a convict with a seven year sentence in 1801,

J. B. East: *Portrait of Billy Blue*

having been sentenced in Maidstone, Kent, in 1796; though another source connects him with the Nore Mutiny of 1797.[20]

In a passage presaging the circumstances of Beck's parents in *The Emigrant Family*, Harris says of Blue:

> The old man – who had a little grant of land at the water's edge, given him, I believe, by one of the governors in those early days when it was considered that a poor man was as entitled to his small grant as the rich one to his proportionately larger – was just come over from the Sydney side with a passenger. He told us, with quite a fatherly sort of authority, that he had been across a good many times that day; that we must pull him over to the other side, and he would take the boat back. The 'Old Commodore' being considered to possess a sort of universal freedom of speech to everybody, no demur was made. We pulled him across in his own boat, and paid him our fares for pulling himself back again.[21]

This passage reveals the accuracy and extent of Harris's knowledge of New South Wales and its personalities. Everything he says about Blue can be verified from other contemporary sources. His nickname seems to date from an earlier period in his life than his long service as the sole licensed ferryman across Sydney harbour from The Rocks to the north shore. In 1811 Governor Macquarie appointed him 'Watchman of the Heaving Down Place in Sydney Cove, to have Charge thereof'.[22] In 1818 he lost his position, and served a year's sentence, through being involved in smuggling rum.[23] This mishap neither removed Macquarie's fondness for him, as is made clear by the subsequent grant of a ferry and, as Harris says, a land grant,[24] nor diminished his great and general popularity with the people of Sydney. In his obituary in the *Sydney Gazette and New South Wales Advertiser* of 8 May 1834, the comment is made that 'as a public functionary, Billy had not the fortune to evade, like his betters, the informers of his day, or to enrich himself by the profits of his avocation'. Like Martin Beck, he was merely emulating the unscrupulous grabbing of wealth by many of the colony's big men. This obituary also confirms Blue's good natured but firm assertion of his own dignity and consequence, if not as one of the rich and powerful, yet certainly as a man. For he was a man:

> To whom the very urchins lifted their caps in token of respect. 'No rows!' 'Go-go my child – true-blue for ever' now and then found utterance as the obsequious citizens struck their ensigns to the Commodore; and if they did not (and the eye of Billy was always at work), the whole street would ring with his screams and abuse. 'You

brute – you long-legged brute – forget the Commodore!' and his stick
would ring upon the stones in cadence to the melodious sound of his
sweet voice, invoking vengeance on the recreant.

Blue's self-assertion against powerful and wealthy men, as well as
ordinary citizens, is shown by his 1823 petitions to Governor
Brisbane, complaining at the attempt by a wealthy settler, Edward
Wollstonecraft, to take over his ferry.[25] It is quite in character that
the 'Old Commodore' would make Harris and his companion row
the ferry *and* pay the fare. The probability is that between 1825 and
Blue's death in 1834 Harris used this ferry many times, and that
like everyone else who lived or sojourned from time to time in
Sydney, he knew much about the ferryman.

If this supposition is true, then it is also likely that Harris was
aware that the old man had a large family of three sons and three
daughters. However, as a model for Beck's family background, the
Blue family has a fatal flaw. For Billy Blue's wife, Elizabeth
William, whom he married on 27 April 1805, was a white
woman.[26] This does not seem to have excited any comment in
Sydney, which suggests that it was regarded as a perfectly
commonplace event. So it can be inferred that Harris was well
aware that a relationship stable enough for the conception and
rearing of six children was possible between an Afro-Black man
and a white woman in New South Wales. To reinforce the point,
some of Blue's children certainly married white people in their turn,
and it would be interesting to know how many descendants of this
remarkable old patriarch are alive in New South Wales today.[27]
Certainly, at the beginning of the century direct descendants of Billy
Blue were proud to be publicly identified as such in the Sydney
press.[28] The inevitability of Martin Beck's social and especially
sexual isolation begins to look rather suspect.

Before anyone, including myself, can pontificate on the sexual,
marital and family life of Afro-Black transportees in New South
Wales, or Australia generally, much genealogical work needs to be
done. But it seems unlikely that Blue was an isolated exception.
After all, a high proportion of the Australian convicts came from
urban Britain's lower classes, and brought with them the attitudes
and values of those classes. We know that by the later eighteenth
century, British racists were beginning to wring their hands about
the association of white women of the lower classes (and some from
high society) with black men, especially in London.[29] We know

"THE OLD COMMODORE,"
BILLY BLUE.

J. Carmichael: 'The Old Commodore'. Billy Blue

that, in not a few instances, black men formally married white women, as well as having casual sexual relations with them, in eighteenth and early nineteenth century Britain. No one has ever found that this kind of thing led to affrays and riots, although riot and affray were then common enough in British towns and cities. We also know that a high proportion of the so-called 'Black poor' of late eighteenth century London lived in precisely those districts, such as St Giles, that produced a constant stream of convict transportees. So the white lower classes in Harris's New South Wales would have seen nothing obnoxious, unnatural or unusual in relationships between Afro-Black men and white women. Thus one of the greatest oddities of *The Emigrant Family* is Harris's assumption that Martin Beck would be unable to find a woman to share her life with him, not because of the comparative dearth of women in the colony, but because of his race and colour. Yet, as we have seen, Harris had recorded one black man in intimate proximity with white women, and in all probability knew about Billy Blue's family. Did Harris find the idea of sexual relations between a black man and a white woman so unpalatable that he strayed from his usual practice, and allowed what he believed to stand in the way of what he observed? Did he, at any rate, believe that the reading public would not stand for a black man with a white sweetheart? Or was it, perhaps, that since his own marriage was running into trouble by 1849, he shared his creation's alienation from women, an alienation which women, not Beck, were responsible for?

If white women's universal aversion to Martin Beck seems fanciful, his career as a bushranger is certainly not. This is not merely because bushranging was then rife. Although the bushrangers most remembered by the Australian people today are all white, it is a striking fact of Australian history that the very first bushranger was an Afro-Black First Fleet transportee, John Caesar. His place of birth is uncertain, but his very name is redolent of the pseudo-classical names imposed by slave masters. He was convicted at Kent Lent Assizes in March 1786 of stealing £12 4d., and sentenced to transportation for seven years (the usual sentence of most First Fleet convicts). At conviction, he was twenty-two years old, and his occupations are recorded as 'black servant' and 'labourer'.[30]

Of all the First Fleet convicts, Caesar was regarded by the powers-that-be in the new colony as the most dangerous and the most intransigent. Within little more than a year of the arrival of the First Fleet in January 1788, Caesar was locked in conflict with colonial authority. James Scott's *Remarks on a Passage to Botony Bay 1787–1792* notes that on 29 April 1789, Caesar, together with another Afro-Black convict only identified by the nickname 'Black Jemmy', was tried for theft. Caesar was evidently considered the more culpable, as he was sentenced to life transportation, while his associate 'only' received 500 lashes.[31] But the most extensive contemporary information on Caesar is to be found in the pages of David Collins's *An Account of the English Colony of New South Wales with Remarks on the Dispositions, Customs, Manners, etc of the Native Inhabitants of that Country* (1, London 1798).[32] Collins was Judge Advocate of the colony, and as such developed an absolute phobia for Caesar, quite different from his comparatively sympathetic and enlightened interest in the Aborigines. To Collins, Caesar was 'an incorrigibly stubborn black' and 'a man, who certainly, during his life, could never have been estimated at more than one remove above the brute, and who had given more trouble than any other convict in the settlement' (pp. 57, 331). Not daunted by the indefinite extension of his sentence, Caesar escaped into the bush in June 1790 'with some provisions, an iron pot and a soldier's musket'; not apprehended till the next month, he lived by raiding the garden plots of the convict settlement (p. 57). This was merely the first of a constant series of escapes by Caesar, including a daring escape in a canoe in December 1789 from Garden Island, across the shark-infested waters of Sydney Harbour (p. 73). He had been sent there after his first escape because:

> He was such a wretch, and so indifferent about meeting death, that he declared while in confinement, that if he should be hanged, he would create a laugh before he was turned off, by playing some trick upon the executioner. Holding up such a mere animal as an example was not expected to have the power or intended effect . . . (pp. 58–9)

Modern readers will, on the whole, suspect Caesar of resolution in the face of the worst that authority could do to him, rather than being a 'mere animal'. Even Ned Kelly could not have showed greater defiance. And even Collins had to admit that Caesar was reputed to be the hardest working in the colony (p. 58). In the end, the authorities decided in February 1796 to offer a bounty of five

gallons of spirits to whoever would apprehend him, since he had 'sent word, that neither would he come in, nor suffer himself to be taken alive' (p. 377). On 15 February 1796 news came that two bounty hunters had surprised and shot Caesar in the bush, and that Caesar had died of his wounds. In his capacity for hard work and his defiance of the world, Caesar resembles Martin Beck. Did Harris have him in mind when writing *The Emigrant Family*? There is no positive evidence to establish this. As an educated and well-read man, Harris might have read Collins. Possibly during Harris's time in New South Wales stories and ballads of Caesar were still circulating among the ageing survivors of the convicts of the 1790s. John McQuilton, a leading modern authority on bushranging, believes that there may well have been such ballads, but that if so, they became supplanted during the nineteenth century by others celebrating the exploits of later bushrangers such as Ben Hall and Ned Kelly.[33]

Another Afro-Black intransigent in New South Wales of whom Harris may have known was the mysterious 'Black Francis', remembered in the early twentieth century reminiscences of an 'old-timer', Charles MacAlister. MacAlister's *Old Pioneering Days in the Sunny South*[34] remembers 'Black Francis' as 'the Goulburn castigator' (i.e. a convict employed by the authorities to flog other convicts) in the years 1838–41. We are told:

> Black Francis used to lay the cat on with a savage ferocity. He met with a sudden and tragic end – being found one morning 'as dead as a doornail', in the bush near Run of Water, with three leaden slugs in his carcase. He used to make it his business to inform on some 'ticket-o'-leave' men who (after sometimes sharing their plunder), were in the habit of robbing teams of spirits, that carriers were taking up-country. On several occasions he had 'tried' and flogged his man for the offence referred to. (pp. 63–4)

I have not been able to identify 'Black Francis' among the several Afro-Black convicts with that forename or surname, of whom I have a record. Nor have I been able to find his death among coroner's inquests for the appropriate period. However, Harris certainly knew the Goulburn area – it is not far from the setting of his fictional Rocky Springs station – and if MacAlister's memory was accurate after a period of over sixty years, Harris could well have known about this man. 'Black Francis' is in some obvious ways unlike Martin Beck, but the general setting of association with bushrangers, treachery and retribution might well have given Harris ideas for his novel. 'Black Francis's' career as a castigator brings out the unexpected in the lives of Afro-Blacks in New South Wales during the convict era. Where else in the British Empire would one have found white men, in a state of bondage, being flogged by a black man? Parallel to this is the fact recorded in the 1828 census of New South Wales that Billy Blue had a number of (presumably white) convicts assigned to his service by the government. This inversion of the usual norms of such places as the Cape Colony, the West Indies and Mauritius, or even of Britain itself where black slavery was only formally ended by the 1833 Abolition Act, is striking. Strange as the fictional figure of Martin Beck in *The Emigrant Family* may seem, aspects of the actual lives of Afro-Blacks in Harris's New South Wales were clearly equally strange. It may well be that the African diaspora that trickled to the Australian colonies had some unique experiences for Afro-Black people in countries of predominantly white settlement. MacAlister himself dryly observes, 'What a short shrift would this negro flogger have had in such a State as N.C.' (evidently meaning North Carolina).[35] The work of Daniel and Annette Potts has shown that black Americans, in the later period of the gold rushes of the 1850s, found Australia a genuine land of opportunity.[36] They do not seem to have faced the racial hostility that notoriously faced the Chinese in the Victorian and New South Wales gold fields. Likewise there are fragments of information from Tasmania, of which the most startling example is the career of Sir Francis Vileneuve Smith, popularly known in the colony as 'Blackie Smith'. Smith served as Chief Justice of Tasmania, and was the son of a French West Indian 'woman of colour'.[37] On a more humble level, 'Black' Dick White, a former highwayman and transportee who died in 1849, became the proprietor of a hotel in Launceston. The hotel still exists, I am told, and still perpetuates his name.[38] In such a thirsty country as colonial Australia, to be perpetuated in this manner suggests local fame and popular acceptance of a very particular sort. Billy Blue, too, long had a public house as his memorial, the 'Old Commodore' in North Sydney, of which the original licensee was one of his sons.[39]

There was plenty of racism in nineteenth century Australia. The evidence of racism of a vicious sort directed against Chinese and Aborigines in particular is overwhelming. As far as Aborigines are concerned, one has to look no further than the works of Alexander Harris, including *The Emigrant Family*. In the episode already referred to, in which Beck incites and organises an Aboriginal raid on Rocky Springs (see volume II of the novel, chapters 8 to 10), Beck manipulates the Aborigines, as he does other men, rather than identifying with them. Only when to restrain them from violence against persons rather than property does he agree that he is 'belonging to black fellow':

> Baal (not) Englishman me . . . Baal I like Englishman. That too much take away black fellow's land. That too much, hunt away kangaroo, 'possum, fish. That jumbuc (sheep) too much drink up all bardo (water). Black fellow, me. Belongin' to 'nother country; but just the same as this black fellow. (p. 224)

All that needs to be added to this list of the reasons for Aboriginal resistance to white settlement is the abuse of Aboriginal women, for it to be an almost comprehensive summary of the grievances modern historians identify as underlying that resistance. Once again, Harris scores high on observation of Australian realities. However, he hated and despised 'myalls', and was outraged by the feeble and ineffectual official efforts to protect them. Aboriginal resistance was undoubtedly fiercer than historians have, until recently, admitted. But when Harris accuses the Aborigines of cannibalism,[40] he is merely mouthing white phobias about 'savages' in general.

For to Harris, the Aborigines *were* savages, and as such they should be treated. In *The Emigrant Family* he manages to slip in a bitter reference to the seven stockmen hanged by the government, in the teeth of white colonial opinion, for the Myall Creek massacre.[41] A little later he puts long speeches in the mouth of Reuben Kable, denying the existence of white violence except in self-defence, and insisting that protection had encouraged Aboriginal violence against whites. Here Harris has clearly put down his pen as a novelist, and is taking it up as a propagandist. Kable's justification of the relentless extension of the frontier is a curious mixture of perception about Aboriginal resentment and unflinching special pleading for the settler as an agent of 'civilisation':

> There was never a clearer case in the world for the white agriculturalist and herdsman in seizing land . . . The fact is this – The savages die off from the effects of various vices, not through want of food . . . Their aggressions are almost wholly the result of ill-feeling, in consequence of

the *invasion of their territory*; but who will say that that invasion is an improper one? . . . The first question is, shall we hold the land or resign it? And, it being decided that we are to hold it, then comes the question, shall we do so, checking intimidation by intimidation, and violence by violence? . . . Public machinery cannot touch the case: the savage flies to his fastnesses and defies the policeman to catch him. Every man must be his own constable who goes to the extreme verge of civilisation; and the retribution enforced must be palpable, prompt and decisive. Indeed, the very best protection for the savage is that the white man must not be afraid of him. (pp. 258–9)

Here, Harris is simply reiterating what he had said at much greater length in *Settlers and Convicts*, and he was to repeat these sentiments all over again in *Religio Christi*. Concerning Aborigines, Reuben Kable is in the crudest way Harris's mouthpiece, not an autonomous fictional character.

Yet, by contrast, Harris allows Reuben Kable to identify to some extent with Martin Beck who is a 'native' in the same sense as himself. To the suggestion by a fellow white Australian that Beck ought to go to America where there are 'plenty of his own people', Kable replies: 'after all, this is home to him'. And, sympathising with Beck's predicament as an Australian, Kable says: 'he is as you may say all alone in the world; the white people think nothing of him. And what else can he do but look out for himself?' (p. 249)

In the end, Martin Beck is perhaps *sui generis* in the fictional portrayal of Afro-Black people by English authors in the nineteenth century. This remarkable figure leads us to the actual historical occurrence of an Afro-Black presence in early colonial Australia, and provokes an analysis of the true nature of that presence in a convict and white settler society. Furthermore, consciously or unconsciously, Harris identifies with Martin Beck. Whether one considers Beck's skills or virtues, they are of a kind that the mature Harris approved, even if the younger Harris did not possess. Harris admired temperance, hard work and sexual self-restraint. At least arguably, Harris resented women as much as he desired them, and certainly he seems to have seen even 'good' women as very silly creatures. Writing under the pseudonym of an 'Emigrant Mechanic' in *Settlers and Convicts*, he carefully describes himself as undertaking the arduous and skilled operations of a bush sawyer, splitter and carpenter. But it is very doubtful indeed that he ever possessed such skills, or performed these tasks.[42] Martin Beck is made a master of such work. Beck has the virtues and skills of native

Australian whites, without most of their vices, and if he lacks their
sense of comradeship that is more the fault of the white world than
of himself. As an English emigrant, Harris himself was perhaps at
best a sympathetic outsider in the world of the bush, or even
Sydney. So, in conclusion, *The Emigrant Family* is perhaps the first
novel in Australian fiction to deal with the theme of the outsider in
Australian society, and so has an unsuspected place alongside such
modern works as Thomas Keneally's *The Chant of Jimmy
Blacksmith*. I would like to think that one day a major Australian
film director will make Martin Beck, as has been done for Jimmy
Blacksmith, the subject of a film.

Notes

1. *Settlers and Convicts, Recollections of Sixteen Years' Labour in the Australian
   Backwoods, by an Emigrant Mechanic* (i.e. Alexander Harris), London, 1847
   and 1852; with foreword by Manning Clark, Melbourne (1953), reprinted with
   new foreword by Manning Clark, Melbourne (1964).
2. *Religio Christi* was serialised in the American journal, the *Saturday Evening
   Post* in 1858. It was republished, with an introduction by Harris's grandson,
   Grant Carr-Harris and a preface by Alec H. Chisholm, President of the Royal
   Australian Historical Society 1959–61, under the title *The Secrets of Alexander
   Harris, A Frank Autobiography by the Author of Settlers and Convicts* (Sydney,
   1961).
3. Alexander Harris (ed. and with intro. by W. S. Ramson): *The Emigrant Family,
   or, The Story of an Australian Settler* (Canberra, 1967), p. 5. All other
   references to *The Emigrant Family* are taken from this edition. I wish to thank
   Professor Russel Ward of the University of New England, Armidale, NSW, for
   suggesting to me the value of examining this work.
4. W. S. Ramson: 'The emigrant family: the delineation of actual life', in Ramson
   (ed.): *The Australian Experience: Critical Essays on Australian Novels*
   (Canberra, 1974), p. 16.
5. Ramson: 'Introduction to *The Emigrant Family*', p. 1, Ramson says of the novel
   itself that it 'remains essentially a handbook of practical information'. In my
   view, this is by no means the whole truth.
6. For a discussion of this kind of Pan-Africanism, see I. Duffield: 'Pan-
   Africanism, rational and irrational', in *Journal of African History*, XVIII,
   no 4 (1977), pp. 597–620.
7. This stereotype emerged early in the history of British abolitionism, and is
   exemplified in Josiah Wedgwood's famous Slave Medallion of 1787, depicting
   an African in chains, kneeling in a supplicant posture, with the legend above
   'Am I not a man and a brother?' Fiona Spiers shows in her unpublished paper
   'Blacks in Britain and the struggle for black freedom in North America
   1820–1870', presented at the *International Conference on the History of Blacks
   in Britain*, London (September 1981) that British abolitionists of that period
   persistently preferred to exhibit Black Americans who fitted the stereotype on
   their platforms. Publication of this is pending.
8. For modern analysis of massacres by Aboriginals, see H. Reynolds: *The Other
   Side of the Frontier* (James Cook University of North Queensland, 1981),
   pp. 78–82; G. Reid, *A Nest of Hornets. The Massacre of the Fraser Family at*

Alexander Harris's *The Emigrant Family*

Hornet Bank Station . . ., 1857 . . . (Melbourne, 1982), *passim*. Both authors reveal a clear pattern; Europeans provoked violent retaliation by seeking to monopolise the use of land resources (often attempting to drive Aborigines into remoter hinterlands); and more generally by violating Aboriginal custom (sometimes unwittingly).

9. By the present author, in archives and libraries in NSW & Tasmania, September to December 1982 and July to September 1983. Gratitude is due to the Carnegie Trust for the Universities of Scotland and the University of London Australian Studies Centre for funding this work.

10. In six days at the Archives Office of Tasmania, Hobart, in August 1983, forty-three Afro-Blacks, mainly convicts, were identified. These were mainly found in vol. 1 of Con/23, *Alphabetical Registers of Male Convicts, 1804–39*. However, as well as the other two volumes of Con/23, many other categories of Tasmanian convict archives promise an abundance of material; as does the fact that convict ships sailed direct to Tasmania from such places as the Cape Colony, Mauritius and Bermuda. Additionally, many ships to Tasmania from Britain will have carried small numbers of blacks among much larger numbers of whites, as was the case for ships from Britain to NSW. Additionally, Ms S. Chamberlain of La Trobe University, who is currently working on the nineteenth-century Tasmanian whaling industry, has evidence of hundreds of black seamen engaged on the whaling ships.

11. I. Duffield: 'History and fiction: Martin Beck and Afro-Blacks in colonial Australia', *Journal of Australian Studies* (forthcoming, 1985), n. 40, lists in detail the Montego Bay rebels who were transported, and Australian and Jamaican sources on them. Seven Muslims convicted of mutiny in Mauritius on 27 February 1837 are listed per *Symmetry*, AONSW, *Printed Indents of Convict Ships, 1838*, pp. 72–3. Caetane, an arsonist from Mozambique, is listed per *Layton*, AONSW, *Printed Indents of Convict Ships, 1840–42*, pp. 6–7. For more information on transportees from the Cape Colony and Mauritius, see V. C. Malherbe: 'David Stuurman: "Last Chief of the Hottentots"', *African Studies*, XXXIX, 1 (1980) and '"Hottentots" and the question of convict transportation from the Cape Colony', *South African Journal of History* (forthcoming). I am grateful to Ms Malherbe for letting me see the typescript of the latter article. Also see I. Duffield: 'Transportation of Indian Ocean peoples to Australia', in J. Gundara, R. Visram and I. Duffield: *Imperialism, Migration and the Indian Ocean*, paper presented at the International Indian Ocean History Conference, Perth, Western Australia, December 1984.

12. This couple, Louis Marcelin and Mary Josephine, were natives of Mauritius, convicted and sentenced on 18 December 1833 to seven years transportation for receiving stolen goods. They arrived at Sydney per *Dart*, 31 December 1833. At conviction, they had five children, and Mary Josephine was pregnant when transported. See AONSW, *Printed Indents of Convict Ships, 1833*, pp. 207–8 and 247–8.

13. See Leslie C. Duly: '"Hottentots" to Hobart and Sydney: The Cape Supreme Court's use of transportation 1828–38', in *Australian Journal of Politics and History*, XXV, 1 (1979), pp. 39 and 44.

14. As well as forming part of the crowd in the streets of later eighteenth- and early nineteenth-century London, some blacks became well-known personalities. For examples, see Paul Edwards and James Walvin: *Black Personalities in the Era of the Slave trade* (London, 1983), pp. 145–237.

15. *Secrets of Alexander Harris*, p. 52.

16. For black bandsmen in the British army, see Peter Fryer: *Staying Power: The History of Black People in Britain*, (London, 1984), pp. 81–8.

17. *Secrets of Alexander Harris*, p. 75. This is strikingly similar to a passage in Pierce Egan's *Life in London*, quoted in Donald A. Low: *Thieves Kitchen: The Regency Underworld* (London, 1982), p. 113. But where Egan sought to titillate, Harris sought to shock.

18. I am grateful to Dr Barry Dyster of the University of New South Wales Department of Economic History for this information.

19. *Settlers and Convicts*, p. 106.

20. Blue was transported per *Minorca*, arriving Sydney 14 December 1801. See AONSW, Microfilm Reel (hence MR) 392, *Indents of Convict Ships, 1801–1814*. His trial at Kent Quarter Sessions for stealing 20 lb. of sugar from a ship at Deptford is mentioned in the *Maidstone Journal*, 11 October 1796. The formal indictment and depositions in relation to his case survive in the Kent County Archives, Maidstone, and reveal that he lived in the Parish of St Paul Deptford, that he was a chocolate maker, and that he also worked as a 'lumper' unloading ships in the Thames. For further information on Billy Blue, see Meg Swords: *Billy Blue The Old Commodore*, North Shore Historical Society, North Sydney (1979); I. Duffield: 'Billy Blue and the African diaspora in Australia', in *History Today* (forthcoming, 1985).

21. *Settlers and Convicts*, p. 90. *Ibid.*, p. 89 speculates that Blue was so-called because he was 'a very black black'.

22. Mitchell Library, Sydney (hence ML), *Sydney Gazette and New South Wales Advertiser*, 17 August 1811, p. 1.

23. ML, *Sydney Gazette*, 17 October 1818, p. 2.

24. Blue petitioned Macquarie for the right to operate a ferry on 7 October 1816. See AONSW, MR/2161, NSW Colonial Secretary's In-Letters, 1816, p. 151. *The Census of New South Wales November 1828* records Blue as holding a grant of eighty acres at Hunter's Hill. By contrast, the wealthy free settlers of the day held grants of thousands of acres, sometimes tens of thousands.

25. For Blue's petitions to Macquarie of 28 October and 17 November 1823, see AONSW, MR/2173, Colonial Secretary's In-Letters, 1823. For Wollstonecraft's answer to the charges contained in these petitions, and counter charges that Blue was involved in aiding and abetting escaped convicts and deserting seamen, smuggling and resetting of stolen goods, see Wollstonecraft to Col. Sec. Goulbourn, 18 November 1823, *ibid.*, pp. 216a, 216b & 216c.

26. For information on Blue's marriage and family, see Swords: *Billy Blue*, pp. 15–17, 40–1, 62–6. Ms Swords' pamphlet, which only came into the author's hands while making final revisions on this essay, is a mine of information; but the author would disagree with her comments on pp. 19–20 on his 'racial background'. Here, Ms Swords seems to give too much credence to fanciful stories from the early twentieth-century Sydney Press, and concludes that he 'must have been' partly of Amerindian descent. One of her grounds for believing this is that his 1823 petitions (see n. 25 above) claimed he had been a spy or guide in Cornwallis's army in Virginia in 1781. In fact, this was a task commonly undertaken by black soldiers in the British army during the American Revolution. For an example, see Fryer: *Staying Power*, p. 192. For further information on black soldiers in the British Army during the American Revolution, see J. W. St G. Walker, 'Blacks as American loyalists: The slaves' war for independence', *Historical Reflections*, II (1975), *passim*, and Sylvia R. Frey, 'The British and the Black: a new perspective', *The Historian*, XXXVIII (1975–6), *passim*.

27. For more information on Blue's descendants, see Swords: *Billy Blue*, pp. 62–6; AONSW, MR/2223, *Census of New South Wales*, 1841, entries 14, 42 & 46, pp. 141, 145; article in *Sydney Star*, 26 September 1908. The latter details many

of the ramifications of different branches of the family; not only Blues, but Lavenders, Schofields, Rogerses and Boyces are mentioned, and their relationship to Blue and his six children explained. All this demolishes Harris's suggestion that an Afro-Black male would be sexually isolated in Australia even if by progressively marrying white of the Blue descendants ceased in time to be perceived as black.

28. Self-evident from the cooperation that the journalists writing for the Sydney *Star* and Sydney *Sunday Times* received from descendants.

29. See J. Walvin, *Black and White: a study of Negro and English Society 1555–1945*, (London, 1973), pp. 52 & 55; Fryer, *op. cit.*, pp. 161–4.

30. See John Cobley, *The Crimes of the First Fleet Convicts* (Sydney, 1970), p. 46.

31. James Scott: *Remarks on a Passage to Botany Bay 1787–1792. A First Fleet Journal*, (Sydney, 1963), p. 47.

32. All refs. to Collins, *Account of the English Colony of New South Wales . . .* are from the edition edited by Brian H. Fletcher (Sydney, 1975).

33. Conversation between author and Dr McQuilton, University of New South Wales, September 1983.

34. Charles MacAlister: *Old Pioneering Days in the Sunny South*, (Goulburn New South Wales, 1907). E. G. Hazell: *Some Came Free 1830–1892. A Story of Early Colonial Life at the Limits of Location* (Canberra, 1978) has refs. to 'Black Francis', partly drawn from MacAlister. Hazell complains: 'While William Hazell walked the beat [i.e. as a constable] at two shillings a day, Black Francis swung his flail for two shillings and eightpence a day' (p. 116).

35. MacAlister, *Old Pioneering Days*, p. 109.

36. E. Daniel & Annette Potts: *Young America and Australian Gold; Americans and the Gold Rushes of the 1850s* (St Lucia, Queensland, 1974) and 'The Negro and the Australian gold rushes, 1852–1857', in *Pacific Historical Review*, XXXVII (September 1968), pp. 381–99. The black people discussed in these works were all free immigrants, though some may have been slaves in the United States. I am grateful to Professor Russel Ward for drawing my attention to these works, and also to those listed in n. 34 above.

37. Information from Mr Geoffrey Stilwell of the Archives Office of Tasmania, 29 July 1983. His knowledge and enthusiasm exemplifies that of many archivists and librarians in Australia, to all of whom I owe a great debt. For an article on Smith which does *not* mention his black ancestry, see *Australian Dictionary of Biography*, VI, *1851–1890, R–Z*, pp. 144–5.

38. Information from Geoffrey Stilwell, 19 July 1938. Also see section on Richard White in H. B. Holmes: *The Claytons of Wickford*, unpub. typescript in State Library of Tasmania (Hobart, 1981).

39. The original license is missing in the AONSW. MR/1242, New South Wales Colonial Treasurer, Publicans' Licenses, 1860–1, has a renewal of license for John Blue *re* the 'Old Commodore' Hotel, North Shore, 31 May 1860. The Sydney *Star*, 6 October 1908, says 'John Blue, "Billy's" son . . . built the Old Commodore Hotel, Blue's Point road, which in its old and reconstructed state, has been conducted by Mrs M'Kay for the last 50 years' and 'John Blue was succeeded by his son John who kept the Old Commodore Hotel prior to Mrs M'Kay'. Mary Salmon, Sydney *Sunday Times*, 9 February 1908 says 'over the door [of the hotel] flapped a signboard with a picture, highly coloured by a local artist, of the original Blue, as tradition always represented him – carrying a sack-like bag'.

40. *The Emigrant Family*, p. 231.

41. *The Emigrant Family*, pp. 248–9. For John Johnstone and the Myall Creek massacre see Part A, *Australian Colonial History Source Material* (University of

New England Department of History, 1982), pp. 92–120.

42. Alec H. Chisholm: 'The odd case of Alexander Harris', in *Meanjin*, XIX, 4 (1960), p. 415, reveals that Harris's self-portrayal as an expert sawyer and splitter in *Settlers and Convicts* is an invention.

5 Reading the novels of empire: race and ideology in the classic 'tale of adventure'

BRIAN STREET

I am concerned with present-day readings of the novels of empire, those 'tales of adventure' in foreign places through which life overseas was brought home in vivid and memorable form to the vast majority of Victorians who never ventured abroad themselves. The works of H. Rider Haggard, John Buchan, Edgar Rice Burroughs, R. M. Ballantyne, G. A. Henty and others currently tend to be classified in school and public libraries as either light 'adventure stories' or 'classics' and are generally read as such. I would like to suggest an alternative approach to reading such material that both retains the ability to appreciate its literary value at the same time as providing a sharper critique of the contribution these works make to contemporary stereotypes and preconceptions of 'race' and culture.

The 'black presence' in these novels is constructed out of nineteenth-century imperialist and scientific thinking, as I attempted to demonstrate in an earlier work.[1] Behind the apparently trivial and harmless exotica of the tales of adventure lie deep preconceptions about the nature of humankind, about how the variety of human societies can be conceived of, described and understood and about the role of different cultures and 'races' in the world order. These preconceptions and in particular the emphasis on 'race' as the ordering category for making sense of human variety, still persist in modern Britain, as I shall briefly illustrate and as numerous recent studies have established.[2] An alternative 'reading' of the novels opens up to question the relationship between the persistence of these notions and the ways in which the novels are currently read. To examine nineteenth-century representations of the 'savage in literature' is not, then, a matter of merely antiquarian interest, irrelevant to modern-day 'race relations'; it is, in fact, the crucial ground on which the symbols and myths of those relations are most clearly exposed and in which, for many members of contemporary British society, they acquire salience.

Before examining the literature itself I will briefly suggest some of the ways in which nineteenth-century preconceptions about culture and society persist in modern Britain. Representations both of contemporary 'Third World' societies and of 'ethnic' groups within Britain draw to a large extent, I suggest, on the same assumptions and beliefs and the same images that underlay representations of 'primitive' society in the last century. The members of these groups and societies may not now, overtly, be referred to as 'primitive' or 'savage', but new coinages and euphemisms, such as 'ethnic', 'underdeveloped', 'backward' and 'simple' often carry the same message. The relationship between the 'racist' language and imagery of everyday life in contemporary Britain and that of the last century, which I am suggesting is maintained and reproduced in the 'ethnographic novel', can be illustrated by a crude and well-known example.

When a football crowd greets the arrival of a black player on the pitch with grunts and mock 'ape' noises, it might seem that the explanation is a matter 'simply' of prejudice and ignorance. White people are expressing their ethnocentric fears and prejudices about blacks. But the question still remains of why they should do so in this particular way; why these particular noises and actions are taken to have that significance; why is it that in this culture these symbols are agreed (by the analysts as well as by the participants) to have these meanings? This is where the evidence from nineteenth-century literature is significant. The symbols and the associated myths have a real history, they are not just invented *ad hoc* to suit immediate circumstances. Their meaning is socially constructed out of a specific past, which means that it is not enough to attend to the present circumstances themselves in order to explain them. We must also examine how they come about and how they work *as* images and symbols. Underlying even such apparently crude and simple activities as the grunts and calls of a football crowd can be found a complex network of ideas and associations fossilised from the theory and ideology of a previous period.

The noises uttered by the crowd are, of course, intended to bring out an association between black people and apes. The significance of this association is that apes represent earlier more 'primitive' versions of the 'higher' races of mankind (an idea adapted, as we shall see below, from Darwinian evolutionary theory). But why should blacks be associated with apes in the first place? If one employed the criterion of coverage of hair, for instance, in order to liken certain human beings to hairy apes, then whites would be 'nearer' according to some scientists. The association depends, then, on which criteria are employed. In contemporary English culture these criteria have been pre-selected by a very specific and relatively recent history of ideas and conceptions about race, evolution and hierarchy. It is these conceptions that order and determine the specific representations familiar in football crowds and elsewhere in contemporary Britain. In examining the nature of these conceptions, then, we are also throwing some light on the ordering processes themselves and learning about the ways in which our deepest assumptions are constructed and legitimised, about how ideology is constructed.

The central ordering device for a long time prior to the nineteenth century in Britain was the concept of a 'chain of being', whereby nature was taken to be a unified whole, ranked in a hierarchy from the angels to the lesser insects.[3] In the nineteenth century this essentially theological notion was adapted to scientific descriptions of nature and refined by Darwinian theories of evolution.[4] The various stages on the 'ladder' were now seen to have emerged out of each other and the superiority of one over the other was, in theory, based on their greater complexity rather than on moral preconceptions. However, the metaphor of the 'chain of being' continued to inform the descriptions of natural processes, so that the 'higher' species were popularly felt to be morally and culturally 'superior'. The application of evolutionary theory to the ladder meant that researchers could expect to find examples of earlier stages of their own development by examining living contemporary societies. The 'comparative method' enabled travellers and scientists alike to examine living creatures and fellow men for evidence of their own past and for criteria by which to rank them on the scale of being.[5]

Those ideas are to be found in vivid form in many nineteenth-century novels that are still popular today. In 'classics' such as Conan Doyle's *The Lost World* (1912), for instance, the plot and characterisation depend crucially on assumptions about social evolution and about the hierarchy of races, with whites at the top

97

and various 'primitive' tribes whom the travellers encounter being at the bottom and no higher than 'apes'. A group of twentieth century adventurers in the South American jungle find a world that has failed to 'progress' in the way it is assumed European society has. The white travellers are able to give it a helping hand by joining in the battles between the apes who inhabit the lost plateau and their cave-dweller opponents, themselves only one stage above the apes and representing the ancestors of modern man. Doyle makes quite clear the 'scientific' assumptions on which the fictional tale is based. Professor Challenger, representing the European scientific establishment comments:

> We have been privileged to be present at one of the typical decisive battles of history . . . those fierce fights when in the dawn of the ages the cave-dwellers held their own against the tiger-folk . . . at last man was to be supreme and the man-beast to find forever his allotted place (*The Lost World*, p. 179)

This notion that living peoples in other parts of the world represent a stage in the history of mankind which Europeans have passed through underlies much of the popular fiction of the period and continues in contemporary Britain, partly perhaps as a result of the continuing popularity of such authors. The representation of 'other' peoples as 'apes', places them in a historical, evolutionary sequence as examples of such an earlier period. John Buchan's popular novels set in South Africa, for instance, describe the Bushman as 'one of the lowest of created types, still living in the Stone Age' (*Prester John*) a description echoed by Bertram Mitford who sees them as 'no more than half ape', a 'descendant of the baboons' (*The Weird of Deadly Hollow*, 1891, p. 199).

The characterisation of foreign peoples as 'apes' in this way also stresses their supposed animal-like qualities and lack of characteristics deemed to define what is 'human'. Vivid descriptions of ape-like peoples provide lasting images that help to confirm the European in their superiority and to distance them from their supposed ancestors. Edgar Rice Burroughs, the inventor of Tarzan, for instance, helps to fix the notion for future generations of young readers that people like their ancestors may still be found in some forgotten jungles, dancing ape-like rituals in ways that European society has left behind. His florid jungle prose transforms the scientific theory of his day into vivid and memorable images, such as in the following description of a ritual dance:

From this primitive function has arisen, unquestionably, all the forms and ceremonials of modern Church and State, for through all the countless ages, back beyond the last uttermost ramparts of dawning humanity, our fierce hairy forbears danced out the rites of the Dum-Dum to the sound of their earthen drums, beneath the bright light of a tropical moon in the depth of a mighty jungle which stands unchanged today as it stood on that long-forgotten night in the dim, unthinkable vistas of the long-dead past, when our first shaggy ancestor swung from a swaying bough and dropped lightly on the turf of the first meeting-place. (*Tarzan of the Apes*, 1917, p. 57)

The images created in such passages are likely to be those brought to mind by contemporary descriptions of blacks as apes and they bring with them the associated notions of social evolution and racial hierarchy of the period in which they were produced. They continue to provide an 'objective correlative' for what might otherwise be obscure and outdated theories.

Against the force of imagery such as this it is difficult for the modern anthropologist effectively to put the argument that social evolution is not the same thing as evolution in nature; that contemporary peoples everywhere have their own history and development; that it is meaningless to try to place them in 'stages'; that the criteria used are inevitably ethnocentric; and that, while apes were indeed the ancestors of men, no one group of living men today is 'nearer' to the apes than any others.

For nineteenth-century scientists and travellers, and the novelist who helped to publicise their ideas, these ideas represented a beginning in putting some order into descriptions of the vast variety of cultures being encountered. In this context, then, the concept of race was seen as a scientific concept for classifying and making sense of such complexity. Banton argues that the idea of race in this 'scientific' sense only emerged recently:

Discrimination against strangers and particularly against dark-skinned people is probably of antiquity. But 'race' as it is known today is a relatively new idea. Only in the last two hundred years has an ideology of race claiming scientific validity been added to the rhetoric of national, economic and social conflict.[6]

The word now has emotive connotations related to exploitation and prejudice, but in the late eighteenth and nineteenth centuries it denoted a supposed 'scientific' category by means of which the variety of human beings could be fitted into a scheme of classification. It was a word of the same type and status as 'species' (which, in fact, many believed races to be). The singular advantage of this criterion of classification was that it denoted physical, tangible and hence measurable characteristics and was thus amenable to empirical 'scientific' enquiry. Furthermore, it provided an external measure of those less concrete 'internal' characteristics such as morality, faith and character which could not otherwise be so easily included within scientific observation. Internal characteristics could be assessed by observation of external ones.

For novelists, of course, this is a common enough device, enabling them to identify their characters' internal qualities quickly and memorably for the reader. In the context of nineteenth-century science, however, this classic device took on a particular colouring and we find writers using racial characteristics to stereotype whole peoples in ways for which they could claim some justification since the scientists were doing the same thing. The writer could refer in passing to primitive peoples' inherent laziness, childishness or cruelty as though these were 'natural', given by racial background and inheritance to all members of a particular race. R. M. Ballantyne, for instance, has his schoolboy heroes describe the natives of a South Sea island as barbarous savages, fighting like demons and then eating their victims, as though this is all that one could expect. His 'classic' *Coral Island* is full of cruelty and atrocities, exaggerated perhaps in order to stress the need for missionaries to bring 'progress' to such benighted lands, but given authority by the racial stereotyping of the period. Similarly the dervishes in Conan Doyle's *The Tragedy of the Korosko* (1898) have their inherent cruelty written on their faces. The Baggara Arabs are 'small, brown, wiry, with little vicious eyes and thin cruel lips'. The habit of associating physical characteristics with internal mental and moral qualities, while a matter of lively debate in scientific circles, passes into popular literature as an accepted fact and provides the novelist with respectable backing for his own generalisations about 'primitive peoples'.

Less virulent, but equally misleading characteristics of simple-mindedness and gullibility are also attributed to foreign peoples in this literature. Rider Haggard, who often wrote remarkably detailed and sensitive accounts of different cultures in Africa, still helps to perpetuate stereotypes of native gullibility through, for instance, his account of the eclipse of the moon in *King Solomon's Mines*. This natural event, which people must have seen frequently, is treated as something that struck fear into primitive souls and can thus be used as a dramatic device, enabling the white men to escape their clutches in a way that appears credible to Haggard's readership (and still to many today).

The use of external characteristics as a means of indicating internal qualities, while ordinary enough in itself for either scientists or novelists, takes on a specific significance in nineteenth-century writing that helps to perpetuate stereotypes of non-European peoples in terms of scientifically authoritative ordering concepts such as race and evolution. The use of the unit of race to place social groups on the evolutionary ladder seemed to offer a fruitful means of making sense of otherwise complex and intractable data. Given the hierarchical nature of the ladder (and of the society in which the scientists themselves lived) it is not surprising to find that the races too were ranked. Given the evolutionary framework for the whole project, it also followed that the 'lower' races of mankind must be nearer to mankind's immediate ancestors, the apes. The judgement as to which races filled this position was, however, more provisional than we might now expect. L. P. Curtis, for instance, shows how many nineteenth-century writers saw the Irish as nearest to the apes, and cartoons of the time (especially those wishing to reinforce a political message regarding English control of Ireland) depicted Irish people as having low foreheads, prognathous features and an ape-like gait which directly associated them with man's immediate ancestors.[7] To many, however, it was the black or 'negroid' races which occupied the bottom rungs of the racial hierarchy and so it was primarily Africans who came to be seen as 'nearest' to the apes.[8]

The criteria for this were generally defined in specific European cultural terms. The Bushmen, for instance, are deemed to be 'primitive' because, amongst other things, their cave paintings appear 'repulsive, grotesque, obscene, the handiwork of bygone ages of the most primitive race in the world'.[9] Rider Haggard explicitly debates within his novel *Allan Quatermain* just how a foreign culture may be classified and concludes that a culture may be 'advanced' in one respect and 'backward' in another, just as his contemporary the anthropologist E. B. Tylor was arguing.[10] Finding the artistic skills of the Zu-Vendi tribe too variable for simple judgement, he tries applying another criterion, that of degree of development of religious thought. The Zu-Vendi are described as having a relatively complex set of ideas about the sun that they embody in imposing rituals. However, this is not really elevating, as religion needs to be for the people to be classified as 'advanced', so he concludes: 'on the whole, I cannot say that I consider this sun-worship as a religion indicative of a civilised people, however magnificent and imposing its ritual'. Conan Doyle, in *The Tragedy of the Korosko*, set in the Sudan, uses as his criterion for judging 'Mohjammedans' the fact that 'they burned the Alexandrian library' and are against representations of the human face. Gilson, writing of the bushmen of the Kalahari, claims that their language 'is just about as comprehensible as the jabbering of apes',[11] which relegates them to the lowest rung of the ladder, and one anonymous writer of a boys' book of adventures declares that 'practical jokes belong only to intermediate stages of civilisation. The English gentleman is above it and the savage intellectually incapable.'[12]

These value judgements are, then, taken beyond the scope of 'normal' ethnocentrism by their location in a supposedly scientific framework of race, evolution and hierarchy that lends respectability and authority to them. That framework underlies the trivial representations of the 'other' that are found in popular novels and everyday representations alike and gives them a significance and an ability to persist that makes them harder to overcome than simple 'prejudice'.

None of this, of course, is going through the minds of the football crowds as they utter their grunts and act out ape-like gestures on the appearance of black footballers; but this particular history of ideas gives meaning, within this particular culture, to activities which would otherwise be arbitrary and 'meaningless'. The meaning is latent in the images and symbols if not consciously present in the minds of those using them. Whatever prejudices they might feel against people of a different colour, hair-type etc., the members of those crowds would not necessarily act them out in these particular ways were it not for the specific history that I have summarised. When I was doing research in the 1970s for a thesis on this topic, I was constantly amazed by the similarity between the popular symbols and myths of race that I would encounter in pubs, etc., and the representations of race in the obscure nineteenth-century anthropology journals that I was consulting in academic libraries (e.g. *Popular Magazine of Anthropology*).

The work of the nineteenth-century anthropologists and others, then, lives on at least in its superficial form in popular ideology. While professional anthropologists have long since abandoned these theories the popular culture has adopted them and continues to represent them in vivid symbolic and mythical form. The persistence of the myths and symbols and their undoubted emotive force, contributes to such perceptions of black people as those I described above for the football crowd. The football crowd may mostly select out blacks because of a perception that in the current economic conditions it is these people who 'take their jobs', squeeze out their social space, or 'swamp' Anglo-Saxon culture, as a British politician recently asserted. But the selection is also conditioned by a perceptual apparatus that is culturally constructed out of the myths and symbols of race described above. That they 'perceive' the *black* player as significantly different from the other players on the field, derives from that specific conceptual framework.

One reason for considering these processes in terms of a 'conceptual framework' rather than simply as 'race relations' is that the ideas and images I have described are not simply confined to an identifiable, minority of 'mindless bigots' but in fact go much deeper in the culture. Recognising them at the level of a framework of thought indicates that they derive from assumptions which a whole range of people might share, including those who consider themselves capable of identifying and condemning the cruder manifestations of it in crowd behaviour. The notion of the African, Pakistani or West Indian as coming from a society that represents an 'earlier' stage of development than European, as lower in the scale of being, whose internal characteristics can be assessed by such external features as colour and head shape and who can be hence classified and put into their appropriate place in a wider scheme – all notions that were familiar to the nineteenth-century anthropologist and to the popular novelist of the time – are ideas that people who think of themselves as 'liberal', 'decent' and 'unprejudiced' still hold in Britain today. The framework underlies not only the crude everyday imagery of the football match but also more ostensibly sophisticated contexts: in literature, drama and schooling.

Many, for instance, who would reject this conceptual framework in the context of 'race relations' in contemporary Britain may nevertheless accept it unthinkingly for describing more distant and alien peoples. The framework can be identified, for instance, as underlying courses in schools and colleges dealing with so-called 'primitive' peoples, in the 'underdeveloped' world.[13] Those who employ it in this way are in fact reinforcing and helping to legitimise a framework whose surface manifestations in terms of everyday 'racist' imagery they spend much of their time trying to eradicate.

I would suggest that one important reason (amongst others) why this is so, why many otherwise liberally-minded teachers are taken off guard, as it were, in their use of nineteenth-century terms and concepts for describing 'other cultures', is that they have learnt that use in the very texture and language of their fictional reading. Many of the popular symbols and myths employed in relations between 'racial' and 'ethnic' groups in contemporary Britain are constructed out of apparently innocuous adventure stories set in foreign lands. The very classification of the stories as 'tales of adventure' or 'children's classics' has helped to avoid the opening up of questions about their relevance to race and ideology today.

In an earlier work I attempted to suggest some of the ways in which the literature could be read with such questions in mind. The novels of Buchan, Haggard, Ballantyne, Mason, Burroughs and countless others, I suggested, brought to a wider public, in vivid imaginative form, the ideas and debates being conducted in scientific circles at the time regarding the nature of society in general and of 'primitive' society in particular. In many cases they drew on the writings of anthropologists for their underlying theory and concepts and they claimed a 'seriousness' and accuracy that was designed to transcend their status as 'fiction'. Writers like Rider Haggard explicitly appealed to 'academic' work to validate their fiction, using for instance the device of footnotes and references to actual scientists to make their characters appear well-informed and authoritative. In this case, Haggard knew practising anthropologists, in particular Andrew Lang and used their work, as for instance in his references to 'totemism' in *Allan Quatermain*; Ballantyne attempted to sound knowledgeable by reference to the concept of 'tabu', while Gilson lends immediacy and realism to his descriptions of the pygmies of equatorial Africa by referring to Stanley's travels.[14] These references also help to facilitate the readers' willing suspension of disbelief, since it is assumed that they share with the author and the scientists preconceptions about 'primitive' life on which the plot hinges. The image of 'other' peoples that these writers helped to construct for public consciousness fitted, then, into a wider system of thought which provided a framework for ordering nature as a whole, humanity in general and 'primitive' peoples in particular. Within an overall framework of the 'chain of being', of racial classification and of evolution that were applied to all societies, there were specific qualities attributed to 'primitive' peoples which were entailed to a large extent by that framework.

> 'Primitive' man, it was assumed, spent his whole life in fear of spirits and mystical beings; his gullibility was exploited by self-seeking priests and kings, who manipulated religion to gain a hold on the minds of their simple subjects; he worshipped animals and trees, tried to control the mystical forces of nature by means of ceremony, ritual taboos and sacrifices, and explained the wonders of the universe in imaginative but 'unscientific' myths. Politically the 'primitive' was in the grip of either anarchy or despotism; social control, if any, was exercised by the most savage tyranny, by the despotism of custom or by religious trickery. Life was a perpetual struggle against harsh nature and harsher men and only the fittest would survive.[15]

This image, I suggested, began to shift towards the end of the century as anthropological theory developed and new ideas began to influence the representation of 'primitive' peoples. The 'ethnographic' novel, while expressing many of the assumptions that lay behind the earlier image, also reveals the importance of the new ideas of scholars and scientists. Late nineteenth century anthropological theory is to be found expressed in vivid, memorable terms and the image of the native developed in this period is given a specific colouring and a supposedly scientific respectability not common in popular representations of alien peoples.

Popular writers like Haggard are perhaps unusual in their knowledge of this anthropological theory, but towards the end of the century a number of 'quality' authors began to make use of it. T. S. Eliot's use of the anthropologist Frazer's *The Golden Bough* is perhaps the best known example, but there is also considerable evidence that D. H. Lawrence read widely in anthropological literature, particularly for his stories of central America, *The Plumed Serpent* and *The Woman Who Rode Away*, while Joseph Conrad made particular use of Wallace's *The Malay Archipelago* for some of his early Malay novels.

Writers of 'ethnographic' fiction are significant for the image of 'other' societies because of their ability to make 'deeply actual'[16] both the scientific theory of the day and their own personal experiences and attitudes. Much of what these writers told of 'primitive' peoples was as a result taken as true by their contemporaries: Morton Cohen, in his biography of Rider Haggard, writes: 'For many Englishmen Africa became the Africa of *King Solomon's Mines*',[17] while Cazamian and Legouis claim 'It is from Kipling that, to the majority of the English, the existence of the Empire dates back'.[18] The image presented by writers such as this, with its attention to the detail of 'exotic' life, its reproduction in popular form of scientific theory and its sense of lived actuality had become hardened by the early twentieth century and has, to some extent, become fossilised since then. It is that image which lives on in representations not only of alien peoples in foreign lands but also of immigrants to this country as I tried to suggest above. The image, then, is not simply an obscure historical quirk, fossilised in a few old-fashioned tales: rather it forms a crucial basis for modern representations of 'other' peoples and it is found within a literature that has a wide and popular readership. Moreover that literature from a previous era has provided the model for contemporary novels of foreign lands and, as Busia has shown, the image lives on in them, modified to present circumstances but remarkably recognisable from its earlier form.[19]

There is, indeed, a close association between the descriptions of fictional societies in nineteenth-century 'ethnographic' fiction and the description of 'real' societies today. The imagery and language through which they are expressed has carried over into contemporary life. The assumptions that underlie the stories also underlie relations between diverse cultures today, whether in terms of relations between the 'British' and peoples in foreign lands or of 'race relations' within these islands. While there are clearly 'material' explanations for the increase of 'racism' during a recession, much more work needs to be done on how the language and imagery through which people learn to represent and describe 'other' peoples affects their *assumptions* about them. The 'ethnographic novel' provides a test case on which we can examine these questions more closely at the same time as it teaches us about the specific ways in which the imagery and symbols of 'race' have been constructed in contemporary Britain.

A crucial factor in this is that nineteenth-century 'ethnographic novels' and modern-day versions of them are not only widely read but that they are read in a way which does not challenge their preconceptions.[20] In many cases the assumptions which underlie the novels are in fact shared by the reader and the author alike. But, more important for their ability to carry language and imagery into everyday usage is the fact that the reader often fails to notice that they are assumptions, and takes them for granted as 'natural'. This is effected by, amongst other things, the very classification of the works. Because the novels are placed in the category 'classics' or 'adventure tales', then they are not approached in terms which would draw attention to the nature of these assumptions. This classification legitimises and validates their status as a particular kind of 'literature' and thereby constrains readers to bring to them that 'willing suspension of disbelief' that might be withheld were they assigned a more problematic status. The question of their underlying framework and assumptions does not arise because that is not how such literature is to be 'read'. The categories are supposedly ideologically 'neutral': they refer to aesthetic theory and to the supposedly harmless 'play of imagination' around fictional texts. As we have seen, however, to 'read' them in this way is to miss a great deal that is crucial to the understanding of present-day society. This direction of focus on one reading and the avoidance of others is part of how a consensus is constructed and developed around a latent ideology. The classification protects the assumptions in such novels and situates them in the mind of the reader in a privileged domain. What should concern us, then, is how we can construct institutional and educational frameworks within which the texts can be approached and 'read' in such a way that this ideology is brought to the surface and made available for critical scrutiny.

The first response has to be to challenge the current classification of such work. One could, for instance, argue that the novels can no longer be read 'straight' as 'children's' books, therefore they should be transferred to the adult section of the library. The shift that is required is not so much in hiding them away (as some would argue) as in bringing them out from the protective umbrella of their status as 'children's classics' or as 'tales of adventure'. The question of their status, which present categories take for granted and therefore tend to disguise, would thus be opened up. Some moves in this direction have been affected by pressure groups such as the Council on Interracial Books for Children (CIBC) and the Writers' and Readers' Publishing Co-operative whose work has influenced both publishers and librarians through, for instance, the recent Library Association Code of Professional Conduct. The Introduction to *Racist and Sexist Images in Children's Books*, for instance, states: 'In face of the widespread dissemination of images about Blacks and the Black experience, we can no longer base critical assessment solely on literary merit. Contents and values, explicit or implicit, deserve similar critical attention. No art or literature can be neutral.' The authors point out 'the need for a critical perspective on children's literature, indeed any literature, that can rely on social factors as well as aesthetics. In particular, we need the tools with which to assess the growing numbers of books in G.B. that deal with Black and minority realities, or have Blacks as the main characters.'[21] The present volume is to some extent a response to such a plea. It will, however, have failed to do justice to the commitment of that early work if it does not also suggest new approaches that take us beyond the simple identification of 'bias' or 'ethnocentricism' that was its main concern. Work in this field has been pitched at the more immediate level of current 'race relations' and has not really examined the deeper framework of thought that underlies not only these relations but general conceptions of culture and identity.

I have been suggesting that the anthropological notion of a 'conceptual system' provides a way of examining this 'deeper framework'. The representations of non-European cultures in nineteenth-century writing were not just a random expression of prejudice but rather cohered together into a system of thought that could be examined in the way that anthropologists investigate the belief systems of the societies they study. One could, for instance, apply to the written literature of our own society the concepts and terms used by anthropologists in approaching oral myth. One could thus elicit the underlying conceptual framework and the hidden contradictions that are perhaps less apparent in the flux of daily experience.

This approach must now, however, be modified in the light of more recent work on language, ideology and literacy.[22] Within anthropology itself, the notion of a 'conceptual system' has been challenged as too 'static' and as failing to take sufficient account of the *processes* whereby a given system or 'ideology' comes to dominate its competitors.[23] The shift to a more dynamic analysis of 'conceptual systems' as forms of ideology is also paralleled in other disciplines in ways that offer fruitful insights for the study of 'ethnographic' fiction.

Jack Zipes, for instance, in *Fairy Tales and the Act of Subversion* (1983) attempts to show that oral folk tales in eighteenth century Europe were

> converted into a type of literary discourse about mores, values and manners so that children would become civilised according to the social code of that time. The writers of fairy tales for children *acted* ideologically by presenting their notions regarding social conditions and conflicts, and they *interacted* with each other and with past writers and storytellers of folklore in a public sphere. This interaction led to an institutionalised symbolic discourse on the civilising process which served as the basis for the fairy-tale genre. (p. 3)

This approach, whose relevance to the content as well as the form of the 'ethnographic' novel is apparent, derives from the conception of a literary work as 'a *symbolic act*'. This definition is, according to Zipes,

> helpful in understanding the origins of the literary fairy tale for children because it immediately perceives the process of writing as part of a social process, as a kind of intervention in a continuous discourse, debate, and conflict about power and social relations.

James Donald, in *Language, Literacy and Schooling* (1981) has suggested a way in which this process can be analysed in relation to written works of the kind I am concerned with here, by placing the emphasis on language as the crucial location for the production and reproduction of ideology. Language, he writes, plays an active role in the construction both of 'ourselves as subjects' and of our relations to others:

> once we get beyond the idea of language as no more than a medium of communication, as a tool equally and neutrally available to all parties in cultural exchanges, then we can begin to examine language both as a practice of signification and also always as a *site* for cultural struggle and a *mechanism* which produces the antagonistic relations between different social groups [p. 4] . . . Language, then 'does not simply reflect reality but always refracts it and constructs it as well.' (p. 7)

In learning to 'read' particular kinds of text one is, then, involved in a process whereby specific language is acquired and specific views on reality constructed. Donald cites the example of the representation of gender but similar processes can be discerned in the construction and representation of cultural 'otherness'. Indeed, Donald's description of the creation of cultural identity in nineteenth-century England has a close bearing on the material which we have been considering. His focus is on 'the contestation around the creation of an *identity* for the English "national popular masses" that can be detected in the reorganisation of cultural hegemony around literacy and education, mainly during the nineteenth century' (p. 5). It is evident from the material I have cited that the 'ethnographic' novel played an important part in this process, with its emphasis on white, 'civilising' heroes encountering 'strange', 'other' cultures in different parts of empire. Such an analysis of the novels, as processes in the construction of an identity for the reader in counterpoint with a vividly realised 'other', may help to throw light on the role of the novels today. They continue to provide readers with an exclusive 'British' identity through reference to a fictitious 'primitive' and 'savage other' and to legitimise the transposition of outdated and virulent myths and symbols of the 'alien' to real peoples encountered in modern-day Britain. We can, then, usefully employ the novels (rather than banning them, for instance) as a means of understanding just how such identities and myths are constructed and of locating immediate 'race relations' within broader perceptions and conceptions of the 'other'. To 'read' the novels of empire as contributions to 'the formation of the subject in language'; as ideological constructions of self and other; as 'discourse and debate about power and social relations'; as *processes* wherein a 'conceptual system' is constructed, may teach us not only about the ways in which relations between 'racial' and 'ethnic' groups in Britain today are actually conducted but, perhaps more crucially in the long run, about how they are constructed.

Notes

1. B. V. Street: *The Savage in Literature* (London, 1975).
2. A. Rampton: *West Indian Children in our Schools* (Interim Report of the Committee of Enquiry into the Education of Children of Ethnic Minority Groups, HMSO, 1981); M. Banton: *Teaching about Prejudice* (Minority Groups Report, no. 59, 1983); ILEA: *Race, Sex and Class*, I–V, 1983.
3. A. C. Lovejoy: *The Great Chain of Being* (Harvard, Mass., 1936).
4. See J. C. Greene: 'Some early speculations on the origins of the human species',

in *American Anthropologist*, LVI, 1954; J. Barnes: 'Anthropology in Britain before and after Darwin', in *Mankind*, V, no. 9, 1960; G. Stocking: *Race, Culture and Evolution* (New York, 1968).

5. J. Burrow: *Evolution and Society* (Cambridge, 1966).
6. M. Banton: *Race Relations* (London, 1967), p. 12.
7. L. P. Curtis: *Anglo-Saxons and Celts* (New York, 1968).
8. See A. Lyons: 'The genesis of scientific racism', in *Journal of the Anthropological Society in Oxford*, I, no. 2, 1970; W. Irvine: *Apes, Angels and Victorians* (Readers Union ed., London, 1955).
9. B. Mitford: *The Weird of Deadly Hollow* (London, 1891), p. 204.
10. E. B. Tylor: *Researches into the Early History of Mankind* (London, 1865).
11. C. Gilson: *In the Power of the Pygmies* (London, 1919), p. 16.
12. G. A. Henty (ed.): *A Boy's Adventures around the World* (London, n.d.), p. 111.
13. B. V. Street: 'Developments in teaching about other cultures in schools', in B. Dufour (ed.): *New Movements in the Social Sciences* (London, 1982).
14. H. R. Haggard: *Allan Quatermain* (London, 1887), p. 157; R. M. Ballantyne: *The Coral Island* (London, 1858), p. 163; Gilson: *In the Power of the Pygmies*, p. 16.
15. B. V. Street: *The Savage in Literature, op. cit.* p. 7.
16. M. L. Cazamian and E. Legouis: *Modern Times* (*A History of English Literature*, II, London and Toronto, 1926), p. 456.
17. M. Cohen: *Rider Haggard – his Life and Works* (London, 1960), p. 95.
18. Cazamian and Legouis: *Modern Times*, p. 456.
19. A. Busia: *Re-Presenting Africa: Patterns of Experiece in British Fiction 1948–1980* (unpublished DPhil diss., Oxford Univ., 1983).
20. See Writers and Readers Publishing Cooperative: *Racist and Sexist Images in Childrens' Books* (London, 1975).
21. *Racist and Sexist Images*, p. 1.
22. See S. Hall *et. al.*: *Culture, Media, Language* (London, 1980); T. Hawkes: *Structuralism and Semiotics* (London, 1977); B. V. Street: *Literacy in Theory and Practice* (Cambridge, 1984).
23. See T. Asad: 'Anthropology and the analysis of ideology', in *Man*, n.s., XIV, 1979; J. Lowry: 'Theorising "observation"', in *Communication and Cognition*, XIV, no. 1, 1981.

6 The dog that didn't bark: the subject races in imperial fiction at the turn of the century

FRANCES M. MANNSAKER

Looking recently through a little children's book called *King Edward's Realm: Story of the Making of the Empire*, written by the Rev. C. S. Dawe for the Educational Supply Association in 1902, I came across the following passage about the early years of the British settlement in South Africa:

> The Governor that did most for the peace of the colony was Sir George Grey, who had already done a good work for the empire in South Australia and New Zealand. He secured the good offices of the Kaffir chiefs by taking them into his pay, and he opened schools where their young men might be trained in some useful occupation, as farming, gardening, and carpentry. But he met with only moderate success. Like the negroes of the West Indies, most Kaffirs hate work, and have no desire to better their condition. Given a noisy musical instrument, a bright sun, and a gaudy dress, and their mirth and gaity seem boundless. (p. 206)

In itself this is not very striking; the picture of the educational benevolence of a wise governor yielding little profit in the face of incorrigible native irresponsibility is what one would expect to find at this date and in this sort of publication. The book begins in 1475 and spans the world, and this paragraph, for all its brevity, is its most extended consideration of what any group of peoples whom the British conquered and ruled were like. The focus of interest throughout is quite other: not with the nature of the ruled but with that of the ruling race. Here, a couple of pages further on, is the British advance into Zululand:

> The invading army crossed the river at a ford called *Rorke's Drift* (1879), and a division of the troops suffered a great disaster, not far from there, as Isandlana. Happily, a small detachment had been left to guard the passage at the ford. The command of this post was in the hands of Lieutenants Chard and Bromhead, whose names deserve an honoured place in our memory. With a force of 104 men they made an

heroic defence against a savage host of 3000 warriors, who had
reddened their assegais in the blood of our countrymen, taken by
surprise, at Isandlana. (p. 208)

The Zulu victory is passed aside to concentrate on the heroic stand
at Rorke's Drift; the British officers are distinguished by name, and
readers are enjoined to remember them; the odds against them are
enumerated. Dawe's story is in fact a succession of daring deeds
performed by the British against the odds; his book is not so much
about the empire as about the greatness of the British as a breed, as
evidenced through their imperial adventure. While his scope and
range remind us today of how relatively long-standing, wide-
reaching and significant was the British empire in the development
of world 'civilisation', in 1902 his is an empire imagined geographically – in terms of physical places providing scope for hero-
adventurers – rather than anthropologically – in terms of peoples to
be discovered and understood. It is this distinctive bias I would like
to try to follow through a little, as it appears in the nation's bedside
reading matter.

Within the range of imperial literature, whether fiction, poetry,
journalist's article or serious history, what interests me most is not
so much what it says as what it assumes. A selection of incidents, a
kind of language used in description, an unexpected omission of
certain details, can suggest for us patterns of attitudes and
preconceptions important for our understanding of our past.
Embedded in the description of Rorke's Drift, for instance, we can
hear certain attendant assumptions: that Briton against Zulu
opposes the brave against the cowardly, the upright against the
treacherous, the justified against the unjustified, the 'white man'
against the 'savage'. Of course, Dawe's book is only a children's
primer, and not to be over-emphasised; also it is written as a patriotic
celebration of the succession of Edward VII, with the Boer war
freshly in mind. I recall its stance, partly because the simplicities and
prejudices stemming from it are possibly too easily dismissed by
scholars; such crudities have considerable power in the shaping of a
national self-consciousness, if only temporarily. But largely because
the same stance, and the same simplicities – albeit honestly enough
held – are so widespread among not only the popular, ephemeral
stories of empire of the turn of the century, but also those books
which try through fiction seriously to tackle the business of the
governance of the empire.

Empire fiction of the latter part of the century is found at its most straightforward in the quantities of boys' adventure stories, from the full-scale yarns of Ballantyne, Henty or Mayne Reid to countless slight magazine tales, snippets and references. The overwhelming appeal of such tales lies in their potential for engagement, for the reader's immediate identification with the hero; and because of the empire, the fiction can involve him in imaginable events in real places, without his having to accept any diminution in strangeness, mystery or excitement. The perennial appeal of *Treasure Island* – adventure and the hunt, lost treasure, faraway places, sea-travel, desperate foes – could become attainable and part of the here-and-now. An explicit connecting link can be found, for instance, in the habit of both Henty and Mayne Reid of copying large chunks of travellers' writings into their tales, and in such productions as the *Boy Travellers* series of Thomas Knox. *The Boy Travellers on the Congo . . . a journey with Henry M. Stanley 'Through the Dark Continent'* (1888) is no more than a condensed version of Stanley's work fictionalised by the addition of two youths supposedly sharing his adventures. Given its base, this tale is very largely concerned with noting the appearance and habits of the various peoples the travellers meet, as well as the usual excitements of shooting rapids and hacking paths through trackless jungle. But the significant premise of its creation remains, like that of the boys' fiction, that such a journey by two dauntless schoolboys is not only imaginatively credible, but actually probable.

When we come to the fiction itself, the emphasis of Dawe's primer asserts itself. With the animating tension of the books between boy reader and boy hero, there are direct implications for what we might call the 'anthropological' elements. Put simply, the native people tend to become one more variety of object against which the boy hero's ingenuity, courage or uprightness can be measured. Savage tribe, mighty waterfall, terrible precipice, unlucky loss of necessary equipment through a sudden storm, all serve the same function in the story, and so tend to receive the same kind of treatment from the author. They are precisely imagined, described in detail, but distanced and made separate. To take an early, very well-known example, in Ballantyne's *The Coral Island* (1857) the boys first have to overcome the physical problems of a deserted island; then the next challenge is to find themselves up against an attack by savages. So two long boats, one pursuing the other and both full of savages, drive onto the beach and

> the battle that immediately ensued was frightful to behold. Most of the men wielded clubs of enormous size and curious shapes, with which they dashed out each other's brains. As they were almost entirely naked, and had to bound, stoop, leap, and run in their terrible hand-to-hand encounters, they looked more like demons than human beings.[1]

The combatant Fijians are distanced from the reader by having the boys watch their fight from behind the bushes, and further by the matter-of-fact style, and, despite dramatic adjectives, the rather prosaically observed detail. As a result they become specimens of savage, undifferentiated and non-human. Then Ballantyne provides Jack, Ralph and Peterkin with an explicitly moral imperative for intervening, which serves to mark them off as of a different kind from those they fight:

> With a savage laugh, the chief tore the child from [the mother's] arms and tossed it into the sea. A low groan burst from Jack's lips as he witnessed this atrocious act and heard the mother's shriek ... The rippling waves rolled the child on the beach, as if they refused to be a party in such a foul murder.[2]

In the opposition of the boys and the natives, the Fijians' savagery, underlined later by their casual cannibalism, is more necessary to the adventure, in both its racial and its moral aspects, than is any truth or otherwise in the depiction of their manners and mores. In other words, the reduction of the native to an object of adventure frees the author from the need for precise and individual examination of his nature. While it must be credible, that credibility is not necessarily closely allied either to historical or anthropological accuracy, or to any sympathetic consciousness of non-European individuality.

Popular boys' fiction deals in simple opposites, uncomplicated moralities and type characters. But it is as well to remind ourselves of their characteristics, I think, because they do mirror, in a simple and direct way, much of what is distinctive and appealing in the more serious books written for adults. It is surely a mistake, for instance, to see Haggard or much of Kipling as making any essentially different appeal to their readers as Henty or Ballantyne do to theirs, whatever might be said of their relative merit as writers, their sophistication of approach, or their literary ambitions. In each case, the required response is so frequently participatory, providing a call to action. And behind the call lies the very real pull of the geographical fact of empire, the heady excitement of its sheer size and space. For the respectable poor of the 1890s, the small shopkeeper and the struggling city clerk, the empire offered an escape in the imagination from the drabness and grind of city life. In one of his most enduringly popular verses, Kipling explicitly exploits the contrasts:

> I am sick o' wastin' leather on these gritty pavin'-stones,
> An' the blasted English drizzle wakes the fever in my bones;
> Tho' I walks with fifty 'ousemaids outer Chelsea to the Strand,
> An' they talks a lot o' lovin', but wot do they understand?
>> Beefy face an' grubby 'and –
>> Law! wot do they understand?
> I've a neater, sweeter maiden in a cleaner, greener land![3]

The cry of Kipling's soldier must have found the heart of innumerable Mr Pollys.

Time and again, imperial adventure fiction presents us with set scenes of some sort of confrontation between the white hero and the savage tribe. Here, for example, are two English officers in the Himalayas, deciding to beard a troublesome rajah in his den, and venturing far into the Hindu Kush to enforce the wishes of the viceroy upon the upstart ruler of Hunza:

> Hasanabad plateau was crowded, with courtiers and citizens; hard-featured mountaineers, in silks or home-spuns, and rolled woollen caps, from which coils of hair, like grotesque ear-rings, hung almost to their shoulders. Tom-toms, kettle-drums, and embryo clarionets, throbbed and wailed like souls in torment; and well ahead of all, the Thum's Wazir, in velvet and kinkhob, advanced to greet the two khaki-clad officers, whose reticent, well-groomed persons stood for that unknown quantity – the Indian Empire. The tenth century confronting the nineteenth, with only bed-rock human nature to bridge the gulf.[4]

This tableau calls up exactly those associations we find in boys' fiction: the few against the many, the civilised against the savage, the purposeful men against the ill-disciplined host, and finally the odds faced and overcome by the call of man to man. But more particularly, the description is shaped precisely to throw the weight of the readers' attention on to the silent but commanding figures of the white heroes; the native serve as some sort of dramatic backdrop. Now such scenes of confrontation do not necessarily involve any actual combat between the opposing forces. They might well take the form of a set occasion contrived to dramatise a contrast in the perceived characteristics of each race. Thus it is as likely that the virtue of the white man is displayed in his superior ability to follow through a task, accept a moral responsibility, take command, or organise a campaign. Even in *Prester John*, Buchan leaves us in no doubt that Arcoll's highly efficient shepherding will in the end defeat Laputa's magnificent charisma, while the more run-of-the-mill novels show this: ' "The Sahib has seen . . . How can the servants of the Maharaj do more? This thing entirely may not be." . . . "Nevertheless, this thing must be", Lawrence asserted quietly.'[5] The distinctive feature of such scenes is the focus on the white man.

As in Ballantyne, with our attention so often directed onto the figure of the hero, those who oppose him tend to lose individual importance. So we read, in a reasonably serious novel, that 'the air itself in India is sensual, if not immoral. Taken with the intercourse with servile natives, the atmosphere is certainly immoral, heavy with intrigue . . .';[6] or note Allan Quatermain's unconsidered acceptance of the sufferings and death of the Hottentot Ventvögel in the Suliman mountains.[7] Of course, many of these novelists are dealing with proper heroes, who are white men, and not with a selection of protagonists of greater or lesser virtue; the lines must remain simplified and clearly drawn; nevertheless, at times it seems that the most striking aspect of the black presence in imperial fiction is its human absence. I do not mean to suggest that the novelists of the empire ignore the black or coloured races – that is patently untrue – but that they are not interested in them as 'characters' in an old-fashioned sense, as individual personalities. They are not, on the whole, accorded the same kind and degree of characterisation as the white men. It is noteworthy that outstanding exceptions to this admittedly crude generalisation – such as John Laputa – tend to be throw-backs to another time, final inheritors of an heroic, lost past, or leaders of hidden peoples. In closer contact with the white hero, natives are more commonly considered in general terms as examples of their race, which is a subject one, and as such differentiated only into one of a limited number of stock types.

Haggard's first popular success, *King Solomon's Mines* (1885), provides four of the five main groups of native type found in the novels of the end of the century. *En masse* they are perceived as overgrown children, and to be dealt with as such. Villains are entire savages, in an almost pantomime sense, like the usurping king Twala and Scragga, his son. More individual attention is given to those of whom the author approves – the faithful servant and the noble prince of his own kind. The warrior chief Infadoos, despite his high status, falls by and large into the first of these groups, as does the devoted Foulata and the hardly considered Khiva, while Umbopa/Ignosi is a complete example of the second. All these have considerable, if primitive, worth, but recognise the intrinsic excellence of the white heroes. The development of Ignosi is typical. We first meet him acting as a servant, but retaining an instinctive pride and self-confidence, and we leave him, not only promising to rule his people according to western notions of justice and morality, but also implicitly bowing to a superior nature: 'I do perceive that thy words are, now as ever, wise and full of reason, Macumazahn [Quatermain]; that which flies in the air loves not to run along the ground; the white man loves not to live on the level of the black. Well, ye must go . . .'[8] Ignosi here is given the usual fictional speech of the good native, African or Indian – the second person singular and the sub-proverbial turn of phrase. Figures such as Ignosi or Infadoos carry a degree of characterisation which is adequate for the purposes of the straightforward adventure tale, where the principal emphasis is necessarily upon the action. Indeed, one can hardly claim that certain of the British heroes have a much more successfully achieved individuality: Captain Goode, for instance, is distinguished by no more than a few rather comic eccentricities of habit. Nevertheless, they each fit into clearly recognisable roles and character types which are reproduced by the hundred throughout the novels of a similar date and kind. Even the most sketchy further reading of Haggard would suggest their individuality to be more apparent than real. Admittedly in part because he figures in so many novels and stories, Quatermain appears a reasonably complex and sophisticated creation, if not always entirely convincing; but is it really possible to distinguish between Infadoos and Billali, or Foulata and Ustane, or Ignosi and Umslopogaas? While they do have different tribal customs, they have not even Captain Goode's selection of singular outward quirks to mark each as separate.[9]

The novelists of the empire as a whole seem to accept a reasonably distinct ranking order among their broad type categories. The natives who are most to be admired are those who come closest to the idea of the English gentleman, the most to be despised approximate to the cad. On the top of the scale, then, is the high caste gentleman of his own kind. In the numerous Anglo-Indian novels of Mrs Penny, he is the English-educated Indian prince, combining western values and eastern courtesy; such a one is Mir Yacoob Ali Khan, 'a man who would grace any society in the East or West'.[10] In the Africa of Haggard, Buchan and Wallace, he is the Zulu, or – as with Ignosi – a prince of an imagined purer breed of the same stock. Such men are immediately recognisable for their innate nobility, as at the meeting of Sir Henry Curtis and Ignosi – 'We are men, you and I', says the native[11] – or Kipling's Colonel's son and border thief in *The Ballad of East and West*. And such a one can be admired, while finally remaining separate and qualitatively lesser than his western counterpart. Next come those simple, honest and child-like people, best if they live far from the centres of British influence and who thus can carry some features of a noble nature unspoilt by contact with the modern world, '[of] simple dignity and single-mindedness and courtesy'.[12] Together with the savage hordes, these tend to be the least differentiated of all, functioning largely as the human ingredient in the exotic landscape. Faithful servants follow closely, though their exact status does to some extent depend on whether they also double as comic figures providing light relief. Below them are the savages, frequently cruel and violent but not necessarily so. Their constant quality is animal-like: they are to a greater or lesser extent sub-human. The eyes, for instance, of the *zenana* ladies of *Maya* (1908) are like the antelope's, full of fear, curiosity and cunning: 'Now fear, curiosity and cunning are to be found in all animals, and also attachment and aversion. If you can find no other senses than these in a human being, you are safe to class him with the animals. He has no soul.'[13] But worst of all and most to be despised is the hybrid, either the half-caste, or the degenerate native who hangs on the fringes of western society, apes the white man's manners and denies his own race.

Within the ranking scale there are specific racial preferences. In the Indian fiction, Muslims, soldiers and hill people are better than Hindus, civilians and those from the plains. In Africa, the warlike Zulu are better than the Basuto and Hottentot. Haggard's Kuluana women are recognisably ladies, distinguished by lips 'not unpleasantly thick as is the case in most African races', while the evil

119

Twala's lips 'were as thick as a negro's, the nose was flat'.[14] The approved ones not only act but also look the most caucasian.

As these examples might indicate, the distinguishable categories of Africa can be paralleled in the fiction of native India. In this period, the prominence within the stories given to each group is a little different, but the changes in emphasis are those, I think, that might be expected, given the more settled and structured Indian raj as against the exploratory and frontier-like expansion into Africa. Thus the noble prince plays less of a part here, and tends to be located among those peoples relatively untouched by British rule – the tribal people of the southern hills or the Himalayas. Indra/ Chandra of Mrs Penny's *Sacrifice* (1910), for instance, is a small scale version of the lost heir to a native kingdom, found at last to bring to his inheritance the proven standards of western civilisation. Like Ignosi, he is helped by the white hero against the more savage elements of his own kind. Likewise, the entire savage is less in evidence, except when some terrible catastrophe arises, such as the Mutiny, to bring out the latent 'black demon' in him,[15] or when an Englishman trespasses too far into Indian concerns. Mallender of *In Old Madras* (1913) has his eyelids, upper lip, nose and ears cut off by outraged Coorgs for daring to elope with one of their princesses.[16] Also to be expected, the faithful servant is very prominent, often in a comedy role, and of course Indian fiction is packed with examples of the ludicrously westernised hybrid – a kind who does not really figure in African stories until into the twentieth century. The Bengali *babu* is sufficiently established a type before 1900 for the journalist Anstey to develop his comic sketches of Baboo Hurry Bungsho Jabberjee, BA for a purely British rather than Anglo-Indian audience.

When I suggest that the imperial novelists describe their native characters as type figures which lack essential individuality, that by and large they are unable to take them seriously as people, I do not mean to claim that in this the black races always emerge as less differentiated than do the white heroes – who, after all, also need to carry a certain race typicality – or that the degree of characterisation they are afforded is not often perfectly adequate for their role within the story. Nor do I wish to suggest that all the types are necessarily inaccurate, unlikely, or in themselves unconvincing. Their acceptability within each novel is largely a matter of the relative skill of the novelist and of the kind of story he is telling. The best of these novels are highly competent thrillers or well-crafted, workmanlike pieces of entertainment; to make too many demands upon them as literature is unreasonable. But while the good novelist will indeed strive, often with apparent success, to endow his central native figures with certain individual traits, their primary significance still remains in their function within the story. In the mass of novels, good and bad, the natives function as types. It is this role typicality which above all contributes towards that curious sense that the natives do not properly exist. They never surprise.

In part, this appears the inevitable result of the novelists' concern to demonstrate the heroism of the hero, and to focus our attention there. If we take the faithful servant group as an example, in many stories it is immediately apparent that he exists because the plot cannot be made to work credibly without him. Thus, a novelist wishes to display the British hero to greatest advantage, so writing an adventure about the Indian Mutiny he depicts India as being totally in revolt; but the more overwhelming the strength of the rebels, the more imperative the faithful servant becomes. How can a fair-haired, white-skinned hero of the Mutiny – for he has to look like an English gentleman – fight his way through rebel-infested territory without the help of one, or often more, trusty servant? The heroine of *The Great White Hand* (1896) is saved by the efforts of Zeemit Mahal from the 'demoniacal-like hatred exhibited by the majority of the natives';[17] no fewer than seven devoted followers are required to help out the plot of a pot-boiler like *Jenetha's Venture* (1899).[18] As an extension of this function, these figures can be made to provide a spurious kind of 'outside evidence' for the worth of the white protagonists. In *The White Lady of the Zenana* (1904), the slave girl Taj Bee tells the captive English heroine that no one will suspect her of helping in the projected escape for 'no one will think that Taj Bee can love you, and do your will against the Lords of the house'; against all previous affection and duty, she risks her life for the sake of the heroine's purity and goodness.[19] The ultimate worth of the protagonist is reflected in the quality of his followers. Hints of this convention, as of so many others, creep even into those few books whose quality stands out for themselves. It is noticeable that John Laputa is served by the likes of the cowardly bully 'Mwanga, while his opponent Arcoll has the unnamed, courageous and resourceful kaffir who saves David Crawfurd.[20]

In the more aggressively imperialist novels, the devotion accorded to the hero or heroine by a native operates explicitly as a justification for the possession of an empire. Henty's *Rujub the Juggler* (1893) has dedicated himself to the expulsion of the hated British from India; just before the rebellion which is to be the fulfilment of his life's work, an English civilian rescues his daughter from the clutches of a man-eating tiger. This single act effects a complete reversal in his sympathies, and an arch-plotter against the raj becomes one of its strongest adherents:

> I saw that, though the white men were masterful and often hard, though they had little regard for our customs, and viewed our beliefs as superstitions, and scoffed at the notion of there being powers of which they had no knowledge, yet that they were a great people. Other conquerors, many of them, India has had, but none who have made it their first object to care for the welfare of the people at large. The Feringhees have wrung nothing from the poor to be spent in pomp and display; they permit no tyranny or ill-doing; under them the poorest peasant tills his fields in peace.
>
> I have been obliged to see all this, and I feel now that their destruction would be a frightful misfortune.[21]

Rujub's rather sentimental conversion is not particularly convincing, and when he has been made to commit himself to the British cause he is dismissed from the scene with hardly a word. But what reads today like a cold and callous ending was surely written as a triumphant vindication of the glory and good of empire. Within the novel, what Rujub was like, how he felt and how he acted, are not significant; his function is to confirm the collective virtue and heroism of the British. Rujub is admittedly an extreme and obvious example. Nevertheless, on the whole the black or coloured figures in popular fiction of this kind function with greater or lesser crudity as foils to enhance the white hero. When I asked earlier whether it was possible to distinguish between Infadoos and Billali or Foulata and Ustane, perhaps I should further have asked whether it was in fact necessary so to do.

Obviously the adventure stories which make up a large proportion of imperial fiction need to some extent to rely upon type characters, as do the less numerous but still frequent comic sketches of native life and manners. In the first, complex characterisation can be dangerous in holding up the action, or simply in fudging the clear-cut moral argument. Haggard himself runs into something of this problem in *She*. In the second, the entertainment often depends upon exaggerated stereotypes, as with Anstey's Baboo Jabberjee. However, it is possible to discern the same types, serving the same functions, though maybe more skillfully disguised, in that other large body of popular fiction which attempts to offer alongside the adventure some more serious comment on Britain's imperial role. Maud Diver's heroes at Hunza, quoted above, are heroic not because they slay wild animals or find gold or prevent a hot-potting, but because they are fulfilling an official imperial task. The distinction is important, for it marks a central division between novels which rely primarily upon more sophisticated versions of the Ballantyne appeal, and those which graft onto this kind of individual adventure the collective heroism expressed through the benevolent government of a subject people. This division is not by any means to be taken as one of quality. While among the second group must be put Buchan, who can be good, and Kipling, who is good, so also, alas, must be Diver and Mrs Penny, who are not good at all. Nor do I intend to denigrate Haggard by calling him Ballantyne for grown-ups. Rather the distinction is one of the approach to the subject matter – and at times, more unfortunately, one of solemnity. At this period, novels of this kind are more often concerned with the older Indian empire than with Africa, and so my examples shall come from there.

The Rev. Dawe again reminds us of a significant assumption: individual acts within the imperial adventure cannot be easily separated from the perceived moral purpose of the whole. Of the Earl of Dalhousie, governor-general of India from 1848 to 1856, he writes:

> though he added to the empire more territory than any other British ruler in India, before or since, he did it all for the good of India as well as for the greatness of Britain. Believing that rulers exist only for the good of the governed, he made it his aim to do away with abuses, to redress wrongs, to deal even-handed justice all round, and to promote the happiness of the people under his care. (p. 172)

Dalhousie's territorial acquisitiveness and aggressively westernising policies, however well-intentioned, did much to pave the way for the Mutiny of 1857; but Dawe writes without a doubt that the agreed worthiness of objective confers some sort of absolute worth on action and event. The same simple premise is evident among many minor novelists of the later part of the century, and it transforms the shape of the imperial adventure. Camilla, in *The Coeruleans* (1887), finds herself for the first time, in a community where everyone was hard at work – work which formed part, however insignificant, of a beneficial enterprise. The nobility of the task seemed to throw a sort of moral grandeur over lives that might otherwise have been commonplace and even ignoble in their dullness. Unconscious as many of them were of the process, it infused an earnestness, a reality, a purposeful steadiness of aim, into the character of the men who took part in it.[22]

The purpose and the adventure have so come together that the purpose is of itself the adventure, and the grandeur, drama, bravery, chivalry, racial pride – the recognised ingredients of the later imperial mode – do not need any specific action or series of events to give them expression. The adventure is simply in *being* the rulers.

In this vein, the most humdrum of novelists can be found tackling large issues of imperial debate. However, they do not seem to have the same scope as the creators of the single, roving adventurers on the frontiers of civilisation to depart from the actual; as I have suggested, the natives of the simple adventure stories have to have the appearance but not necessarily the substance of anthropological accuracy. The 'adventure of government' novelists, on the other hand, must conform more closely to the known. It is all the more interesting, then, that they tend to remain wedded to the conventional.

The City of Sunshine (1877) is an attractive book which deliberately sets out to describe the business of governing alien peoples. Unlike the adventure stories, its concentration is not on a conventional hero, and there is only one white character in the whole. Mr Eversley, the local magistrate, is a kindly old official, who loves his charges as children, speaks their language, and defends them against the unthinking regulation of his superiors. For the author, his paternalism is patently the right approach. The Indian villagers are the typically indistinctive, childlike, dignified gentlemen, who recognise his innate quality as a *pukka sahib*, accord him simple devotion, and scorn the jumped-up *babu* deputy; as the village headman says, using the novelists' traditional turn of phrase associated with non-whites,

> If a dog makes a pilgrimage to Kasi, he is still but a dog when he comes back again . . . Our Dipty, though he has got all the learning that the Calcutta sahibs can put into him, is still no more of a gentleman than his old father Ram Lall, the oilman. You noticed, Huree – you saw, Lutchman – how politely the Huzoor Magistrate Sahib Bahadoor spoke

to me. He is a great man, and of good caste of Englishman, and knows what proper manners are . . .[23]

Once again, the characterisation is such as to throw the quality of the Englishman into sharp relief.

For Maud Diver and Sidney Grier, both explicitly political writers, the Indians hardly exist except as tribes for the hero to subdue, or soldiers to support him loyally in his task. For Henry Bruce, all Indians are defined in their role as part of 'the great system of collusion that unites all natives against all Europeans'.[24] For Edmund Candler, the Indian official must be the instantly recognisable *babu*

> of the hybrid Cambridge type, with the veneer fast wearing off, – a prig preternaturally fat, and a bundle of touchiness. He welcomed Dick with disconcerting familiarity, adopting the spurious, pseudo-jolly-good-fellow-well-met air which sits as well on men of his type as clothes on a scarecrow . . .[25]

And so it goes on.

Of all the Anglo-Indian novelists of the time, Flora Annie Steel is one of the most highly regarded, then and now.[26] Her books deal with petty near-mutinies, local disturbances narrowly averted, and everyday troubles arising reasonably credibly from the everyday business of running the empire. *The Potter's Thumb* (1894) tells of the battle of wits between the Diwan of Hodinugger and the local officials over the opening of the sluice gates on the canal below the town; *The Hosts of the Lord* (1900) describes the difficulties of keeping the peace in a town of pilgrimage between various religious factions; *Voices in the Night* (1900) deals with the problems of imposing sanitary regulations in time of plague on people who do not understand how the illness spreads. In each case modern policy, seemingly necessary for the good of India as a whole, is faced with local opposition based upon traditional custom. The result is in compromise, for Anglo-India makes mistakes and conservative India is sometimes right. The books are thoughtful and complex; nevertheless, they are based on the premise that violent opposition to the British rule is an ever-present probability. Mrs Steel's analysis of this incipient violence suggests that it springs inevitably from the clash of mutually alien peoples, and in detail, her Indians are not far removed from the conventional notions of native character I have been sketching out.

In *The Hosts of the Lord*, the hero is saved and order reasserted through the devotion of the aboriginal Am-ma to the heroine, and his simple conviction that as the British have the power of the *dee-puk-rag*, the miraculous electric light, then they are the true masters of India. Am-ma combines the near-animal specimen with the loyal follower of the superior race; his opposite is Gogol, the evil savage who hits out blindly against the civilising white man. In the same novel we have a type of noble native in Roshan Khan, a rising young *risaldar* barred from advancement because of his native birth; he finds himself leading a little rebellion which he knows cannot succeed, because of his loyalty to his own people. Roshan Khan is destroyed because his affections and duties as an Indian dictate a doomed course of action, while those same excellent qualities force him to acknowledge the superiority of western ideals. Further, Mrs Steel has all the usual contempt for the followers of Young India, the *babus* who advocate social progress and marry children of ten, and preach the doctrine of complete independence in bad English prose. Her *babu* Ramanand is only a 'pestilential little fool'.[27]

For Mrs Steel, the British were not individually superior to the Indians, but as a race they were more advanced; they thus had a duty to teach their subjects their customs and beliefs. Culturally separate, it did not do for the races to approach too closely. At the beginning of *The Hosts of the Lord*, the shrewd prison governor of Eshwara says bluntly

> So long as we don't understand [the Indians] . . . and they don't understand us, we jog along the same path amicably, like – well! like the pilgrims to the 'Cradle of the Gods', and the telegraph posts to the Adjutant-General's office up to the road yonder . . . No! It is when we begin to have glimmerings that the deuce and all comes in –

The structure of the story subsequently suggests he is right. The Indians are still, for the most part, children who must be coaxed towards the light. Her Anglo-Indian officials are not always as wise, as courageous or even as honest as the British heroes of the adventure novels; but at their best they offer India's only hope for the future. Such a one is Lance Carlyon, the hero who succeeds where Roshan Khan fails:

> boyish, almost thoughtless as he was, puzzling himself not at all with the problems of life, you could never dip below the surface without

126

finding him, as it were, there before you; finding him clear-eyed, ready to treat the shady side of things as he treated the light side; that is, with an absolute limpid honesty.[28]

And with Lance, we are back with Sir Henry Curtis, almost indeed with Ballantyne's Jack Martin, Ralph Rover and Peterkin Gay.

The native figures, then, by and large remain within certain clearly defined limits, and maintain a distinctive relationship with the white man. If we abstract what appear to be conventions in the tone, structure and characterisation of these imperial stories, the similarities between them are insistent, whether the tale be boys' adventure, grown-up romance or fictionalised explanation of government. Such conventions are often unobtrusive in books considered individually, and become apparent through a more general over-view. However, there is a further feature to be noted. Mid-century writers such as Ballantyne, Mayne Reid or Henty were at least in part adventurers themselves; they travelled the world and delighted in the excitement of strange places. The writers of the end of the century, still imbued with that sense of the wide, wide world, came from very different stock. In India, for instance, Mrs Steel was the wife of an ICS official, and while she laboured mightily for the education of Indian girls and fought many a battle with bureaucracy, remained always on the inside of official life. Maud Diver sprang from an old Anglo-Indian family, related – albeit distantly – to the great Lawrences; Bithia Croker spent fourteen years as an officer's wife in India and Burma; Mrs Penny was the wife of the Madras chaplain. In Africa, Haggard took part officially in the annexation of the Transvaal in 1877, and devoted much of the latter part of his life to official welfare throughout the empire. Buchan was an assistant private secretary to Lord Milner in South Africa and ended life as governor-general of Canada. In other words, many of the obvious names are directly connected with the official imperial machine. Their apparent inability to perceive the empire except in terms of the British adventurer hero, with the native peoples fixed in recognised postures according to category, is, then, the more interesting. It stands out, moreover, in distinction to the range of sympathy found in Kipling's Indian stories and in *Kim*. Kipling, of course, was the son of a merchant and himself a journalist, and never quite a part of official Anglo-Indian society.

Before considering why these later writers remain so tied to established conventions, it might be useful to remind ourselves of the context in which their novels were written and became so popular. In the first place, current scientific speculations concerning species and race were such as to encourage rather than discourage racial stereotyping and comparative assessments of worth and quality. The second half of the nineteenth century was dominated by various evolutionary theories of human development in almost all areas of study – the political, ethnological, anthropological, psychological, sociological, religious – which carried certain corollaries in the discussion of racial characteristics. To describe an evolutionary process, it is almost impossible to avoid such words as 'progress', 'development', 'fittest'. However much Darwin, for instance, or Wallace, might insist that he handled such notions neutrally, that such words carried only a functional connotation, they could so easily be translated into moral and value-laden terms, particularly when applied to people and to societies. Indeed, the investigations themselves were often of a kind that made such an extension difficult to avoid. The anthropologist Edward B. Tylor, for example, propounded a well-regarded theory that the human race as a whole followed a certain sequential pattern of cultural development.[29] Therefore, it had to be possible to devise some sort of progressive scale of development from the primitive to the civilised, and further to classify contemporary societies according to the stage along the scale to which they had reached. The American L. H. Morgan described such a scale in his *Ancient Society, or, Researches in the Lines of Human Progress from Savagery through to Civilisation* of 1877. In this kind of classification, it is extremely difficult to avoid terms which themselves suggest a moral dimension, even where such connotations are not – as they often were – deliberately encouraged.

Further, it was possible to see the political rise and decline of empires in Darwinian evolutionary terms. As early as 1868, Charles Dilke had so described the British empire.[30] In 1894, Benjamin Kidd in *Social Evolution* predicted that the internal competition of a nation would be replaced by a 'rivalry of nationalities' in which the Anglo-Saxon race would emerge at the top.[31] Such a crude social Darwinism could, in the context of the turn of the century political anxieties, encourage the kind of hysterical oratory which assigned to the British race a divine right for waging war on the Boers: 'Never since on Sinai God spoke in thunder has mandate more imperative been issued to any race, city, or nation than now to this nation and to this people'.[32] There was, that is to say, a recognised pattern of thinking which encouraged the idea of a racial separateness and which could be called into play to defend the special fitness of the British for imperial rule.

But the idea of evolution could be used in very many different ways and was open to many different interpretations. What, for instance, did 'fittest' mean? It might not necessarily be equated with a western European definition of 'best'; the civilised might not be those most fitted to survive. Indeed, it was argued that the white races, being of a superior civilisation, were in fact less well equipped to survive than the black or the yellow:

> there seems ... good warrant for assuming that the advantage has already passed to the lower forms of humanity, and indeed it appears to be a well-ascertained law that the races which care little for comfort and decency are bound to tide over bad times better than their superiors, and that the classes which reach the highest standard are proportionately short-lived.[33]

The idea of the 'survival of the fittest' has here turned against the civilised.

Again, was 'best' to be interpreted individually or for whole societies? There were many observers who looked at the condition of the populace in the over-grown and over-crowded city slums and concluded that the British race as a whole was already in decline. From the medical profession came dreadful warnings that the British stock was degenerating, both physically and morally, in such conditions:

> the close confines and foul air of our cities are shortening the life of the individual, and raising up a puny and ill-developed race ... It is beyond prophecy to guess even what the rising generation will grow into, what this Empire will become after they have got charge of it.[34]

The recognised extent and importance of the problem is evidenced by the many efforts in the years immediately after 1900 to improve the physical welfare of the nation through the school system, with school meals, domestic science and hygiene classes and regular medical inspections. At the end of the century, the condition of city children could most powerfully suggest a race in decline.

The prevalence of the evolutionary model, then, could enhance a conviction of British superiority, suggest its vulnerability, and support fears of British decline. The extent and pervasiveness of these fears can perhaps best be seen in the countless opportunities taken for claiming that Britain was still capable of producing heroes, despite all. The *Blackwood*'s review of Lord Robert's *Forty One Years in India* (1897), for instance, finds in him a man whose deeds should convince the world 'that a nation which can produce such men has not entered yet on the period of its decline, has not yet had its energies and spirit sapped by peace and prosperity, but is still capable of vindicating its Empire in all parts of the globe'.[35] This claim is echoed again and again in the imperial adventure stories. Throughout Maud Diver's novels of frontier wars runs the message that the empire needs great men, and the empire breeds them itself in its own especial way. Repeating those fears for the degeneration of England – a degeneration that is for her explicitly moral – she writes that

> Even in an age given over to the marketable commodity, England can still breed men of this calibre. Not perhaps in her cities, where individual aspiration and character are cramped, warped, deadened by the brute force of money ... but in the unconsidered corners of her Empire, in the vast spaces and comparative isolation, where old-fashioned patriotism takes the place of parochial party politics, and where, alone, strong natures can grow up in their own way.[36]

Here, in the empire, the race will find the necessary space to breed the heroes which it should innately bring forth, and possibly no longer can in the tainted atmosphere of Britain.

And even if the race being raised in Britain were physically in decline, the hero of the imperial adventure could, individually, stand against the tide. In England, we find Allan Quatermain rejecting the 'prim English country, with its trim hedgerows and cultivated fields, its stiff formal manners and its well-dressed crowds', and vowing to 'go and die as I had lived, among the wild game and the savages'.[37] Free from the restrictions of late Victorian respectability, Haggard's heroes are allowed to take on the savage races on their own terms, and to win through because to their own strength is added the understanding and control of the civilised, and the distinctive, indefinable quality of Britishness.Sir Henry can defeat Twala in single combat, but Captain Goode can use his almanac to predict a miracle, and Quatermain can insist on King Ignosi's adoption of western justice. The adventure stories, with their white heroes and clear-cut moral issues, could thus themselves operate as some sort of evidence – certainly imagined, but at least imaginable – that the British race was still in the ascendent. They could provide an answer to horrid imaginings of decline.

By the end of the nineteenth century, racial theories of many provenances seemed to support notions of separation and mutual struggle, and could be used in support of a belief in white supremacy. Evolutionary theories derived from Darwin prompted, as well as optimism, fears of racial decline and possible extinction. But while writers could suggest that the empire-builders belied those fears, the empire itself was increasingly called into question in a Europe moving politically towards a wider and less authoritarian model of government. The possession of empire itself needed defending.

In part the defence made was political and economic; the empire was seen as necessary to enable Britain to maintain a world power and prestige perceived to be already slipping from its grasp. In the mid-century, J. A. Froude had suggested that the survival of Britain as a great power depended upon imperial development:

> Other nations, once less powerful or not more powerful than ourselves, are growing in strength and numbers, and we too must grow if we intend to remain on a level with them. Here at home we have no room to grow except by the expansion of towns which are already overgrown . . . our greatness will be held by a tenure which in the nature of things must become more and more precarious.
>
> Is there no alternative? Once absolutely our own, and still easily within our reach, are our Eastern and Western colonies containing all and more than all that we require . . .[38]

By the turn of the century, such arguments provided many with the justification for the undignified African scramble in which Britain, France and Germany were currently engaged: 'It is said that our Empire is already large enough and does not need extension. That would be true enough if the world were elastic, but, unfortunately, it is not elastic, and we are engaged at the moment in the language of mining in "pegging out claims for the future".'[39] But more powerfully, the vindication of the empire was couched in terms of the peculiar British ability to fulfil a most seriously-conceived, parental, educative trust:

> In Asia and in Africa great native populations have passed under our hand. To us – to us, and not to others, a certain definite duty has been assigned. To carry light and civilisation into the dark places of the world; to touch the mind of Asia and of Africa with the ethical ideas of Europe; to give to thronging millions, who would otherwise never know

peace or security, these first conditions of human advance: constructive endeavour such as this forms part of the function which it is ours to discharge.[40]

In this kind of argument, the white heroes were both necessary for the fulfilment of the trust, and the reason for its existence.

Here, surely, the significance of the boys' adventure story model becomes apparent for even the sober-minded 'adventure of government' novelists. It is at least plausible to suggest that writers who were themselves of the empire establishment found in the boys' adventure stories a set of conventions which could readily be used to carry their explanations of the British imperial role. They inherited from their schooldays a language which offered a description of the British national character as active, moral and heroic, and which, translated into the business of governing the empire, provided an apparently convincing justification for its continuance. But at the same time, the particular image of the white hero this required was largely dependent upon the reverse image of the native as either savage and uncivilised or child-like and unsophisticated. It should not be surprising, then, that the native figures are treated in the way I have described.

Interestingly, in the 1890s, after years of comparative neglect, the Indian Mutiny suddenly becomes 'one of the two epochs in history on which every young writer feels irresistibly impelled to exercise his 'prentice hand'.[41] The novelists of the Mutiny describe, not the messy business of history, but a simple epic struggle between white men and black, good and evil. The subject, wrote Mrs Steel of her own Mutiny novel, 'was one to touch all hearts, to rouse every Britisher's pride and enthusiasm ... it was then the Epic of the Race'.[42] The phrase, and the stance, were repeated in G. W. Forrest's monumental *History of the Indian Mutiny* of 1904.[43] As a body, the imperial novels constitute a similar kind of 'epic' for the British. And given the circumstances surrounding their production, the angle of vision of many of their authors, and their literary inheritance, it is surely unsurprising to find explicitly British heroes proliferating, and that few really wished to look too closely at the empire's subject peoples.

Notes

1. R. M. Ballantyne: *The Coral Island* (Blackie's Modern Reprint ed., London, 1965), p. 169.

2. *Coral Island*, p. 173.
3. R. Kipling: 'The Road to Mandalay', in T. S. Eliot (ed.): *A Choice of Kipling's Verse* (London, 1963), p. 189.
4. M. Diver: *Candles in the Wind* (London, 1909), p. 191.
5. *Candles in the Wind*, pp. 13–14.
6. H. Bruce: *The Eurasian* (London, 1913), p. 67.
7. H. Rider Haggard: *King Solomon's Mines* (Harmondsworth, 1970), pp. 79–81.
8. *King Solomon's Mines*, p. 245.
9. Billali and Ustane appear in *She* (1887); Umslopogaas figures in the exceptional *Nada the Lily* (1892) and in *Allan Quatermain* (1887).
10. F. E. F. Penny: *A Mixed Marriage* (London, 1903), p. 100.
11. Haggard: *King Solomon's Mines*, p. 44.
12. B. M. Croker: *A Family Likeness* (London, 1892), i, p. 250.
13. P. L. Oliphant: *Maya, A Tale of East and West* (London, 1908), p. 306.
14. Haggard: *King Solomon's Mines*, pp. 106, 115.
15. E.g. J. E. Muddock: *The Great White Hand; or The Tiger of Cawnpore* (London, 1896), pp. 233–7.
16. B. M. Croker: *In Old Madras* (London, 1913).
17. Muddock: *The Great White Hand*, p. 199.
18. A. F. P. Harcourt: *Jenetha's Venture: A Tale of the Siege of Delhi* (London, 1899).
19. H. Bourchier: *The White Lady of the Zenana* (London, 1904), p. 83.
20. J. Buchan: *Prester John* (Harmondsworth, 1956), pp. 115–16, 122.
21. G. A. Henty: *Rujub the Juggler* (London, 1893), iii, p. 33.
22. H. Cunningham: *The Coeruleans: A Vacation Idyll* (London, 1887), ii, p. 24.
23. A. Allardyce: *The City of Sunshine* (London, 1887), i, p. 185.
24. Bruce: *The Eurasian*, p. 106.
25. E. Candler: 'Probationary', *The General Plan* (London, 1911), pp. 23–4.
26. For an excellent introduction to these novelists, see Benita Parry: *Delusions and Discoveries: Studies on India in the British Imagination 1880–1930* (London, 1972); also Violet Powell: *Flora Annie Steel: Novelist of India* (London, 1981).
27. F. A. Steel: *The Hosts of the Lord* (London, 1900), p. 80.
28. *The Hosts of the Lord*, p. 169.
29. E. B. Tylor: *Researches into the Early History of Mankind and the Development of Civilisation* (London, 1865); *Primitive Culture* (London, 1871).
30. C. Dilke: *Greater Britain* (London, 1868), I, pp. 391–2.
31. B. Kidd: *Social Evolution* (London, 1894), pp. 45–6.
32. J. A. Cramb: *Reflections on the Origin and Destiny of Imperial Britain* (London and New York, 1900), p. 315.
33. C. H. Pearson: *National Life and Character: A Forecast* (London, 1893), pp. 341–2.
34. J. Cantlie: *Degeneration Amongst Londoners* (London, 1885), pp. 35, 52.
35. *Blackwood's Edinburgh Magazine*, 1897, CLXI, p. 313.
36. M. Diver: *The Great Amulet* (Edinburgh & London, 1908), p. 211.
37. H. Rider Haggard: *Allan Quatermain* (Hodder & Stoughton ed., London, 1966), p. 9.
38. J. A. Froude: *Short Studies on Great Subjects* (second series, London, 1871), pp. 171–2.
39. Earl of Rosebery: 'Speech at the Anniversary Banquet of the Royal Colonial Institute', *The Times*, 2 March, 1893.
40. H. F. Wyatt: 'The ethics of empire', in *Nineteenth Century*, 1897, XLI, p. 529.

41. 'The Indian Mutiny in fiction', in *Blackwood's Edinburgh Magazine*, 1897, CLXI, p. 218.
42. F. A. Steel: *The Garden of Fidelity* (London, 1929), p. 226.
43. G. W. Forrest: *A History of the Indian Mutiny* (Edinburgh & London, 1904), I, p. 362.

7 Buchan and 'The Black General'

DAVID DANIELL

John Buchan is still most widely known for *The Thirty-Nine Steps* (1915) though it was his twenty-seventh book – he wrote over a hundred – and the second of his six 'shockers'. The reputation of that book does little justice to him, and the three films under its title have not helped, having either no connection with Buchan's book at all or so little as hardly to count. He was, by his own estimation of himself, primarily a classicist and historian: his biggest work was a twenty-four volume history of the first world war, written as it was fought, and his most outstanding books were lives of Sir Walter Scott, Cromwell, Augustus and Montrose, and serious novels like *Witch Wood*. He was barrister, publisher, wartime director of information, director of Reuter's, MP, high commissioner for the Church of Scotland and governor-general of Canada as Lord Tweedsmuir. Born five years after Dickens died, he died in 1940; his posthumous autobiography, *Memory Hold-the-Door*, is regarded by many as his finest book.

Two years after going down from Oxford, with London at his feet, he sailed to South Africa to work with Milner. He was there from October 1901 to August 1903, and was chiefly concerned with resettlement programmes after the Boer war. He travelled extensively, much on horseback, and found that large areas of upland Africa bit deeply into his imagination. Several books came out of his African experience: a big analytic account of the history, geography, economics and politics called *The African Colony: Studies in the Reconstruction* (Blackwood's, November 1903); a curious and not yet fully understood fictional study of political and social thought, particularly about the empire, called *A Lodge in the Wilderness* also from Blackwood's, in November 1906; and a boys' adventure story, *Prester John*, published by Nelson in August 1910.

135

It is this latter book, and especally its serial publication in a boys' magazine, which is my subject here.

Prester John was popular, and still is; it has been, and still is, frequently reprinted. It tells the story of a young Scots boy, drawn very much in the tradition of R. L. Stevenson, who finds himself in South Africa at the time of a great native rising against the whites. After heroic adventures he defeats the black leader of the rising, a christian minister whom he had already watched, by chance, in Scotland, performing secret unchristian rites. This black leader, Laputa, sees himself as the reincarnation of the ancient and legendary African (and long before that, oriental) priest and king, Prester John, and his talisman is a gold and jewelled necklace supposed to have been handed down from the Queen of Sheba. Though the book is for boys, it is rich, allowing the African leader great stature, and setting him in a kaleidoscopic context of lightly-touched interests, historical, social, literary, geographic and above all religious. The downfall of Laputa is a matter of personal grief to the hero who clearly sees in him a lost, if flawed, father figure. The book owes more to Stevenson, Bunyan, Milton and Buchan's Montrose studies than it does to such apparently obvious predecessors as Rider Haggard, whose *King Solomon's Mines* was, by the time of *Prester John*, a quarter of a century old. It also owes a good deal to Buchan's own observation and knowledge. It still awaits adequate critical treatment.[1]

Prester John was welcomed and praised when it first appeared, and it was usually and rightly associated with Stevenson. It had, however, a second life – a third, if the American edition under the title *The Great Diamond Pipe* is included – in that it ran in the Newnes boys' magazine *The Captain* as the principal serial from April to September 1910 (XXIII, nos. 133–8) under the title 'The Black General'. Not only the title, however, was changed: a very large number of alterations, some major, appear in *The Captain*'s version. I have not been able to discover whether these had John Buchan's permission: the evidence points clearly to him not being the reviser. Using parallels from elsewhere one can reasonably deduce that he did not feel himself involved in the alteration.[2] Though I believe it is wrong to see in *Prester John* simply the outcropping of familiar, and now hateful, notions about white and black in the Africa of the time – as it is less wrong, for example, with Rider Haggard – I do detect in *The Captain*'s altered version, in the very nature of the changes themselves, something altogether different. There, trimmed and differently tinted, is a version of the Buchan story to which serious objection may be taken, as I shall show.

The title of the book, *Prester John*, is one that commands respect. The very long history of the legend contained in those two words, and their association with matters of the highest value – right rule, true religion, justice and myth – are appealed to. The magazine's title, 'The Black General', is by contrast diminishing, even I suspect intended to oxymoronic. In *Prester John*, the Reverend John Laputa is noble, ambivalent, learned and aristocratic: flawed, of course, but greatly flawed. In 'The Black General' he is shorn of almost all his tragic resonance, and is little more than a peculiar black man, to be exterminated.

To understand the full significance of this, more needs to be said about Buchan's original book, about the imperialist trend in popular literature of the time, and about *The Captain* in particular.

The book belongs to a genre which is only now, in the last quarter of the twentieth century, coming into focus, that of popular literature of the empire. There are incidental remarks in it to which objection must now be taken. Laputa's face is contrasted with 'the squat and preposterous Negro lineaments': a character, admittedly the least important in the book, refers to 'niggers' twice, and so on: selective quotation can multiply such items, though I have quoted the worst.[3] While not excusing these, I feel the point is worth making here that the very survival of Buchan has done him unintentional harm. He has a thousand readers, still, as paperback sales figures show, for every one who reads Haggard, or even Conrad, in whose pages more objectionable remarks can be found; and this is to say nothing of that vast hinterland of popular fiction of the early 1900s, now totally forgotten. It is, surprising as it may seem, the very moderation of Buchan's incidentals which should first of all be noted.

Of course, it is a white man's view of Africa, with the marks of empire upon it. But again, what is to be noted is that Buchan's empire ideas are, as he shows elsewhere, unusual for the time. The celebrated passage in the penultimate chapter in *Prester John* about 'the white man's duty' does now read badly:

Yet it was an experience for which I shall ever be grateful for it turned me from a rash boy into a serious man. I knew then the meaning of the

137

white man's duty. He has to take all risks, recking nothing of his life or his fortunes, and well content to find his reward in the fulfilment of his task. That is the difference between white and black, the gift of responsibility, the power of being in a little way a king; and so long as we know this and practise it, we will not rule in Africa alone, but wherever there are dark men who live only for the day and for their own bellies. Moreoever the work made me pitiful and kindly. I learned much of the untold grievances of the natives, and saw something of their strange, twisted reasoning. Before we had got Laputa's army back to their kraals, with food enough to tide them over the spring sowing, Aitken and I had got sounder policy in our heads than you will find in the towns, where men sit in offices and see the world through a mist of papers.

But anyone who is familiar with popular imperialist writing between 1890 and 1910 must find this passage positively sensitive by contrast. (It was cut from *The Captain*'s version.) Buchan's very survival has done him, again, disservice. The emphasis we ought to be noting is on the 'sounder policy', even if carried out in the offensive manner of being 'in a little way a king', which is learned through direct contact, not 'through a mist of papers', and at the risk of losing all.

Prester John belongs to that class of empire literature which sees the frontier as a place of physical, moral and spiritual renewal for a young British male, and as such has links with an older romance strain which goes back through Scott to Defoe and far beyond.[4] At the climax, David Crawfurd, the hero, emerges, after almost miraculous feats of climbing skill, from the cave with the underground waterfall, the place of wealth and ritual and death, into what is effectively a Scottish moor.

It was little more than dawn, such a dawn as walks only on the hilltops. [*The Captain* removed the last nine words] Before me was the shallow vale with its bracken and sweet grass, and the shining links of the stream, and the loch still grey in the shadow of the beleaguering hills. Here was a fresh, clean land, a land for homesteads and orchards and children. All of a sudden I realised that at last I had come out of savagery.

The burden of the past days slipped from my shoulders. I felt young again, and cheerful, and brave. Behind me was the black night, and the horrid secrets of darkness. Before me was my own country, for that loch and that bracken might have been on a Scotch moor. The fresh scent of the air and the whole morning mystery put song into my blood. I remembered that I was not yet twenty.

138

Buchan is much on record as finding the South African uplands 'like Scotland', but it is important to recognise that 'savagery' was as much present there in his own fiction of Convenanting times written before and after *Prester John*. Here he is in a sense using his own Scottish boyhood to mark the conclusion of a rite of passage. Though it is possible to go on to analyse many other features of the book in their empire-romance characteristics – the working-out of the various, and shifting, significances of all the meanings of the word 'intelligence', for example – one matter presents itself for attention continually. This is the steady beat of religious, particularly biblical, reference. The opening pages are set in, or just away from, a Scottish kirk on the sabbath of the spring communion: the hero is the minister's son (as Buchan was). The Reverend John Laputa, visiting preacher that day in the town's Free Kirk, was also a minister, and so the christian and biblical references have an acceptable context. Crawfurd has *Pilgrim's Progress* and the Bible steadily in mind, particularly in moments of great weakness or need. Such imagery and reference rise to control the action in a great scene of ritual at the heart of the book, when Laputa, standing by a fire next to a wall of descending water in the cave shut in the mountainside, is dedicated to the leadership, and passes as it were from priest to king, which reminds Crawfurd of 'a picture of Samuel anointing Saul king of Israel'. Spoken texts from Isaiah and Psalms and the gospels and Revelation dominate the action in a way which is not at all common in boys' literature of that period, though it had been fifty years before. (Almost all the religious reference is cut in *The Captain*'s version of that scene, in a wholesale pruning.) This use of the Bible is very different from the pseudo-biblical, pseudo-blank-verse rhythms normal to Rider Haggard, for example, particularly at moments of slaughter. In *Prester John* a mind steeped in the Bible is presenting a hero, a noble enemy and an action all themselves steeped in the Bible.

This very fact, with two others which I can adduce, fix *Prester John* in the setting of empire rather than imperialist fiction, a point I shall elaborate presently. The first of the two further qualities to notice is the whole range of sensibilities of the hero. He is unusually observant, and knowledgeable about and responsive to the countryside he passes through. Most paragraphs are illuminated by a touch of detailed observation which lifts the narrative up into the world of romance of Stevenson and Scott. I quote absolutely at random, as the book fell open: 'Only a desperate resolution took me through the tangle of juniper bushes into the red screes of the gully'. Crawfurd knows the bushes, notes the screes. (The sentence is cut in *The Captain*.) The landscape comes clean off the page, even if it has a tendency to be Scotland with different kinds of African blacks instead of Highland clansmen. But more than that, the hero's sensibilities extend to his own sensations across a very wide spectrum of feelings indeed, with an unusual attention to the weaker end. David Crawfurd is more frequently weak, defeated, collapsed, cowardly, in pain and need, desperate for relief from thirst or bonds, than is permitted in all the other popular imperialist literature of the time that I have read. He is no epitome of the 'manly' – that is to say, he is more recognisably human than the very 'macho' heroes of boys' fiction would ever allow.

As I shall show, the adaptation into 'The Black General' systematically removed both the detail of the hero's observation and his weakness and humanity. This has the effect of dehumanising everyone in the book, particularly the blacks. The hero is subtly turned into a cardboard hero: the people among whom he moves are thereby, even if not always overtly, robbed of their humanity as well. This is true of no one so much as Laputa: robbed of his biblical and historical reference, and not allowed his Bunyanesque, Scott-ish, Stevensonian setting, he becomes that much more an ogre from a book of fairy-tales rather than a recognisable likeness of the great priest-king of most ancient legend, Prester John himself. More of this anon.

I return for a moment to the very necessary distinction between empire and imperialist literature, and my claim that *Prester John* belongs to the empire, and more benign, strain, whereas 'The Black General' has been transformed into a more hard-nosed imperialist document (almost certainly without Buchan's consent).

Popular literature of empire goes back at least four hundred years. The excitement of a remote frontier, of British possessions overseas, engagement in small, distant wars, the paramount importance of a navy, pressing problems of peace-keeping, and union, both overseas and at home, can all be found in Elizabethan writers and fairly continuously afterwards. It has to be said clearly, at a time when it can be unpopular to say so, that some of this literature is very far from reprehensible. Coinciding with it, and overlapping to a great extent, is a vast field of popular Protestant literature, in which the Empire can be seen as something as attractive as simply the extension of the family overseas: the British Navy is important only as the means of preserving communication, its glamour chiefly because of the rigours of that work in far-off places, (an aspect of the Navy which brings romance to – of all writers – Jane Austen, as in *Persuasion*). Best-selling works of non-fiction, like David Livingstone's *Travels* (1857, 1865), which are still in print and selling well, or missionary biographies, very often of women, or the accounts of engineers, might now be frequently found to be patronising; but they are not vicious. Empire could, even in the mid-nineteenth century, mean exploration, or what was understood to be so, map-making, engineering, medicine, and special interests in literatures, languages and the problems of translation. Much of the writing about all this was inspired by, and often a part of, the growth of literature for children, without distinction of sex, from the middle of the century. It can be charted through a study of the founding, and success, of children's magazines after about 1830. A great deal of it now unreadable, being both tedious and pious: some of it is neither.

Then, late in the century, a change quite clearly comes over the popular literature of all kinds: it becomes aggressively, and defensively, imperialist. It leaves the christian family ambience and becomes all-male and public school: military values invade and take over the stories; religion is subordinated to fighting; weakness is at best discounted and at worst punished. White dominates black with cool superiority and a god – now in the name of something called civilisation. This quite sudden sideways shift, distressing to watch, dominates, in songs as well as novels, in encyclopaedias and newspapers. The Navy is preparing for some great killing. The move can be seen most clearly in the children's journals, which from about 1860 had begun to focus on boys; and between 1880 and 1900 a hundred children's journals were founded, over half of them devoted to 'manly' adventure for boys – privileged boys at public school, preparing to be officers in the armed forces. The major issue has shifted over several decades from the spiritual one of what is 'holy' to the physical one of what is 'manly'.

This move to imperialist values, all across the popular literature, is disturbing. I take as illustration pages pretty well at random from *The Captain* (the name of which can now be seen as significant). The magazine, around 1910, had a long-running series about

successful and admirable men, inviting emulation, under the title
'How I began'. The May 1910 number opens with a long piece in
lavish praise of Sir Hiram S. Maxim and his famous invention.

> That was the gun which stopped the rush of Fuzzywuzzies at
> Omdurman, winning back the Soudan to civilisation . . . the war-
> correspondents . . . all agreed that it cut the Soudanese down like grain
> before the reaper, and that a perceptible wave of death could be seen
> passing over their ranks . . .

In the November 1911 number a full-page has the caption 'I picked
up a stick, and laid about me for all I was worth. Maskey struck out
with his huge fists, and niggers went down right and left.' The
picture shows two white men winning a vicious fight with four
black men armed with clubs and a sort of pickaxe: the whites are
fully clothed, the blacks naked except for animal skins which give
them the appearance of having tails. A page before this, the text has
'. . . before Maskey was secured he had made shuttlecock of several
black fellows, and knocked them about in a manner that it is safe to
say they would remember as long as they lived'. What is remarkable
about these things is that they are not at all remarkable in context.

The Captain gave good value to its readers. Every monthly issue
was fully illustrated, well printed, with many stories (mostly public
school stories) and attractive articles in the how-to-do-it vein.
There are stories by P. G. Wodehouse and Percy F. Westerman. It is
all, however, exclusively, and presumably comfortingly, male. The
editor (most unfortunately called 'The Old Fag') occasionally
prints, at the back, a letter from a girl, or advises his readers to stay
away from girls who smoke. Each month's number is given wholly
to 'adventure', which means boys and men being 'manly' together,
which means generally being vicious from lofty 'patriotic' or 'loyal'
motives. The cultivation of such knee-jerk responses can now be
seen as primarily defensive. Rightly or wrongly, the empire was
seen as under threat, principally from Russia, especially in northern
India, but also from secretly organised hordes of 'natives'. The
popular literature, for everyone, exhorted the nation to be
'patriotic', to yield consciously to simple expressions of loyalty to
'The Old Flag' or similar ikons. (Buchan clearly hated such
jingoism, and he mocked and dismantled it in *The Lodge in the
Wilderness* and elsewhere.)

John de Walton: illustration for 'The Lost Explorer'

It is in *The Captain* that Buchan's *Prester John* finds itself as 'The Black General', and it is to that transformation that I now turn.

The change of title has one more significance. In a work of fiction called *Prester John*, the delay in the recognition of the leader of the uprising has a certain likelihood: under the title 'The Black General' such delay looks like incompetence. But going beyond the title, I have listed over five hundred alterations from book to magazine, some as small as the removal of a few words, some as large as the cutting of half-a-dozen pages at a time. Abridgement is constantly taking place, with large cuts in the religious details of Laputa's dedication, and the removal of most of the last three chapters of the book. In all, the book is reduced by one-fifth. The effect, as these cuts are in certain observable directions, is of wholesale alteration.

In addition to the cuts there is steady alteration of the text and some re-writing. It has the appearance of having been given to an 'old Africa hand' for 'correction', as there are numerous changes in Buchan's spellings of African names. As these vary so widely between all written accounts of African affairs at this time that I have seen, I feel these hardly qualify as corrections. Buchan's Boer words are usually silently replaced, as 'horse' for '*Schimmel*', unnecessarily. His Scotticisms are silently replaced, with 'thrill' for 'grue' and so on; two are worth noticing: Crawfurd's wry comment on the schoolmaster's sense, 'He did not come out of Aberdeen for nothing' is deleted; and at his removal of the native servant girl Zeeta when he shifts his quarters, 'I carried Zeeta with me' becomes 'I took Zeeta with me' as if 'carrying', though good Scots, was perhaps a mite too physical. More irritating is the pedantic 'correcting' of Buchan's grammar and syntax, of which I noted a score of examples, none of them improvements. In other words, the text is, even superficially, being made to fit an English schoolboy. That this is part of a general process of flattening says a great deal about the reader of *The Captain* in 1910.

More alarming is the alteration of Buchan's text to fit some standard of taste. Thus, all kinds of oath are carefully removed, as are any references to God and heaven. 'God pity his slaves, then' becomes 'Pity his slaves, then'. Colin, the dog, is a mongrel 'in whose blood ran mastiff and bulldog and foxhound and Heaven knows what besides' – the last five words are deleted. 'It was my only hope . . . Thank God, it held': 'Thank God' is removed. And so on, often ridiculously: 'and roundly I cursed him' becomes 'I soundly upbraided him'. The silliest are the replacement of 'hell-for-leather' with 'at top speed' and 'the jog of that accursed horse' with 'my uncomfortable ride'. There are two dozen examples of this. 'Manliness' of course, is all. Consider the rewriting here. First, in *Prester John*, Buchan describing how the villainous Portuguese Henriques has suffered at Crawfurd's hands:

> Henriques looked ghastly in the clear morning light, and he had a linen rag bound round his head and jaw, as if he suffered from toothache. His face was more livid, his eyes more bloodshot, and at the sight of me his hand went to his belt, and his teeth snapped.

In *The Captain* this has been re-written: 'Henriques stood beside him. My blow had been harder than I had imagined; he bore the marks of it.'

The Captain's editor has had to be careful. Laputa's cry of 'What have ye gained from the white man? A bastard civilisation' has become 'a so-called civilisation', which is more 'tasteful'. Even as, by cutting and alteration, he reduces the central black figure to caricature, he removes 'offence' by removing the last four words of a description of hair 'long and curled like some popular musician'; removing 'stinking' from 'I hate this stinking place'; removing Crawfurd's description of himself as 'a specimen of debauchery which would have done credit to a Saturday night's police cell', and his 'drunken' speech; deleting 'you brute' as an address to Colin the dog, carefully altering 'Portugoose' to 'Portuguese' every time, except when he substitutes 'rascal'; changing 'Mwanga's 'joke' to 'jest'; changing 'Get out of my sight, you swine', to 'Get out of my sight, you dog,' and altering Henriques' reply '"Stew in your own juice," he said, and spat in my face' to 'Dealing me a savage kick'; 'correcting' 'The place stank of crocodiles' to 'The place spoke of crocodiles'. And so on, through many more illustrations. The clearest example of the work of this anonymous ancestor of Mrs Mary Whitehouse is at the very moment before the dying Laputa's leap to death. Here is Buchan: '"Unarm, Eros," he cried. "The long day's task is done." With the strange power of a dying man he tore off his leopard-skin and belt till he stood stark as on the night when he had been crowned. From his pouch he took the Prester's Collar.' This is too much for *Captain* readers. 'Stark' is qualified to 'all but stark': and 'Prester's' is removed.

Some pages before, the editor has removed '. . . I could feel that the steps were wet. It must be Laputa's blood'. This is characteristic of the shrinking of the hero's sense-impressions and responses to a flatter lever of 'heroism'. His pain and weakness are systematically taken out. Consider this deleted passage:

> Also, before we had gone a mile, I began to think that I should split in two. The paces of my beast were uneven, to say the best of it, and the bump-bump was like being on the rack. I remembered that the saints of the Covenant used to journey to prison this way, especially the great Mr. Peden, and I wondered how they liked it. When I hear of a man doing a brave deed, I always want to discover whether at the time he was well and comfortable in body. That, I am certain, is the biggest ingredient in courage, and those who plan and execute great deeds in bodily weakness have my homage as truly heroic. For myself, I had not the spirit of a chicken as I jogged along at 'Mwanga's side.

I counted over thirty occasions on which what was deleted in an incident, sometimes the only cut, was the hero's incapacity or hurt, despair or failure. The serial (not Buchan) summarises him as 'a sturdy young Scot'. Deleted is his response to the death of Laputa: 'I remember that I looked over the brink into the yeasty abyss with a mind hovering between perplexity and tears. I wanted to sit down and cry – why, I did not know, except that some great thing had happened.' Such a tearful, and complex, response is necessary if Laputa has had his stature. But it was deleted. So was 'There were tears of weakness running down my cheeks' and 'I was in a torment of impotence' and 'I could only lie limply on the horse's back, clutching at his mane with trembling fingers. I remember that my head was full of a text from the Psalms about not putting one's trust in horses.' This is a serious loss, for with the pain goes not only humanity, but romance. Buchan was, by *Prester John*, his nineteenth book, an old hand at romance and the one he wrote four years later, *Salute to Adventurers*, set in seventeenth-century Scotland and Virginia, is one of the finest modern romances written. But such greatness was not for *Captain* readers, evidently.

Equally damaging is the systematic and very obvious secularisation of what had been a biblically-based, profoundly religious book, allowing the great archetypal movements between death and rebirth, between black and white, between king and priest, between father and god, a full and satisfying play. Without this context, the adventure shrivels to a prefects-study game, with religion as a crude militaristic 'christianity'. I suppose there might just be sense in the removal of all the inside references to the kirk in the opening chapters, the 'correction' of the boys' Sabbath 'play' to 'idle play' and so on. But the deletion of all the religious significance of the dedication and crowning scene in the cave in the centre of the book (Chapter XI, of which a total of five pages of text, out of twelve, have been removed) is desecration of the priest-king, and indeed removal of that aspect of him entirely, as if a black priest-king, a Prester John in truth, had to be kept from the consciousness of *Captain* readers in July 1910. That this loss is not an accident, or a simple victim of abridgement, is shown by the similar removal of such material elsewhere, and a telling cut early in Chapter XVIII. From the following: 'I was always a fatalist, and in that hour of strained body and soul I became something of a mystic. My panic ceased, my lethargy departed, and a more manly resolution took their place' the first sentence has been removed.

All this, of course, reflects a different light on to Laputa. So does the systematic removal of many kinds of wider reference, of which I counted fifty clear examples before I gave up, some of them major: observation of the country and its wild life, of references to and quotations from literature, the Buchan trick of noting a landscape from the fall of its rivers. The book suggests a priest-king whose significance rises to great heights, lifted by a breadth of view and reference. Some of this has survived: he is allowed in the boys' serial the quotation (not ascribed) of some lines of Virgil, before going on to speak briefly of his version of christianity, which feels odd, when the story has been largely shorn of its other references. A following remark about Oliver Cromwell is removed.

For what has been taken out, as perhaps too dangerous, is admiration for the black leader. This admiration is not just, of course, for his animal power, though the following passage has been cut:

> The pace at which he moved must have been amazing. He had a great physique, hard as nails from long travelling, and in his own eyes he had an empire at stake. When I look at the map and see the journey which with vast fatigue I completed from Dupree's Drift to Machudi's, and then look at the huge spaces of country over which Laputa's legs took him on that night, I am lost in admiration of the man.

Also deleted is 'I was hypnotized by the man. To see him going out was like seeing the fall of a great mountain' and much else, including the sentence just before his death, 'I found myself giving my arm to the man who had tried to destroy me'. That ambivalence resonates through the book, to include, at the heart, a true ambivalence over black and white, which undercuts the then unthinking and now problematic offensive incidentals. Even in such a matter as military strategy (since Buchan's childhood admiration for Montrose a matter of keen interest to him) Laputa is reduced, as almost all explanation of the grand movement has been taken out. Indeed, grandeur is what is largely being removed from Laputa, whether it is his simple password ('Immanuel' in the book; avoided in the serial) or more richly suggestive matters. Consider the following complete paragraph: Crawfurd, just before he sets out for the final encounter, notices in a looking-glass the splash of goat's blood on his left temple received 'that night at the cave' i.e. at the dedication and crowning: 'I think that the sight of that splash determined me. Whether I willed it or not, I was sealed of Laputa's men. I must play the game to the finish, or never again know peace of mind on earth. These last four days had made me very old.' A previous paragraph explaining his appearance and the goat's blood has been removed; and from that paragraph everything has gone except 'I must play the game to the finish'. The complexities involved here, the Calvinism, to say nothing of the involved psychology underlying most of it, are cut clean away. This makes 'I must play the game to the finish' into something quite different. The argument that such matters must be pruned because young minds cannot take in theological dimensions is of course both foolish and dangerous. The steady erosion of imaginative colour is as dangerous, whether slight, as in the deletion of 'whinnying' in 'Nay, if I wanted a mount, there was Henriques' whinnying a few paces off', or more significant, as in the loss of: 'They cheered me, those stars. In my hurry and fear and passion they spoke of the old calm dignities of man. I felt less alone when I turned my face to the lights which were slanting alike on this eerie bush and on the homely streets of Kirkaple.'

Whatever happened, it seems, the young *Captain* readers were not to use their capacity for imaginative understanding of the root of Laputa's position. Like Milton's Satan, he is an archangel fatally and dangerously flawed: his flaw is not his blackness but his pride, a theological not a racial concept. At the crowning, Laputa who, as Crawfurd says, 'had some of the tones of my father's voice' so that 'I listened spellbound as he prayed' (the last four words deleted) is in nine lines explained. The man is not dangerous because he is

George Soper: illustration for 'The Black General'

George Soper: illustration for 'The Black General'

George Soper: illustration for 'The Black General'

David Daniell

crazy, powerful and black, but because he is human, and proud. But the nine lines are deleted.

Something remains to be said about the illustrations (Figs. 8–11). The serial has twenty eight pictures by George Soper, four of them whole-page and none of them smaller than one-third page. I have seen more objectionable pictures in early cheap Nelson reprints of the book, where Laputa, and every other black, are pantomime grotesques: but it is clear that Soper had a problem in trying to portray men of various tribes without enough information, and especially to reconcile blackness and nobility. He never solved it. The best he can do is to reproduce the old devices of eighteenth and early nineteenth-century illustrators of travel books, especially books about the South Seas, whereby the women were made Polynesian and the men Melanesian – that is, the women, ('dusky Venuses') had straight hair. So here Laputa has straight hair, while all the other blacks do not, and have a bone in an ear, or a ring on their heads, and 'the old Kaffir' who is really white made up appears in Soper's picture virtually Chinese. Laputa, in the whole page illustration to what is left of the crowning scene, wears a grass skirt as he holds up the necklace. (Buchan's story failed to get a mention in the annual competition among *Captain* readers for the twelve best stories in the magazine, but this picture tied first place in the illustration section.) Crawfurd, in a half-page picture of him crossing the river at night and dropping the pistol, looks uncannily like Laputa, who is made Caucasian in several pictures. The death of Colin happens in the presence of various maddened savages. Nowhere does the illustrator suggest a black leader who, in Buchan's words, 'might have sat for a figure of a Crusader', whose voice 'was the most wonderful thing that ever came out of a human mouth'.

Notes

1. My own book on Buchan, *The Interpreter's House* (London, 1975) has a few pages on *Prester John*. The most extended treatment I have come across is T. J. Couzens' perverse article '"The old Africa of a boy's dream" – towards interpreting Buchan's "Prester John"', *English Studies in Africa*, XXIV (1981), pp. 1–24. Here are some interesting, though biased and sketchy, evidences of some of the native risings of the time and their religious background. The tone of the essay is marred by shrillness, and Couzens has little idea how to use literary evidence. Nor, unfortunately, has Alan Sandison, whose otherwise helpful and interesting study of four writers in *The Wheel of Empire* (1967) is marred by

152

inability to understand characterisation (he says virtually nothing about *Prester John*).

2. See William Buchan: *John Buchan: a Memoir* (London, 1982), pp. 212–13 for Buchan's reactions to Hitchcock's film.

3. T. J. Couzens objects to 'beastly food' for example. In context, the remarks is as follows: 'Such porridge without salt or cream is beastly food, but my hunger was so great that I could have eaten a vat of it'. This is considerably less offensive than Couzens implies, if it is offensive at all. Most of Couzens' evidence for such offence comes from outside *Prester John*, and not even from Buchan.

4. The uniqueness of popular literature of empire in British literature is something which has, as far as I know, received little attention. The post-Renaissance empires of Spain, Russia, Germany and Japan produced nothing, I believe, in the remotest way comparable, though the literature of the American frontier has some resemblance, of course.

8 Problematic presence: the colonial other in Kipling and Conrad

JOHN McCLURE

Serious fiction, as M. M. Bakhtin tells us, dramatises the play of discourses, the competition between different ideologically loaded 'languages' each attempting to set its mark on the world, establish its definitions as authoritative. At the end of the nineteenth century, when Kipling and Conrad were writing some of the most impressive colonial fiction in English, the ethics of imperial expansion was being seriously debated. One issue in the debate was the status of the colonised peoples, the Indians about whom Kipling wrote, the Malays and Africans of Conrad's fiction. Social scientists, liberal humanitarians, missionaries, colonial administrators and planters – each group defined the subject peoples of empire in its own way. But a strong consensus in the west held all peoples of other races to be morally, intellectually and socially inferior to white Europeans, and saw their ostensible inferiority as a justification for domination.

Artists tend to write both within the conventional discourses of their times, and against them. So it is with Kipling and Conrad. Their portraits of other peoples are, to borrow a term from *Heart of Darkness*, inconclusive: drawn now in the conventional terminology of racist discourses, now in terms that challenge these discourses and the image of the other they prescribe. Conrad's especially, is what Kenneth Burke calls 'a disintegrating art': it 'converts each simplicity into a complexity', 'ruins the possiblity of ready hierarchies,' and by so doing 'works corrosively upon . . . expansionist certainties'.[1] Conrad persistently questions the two basic propositions of European racism: the notion that, as Brian Street puts it, 'a particular "character" could be attributed to a whole people . . . a "race" might be gullible, faithful, brave, childlike, savage, bloodthirsty';[2] and the notion that the races are arranged hierarchically, with the white race, or perhaps the Anglo-

154

Saxon race, at the top. In novel after novel Conrad breaks down the crude dichotomies (white/black, civilised/savage, benevolent/blood-thirsty, mature/childish, hardworking/lazy) of racist discourses, ruins the ready racial hierarchies they underwrite, and so under-mines the expansionistic certainties of imperialism. In his stories, written in the 1880s and '90s, Kipling uses many of these same crude dichotomies to defend imperialism, but in *Kim* (1901) he breaks with convention, offering instead a powerful criticism of racist modes of representation. In both Kipling's *Kim* and Conrad's Malay novels, we find powerfully persuasive representations of the colonised peoples, representations that identify them neither as innocents nor as demons, but as human beings, complex and difficult, to be approached with sympathy, respect, and caution.

In the much neglected 'Author's Note' to his first novel, *Almayer's Folly* (1895), Joseph Conrad describes a project of representation that informs much of his colonial fiction. Europeans, he insists in the 'Note', have the wrong picture of 'strange peoples' and 'far-off countries.' They 'think that in those distant lands all joy is a yell and a war dance, all pathos is a howl and a ghastly grin of filed teeth, and that the solution of all problems is found in the barrel of a revolver or in the point of an assegai.' But 'it is not so': the 'picture of life' in these far-off lands is essentially 'the same picture' as one sees in Europe, equally elaborate and many-sided. And the 'common mortals' who dwell there deserve respect and sympathy. In short, the fashionable European 'verdict of contemptuous dislike' for these peoples 'has nothing to do with justice.'[3]

The far-off land that Conrad portrays in *Almayer's Folly* is the Malay Archipelago, the strange peoples Malays and Arabs. In spite of its ringing preface, *Almayer's Folly* is full of conventionally dismissive descriptions of these peoples: the omniscient narrator makes much of their 'savage nature' (p. 69) and 'half-formed, savage minds' (p. 116), and uses 'civilised' as if the word referred to a radically different and manifestly superior mode of existence. But the story related by the narrator tends to cast doubt on such dismissive characteristations. The novel's protagonist, a Dutch colonialist named Almayer, prides himself on being, as a white, infinitely superior to the Malays among whom he dwells. But the story is about Almayer's folly, and events show him to be intellectually and psychologically weaker than the Malays who oppose him.

Almayer's daughter Nina, whose mother is a Malay, occupies a pivotal position between the two opposed communities. She has been given 'a good glimpse of civilised life' (p. 42) in Singapore and an equally intense exposure to Malay culture in the up-river settlement where Almayer works as a trader. Conrad, having established her divided allegiance and unique authority, uses her to challenge Almayer's claims of superiority. Comparing the two communities, Nina at first fails to sees any difference: 'It seemed to Nina', the narrator reports, that 'whether they traded in brick godowns or on the muddy river bank; whether they reached after much or little; whether they made love under the shadows of the great trees or in the shadow of the cathedral on the Singapore promenade' there was no difference, only 'the same manifestations of love and hate and of sordid greed' (p. 43). If Nina has, as the narrator claims, 'lost the power to discriminate' (p. 43), she has gained the power to recognise essential similarities that Europeans such as the narrator are anxious to overlook. This passage is the first of many in Conrad's fiction that insist on the existence of such similarities and dismiss European claims to all but absolute difference and superiority.

Although Nina can find at first no essential difference between 'civilised' and 'savage' ways of life, she ultimately comes to prefer the latter, and her choice has the force of a judgement against European pretences. Nina's mother, who influences her decision, makes her own articulate case against these pretences. Her bitter accusations, dismissed by the narrator as 'savage ravings' (p. 151), reveal the prejudices of the oppressed as well as those of their oppressors. Whites, she tells Nina, '"speak lies. And they think lies because they despise us that are better than they are, but not so strong"' (p. 151). Racism, Conrad suggests, is not an exclusively white phenomenon; but the distinction between speaking lies and thinking them marks Nina's mother's speech as something more than savage raving, and the narrator, by dismissing it as such, only lends weight in the woman's charges.

Almayer's Folly is something of a literary curiosity: I can think of no other novel in which an omniscient narrator's commentaries are consistently undermined by the actions and observations of characters he disparages. Whether Conrad intended to produce this effect or not, he never produces it again. In the novels that follow *Almayer's Folly* the narrators distance themselves from the discourses of racism, adopting them, when they adopt them at all, only provisionally.

An Outcast of the Islands (1896) is set like its predecessor in the remote Malayan settlement of Sambir. Once again the action centres on a successful Malay counter-offensive against western domination, and once again Conrad depicts the Malays who lead the campaign as patient, resourceful and determined men. Babalatchi, who plans and directs the campaign against Captain Tom Lingard, the English adventurer who monopolises commercial and political power in Sambir, is richly and respectfully drawn. He has been a pirate, his methods are unscrupulous, but they are also brilliantly effective. When Conrad calls him a 'statesman', then, there may be a slightly ironic inflection to his voice, but the irony is pointed at the western reader, not at Babalatchi. Syed Abdulla, Babalatchi's Arab ally, is even more impressive. Conrad speaks of 'the unswerving piety of his heart and . . . the religious solemnity of his demeanour', of 'his ability, his will – strong to obstinacy – his wisdom beyond his years', and of his 'great family', which with its various successful trading enterprises lies 'like a network over the islands'.[4] Thus when white characters refer to Asians as 'miserable savages' (p. 126) and boast of their own 'pure and superior descent' (p. 271), the vicious stupidity of racist discourse becomes evident.

Once again in this novel Malay characters offer eloquent and devastating assessments of the white men who rule them. Aissa, a Malay woman courted, compromised and then scorned by Willems, the European 'outcast' of the novel's title, refers repeatedly to Europe as a 'land of lies and evil from which nothing but misfortune ever comes to us – who are not white' (p. 144). Babalatchi's rejoinders to Captain Lingard are even more corrosive of European certainties. Lingard, defending his domination of Sambir, asserts that if he ever spoke to its nominal Malay ruler 'like an elder brother, it was for your good – for the good of all'. 'This is a white man's talk', responds Babalatchi, 'with bitter exultation',

> I know you. That is how you all talk while you load your guns and sharpen your swords; and when you are ready, then to those who are weak, you say: 'Obey me and be happy, or die!' You are strange, you white men. You think it is only your wisdom and your virtue and your happiness that are true. (p. 226)

Babalatchi's searing indictment of European hypocrisy and ethno-centricism is corroborated in a number of ways. The narrator makes it clear, for instance, that Europeans do feel racial antipathy and that the sources of this feeling are irrational. Thus when Willems dreams of escaping from Sambir, his desire is attributed to 'the flood of hate, disgust, and contempt of a white man for that blood which is not his blood, for that race that is not his race' (p. 152). This flood of feeling, which overmasters Willems' 'reason', resembles the 'feeling of condemnation' that overcomes Lingard when he imagines Willems' illicit relation with Aissa. And this reaction, too, is described as 'illogical'. It is an 'accursed feeling made up of disdain, of anger, and of the sense of superior virtue that leaves us deaf, blind, contemptuous and stupid before anything which is not like ourselves' (p. 254).

If Conrad challenges the European representation of Malays as uniformly savage and inferior, he does not do so in order to replace that representation with an idyllic one. Babalatchi and his comrades, Lakamba and Omar, are Malay adventurers, blood-thirsty, lawless men who consider 'throat cutting, kidnapping, slave-dealing' to be 'manly pursuits' (p. 52). The peace Lingard enforces seems in many ways preferable to the anarchy they admire. But Lingard's peace is also a kind of tyranny, and Adulla's ascension to power seems to restore some degree of freedom without destroying that peace. In the end, then, Conrad suggests that any generalised ennoblement of one race or another is as inappropriate as generalised dismissal: there are certainly differ-ences of custom and belief between cultures, but the most important differences cut across racial lines and render racial affiliation meaningless as an indicator of intelligence, character, or virtue.

This same line of argument is developed in *Lord Jim* (1900),[5] which explores, among other things, the relation between a Malay community and its genuinely popular English ruler. When Jim, another European outcast, arrives in Patusan, another upriver settlement in the Malay Archipelago, three local factions are struggling for dominance: Rajah Allang's local Malays, Doramin's party of Malay settlers from Celebes, and Sherif Ali's forces, drawn from the tribes of the interior. Ambitious and utterly reckless, Jim quickly earns a reputation for valour, allies himself with Doramin's faction, and engineers a military victory over Sherif Ali so dramatic that no second campaign is necessary. By this means he becomes the actual ruler of Patusan, and a widely admired ruler. As a white, a member of the race which has conquered the Archipelago, he is automatically feared and, however grudgingly, respected by the Malays. As a fearless warrior, a successful military leader, a peacemaker, and an even-handed governor, he is widely venerated. Conrad describes Jim's triumph, then, in a manner that makes the Malays' acquiescence and approval seem reasonable, a sign not of innate inferiority but of a reasonable reaction to a complex situation. If a 'Jim-myth' (p. 171) arises, it does so because Jim has saved the community from the bloody deadlock of factional strife, in which 'utter insecurity for life and property was the normal condition' (p. 139).

But Conrad, having exposed the logic of colonial acquiescence, goes on to elucidate the logic of rebellion. Like Lingard in *An Outcast of the Islands*, Jim proclaims his unqualified dedication to the Malay community he rules: 'He declared . . . that their welfare was his welfare, their losses his losses, their mourning his mourning' (p. 238). And once again, Conrad tests and refutes this claim to absolute identification. Jim, for reasons that include a misguided sense of racial allegiance, refuses to lead a necessary campaign against piratical white intruders, and these intruders, set free, slaughter a company of Malay warriors, including Doramin's noble son. Conrad's point here, as in *An Outcast of the Islands*, is clear: even the most well-intentioned white ruler will experience a conflict of cultural interests, will be torn between allegiance to his native European community and allegiance to the community he rules. And the resolution of that conflict will be at the expense of his subjects, will justify, ultimately, their resistance to his continued domination.

Conrad makes this point once again in *Heart of Darkness* (1902), but in a most unfortunate way. For here it is the European novelist, Conrad himself, who succumbs to the interests of his own community and betrays his colonial subjects, the Africans he 'represents'. Speaking through Marlow, Conrad identifies the Africans, not consistently but emphatically, as demons and fiends, insists that 'the picture of life' in the Congo forests is appallingly different from the picture in Europe.

In the early stages of Marlow's narrative, the familiar invitations to sympathetic identification with the colonised are still in play. The Congolese are described as victims of a particularly brutal imperialism, compared favourably to their European masters, depicted in ways that stress their kinship with other men. Noting that the villages along the trail to the Central Station are deserted, Marlow remarks, 'Well, if a lot of mysterious niggers armed with all kinds of fearful weapons suddenly took to travelling on the road between Deal and Gravesend, catching the yokels right and left to carry heavy loads for them, I fancy every farm and cottage thereabouts would get empty very soon'.[6] And he suggests that African drumming, 'a sound weird, appealing, suggestive, and wild', may have for Africans 'as profound a meaning as the sound of bells in a Christian country' (p. 20). This is identification with a vengeance.

But as Marlow recounts his voyage up the river to Kurtz at the Inner Station, these familiarising comparisons cease and the emphasis falls more and more emphatically on the savage otherness of the Congolese. Their speech is described as a 'fiendish row' (p. 37) and they are no longer represented as individuals, but rather as 'a whirl of black limbs, a mass of hands clapping, of feet stamping, of bodies swaying, of eyes rolling' (p. 36). When the idea of kinship is suggested, it is with horror: 'No, they were not inhuman. Well, you know, that was the worst of it – this suspicion of their not being inhuman' (p. 36).

The last images of the Congolese are the most thoroughly distancing: 'Deep within the forest, red gleams partially illuminate many men chanting each to himself some weird incantation' (p. 65) and 'a black figure', a 'sorcerer' with 'horns – antelope horns, I think – on its head' (p. 66). This nightmare vision of 'horned shapes' and the equation of the Congolese with a 'conquering darkness' (p. 75) haunt Marlow long after his return to Europe, and they seem intended to haunt the reader as well.

One could attribute the difference between Conrad's representation of the colonised peoples in the Malay novels and his treatment of them in *Heart of Darkness* to social and biographical factors. The Congo basin, ravaged by centuries of slaving, was undoubtedly horrific, and Conrad seems to have had little opportunity, while he was there, to familiarise himself with the Congolese. Certainly Marlow does not: he insists on more than one occasion that he could not get a clear picture of the Africans, the kind of picture, in other words, that might have enabled him to do justice to them as fellow mortals.

But if Conrad cooperates in the familiar misrepresentation of Africans as demonic others, he does so too, I think, because his commitment to accurate representation comes into conflict with another commitment. The nature of that commitment, which has only recently been recognised by Conrad critics,[7] is best brought out in two passages, one from the manuscript of *Heart of Darkness*, the other from the novel itself. The first has to do with events on board the yacht 'Nellie', where Marlow tells his tale. Just before Marlow begins, the frame narrator recalls,

> A big steamer came down all a long blaze of lights like a town viewed from the sea bound to the uttermost ends of the earth and timed to the day, to the very hour with nothing unknown in her path, no mystery on her way, nothing but a few coaling stations. She went fullspeed, noisily, an angry commotion of the waters followed her ... And the earth suddenly seemed shrunk to the size of a pea spinning in the heart of an immense darkness (p. 7 n.)

The steamer makes a perfect figure of the forces of rationalisation: of science, industrial technology, planning and regimentation. And its voyage offers a poweful image of the consequences of these forces. The ship produces, by its precisely calculated passage to the very ends of the earth, the effect that Max Weber called 'disenchantment': it erases from the world, or from the narrator's imagination of the world, all sense of 'mystery' and wonder, leaves it barren and diminished. Marlow's story, which follows immediately, seems designed as an antidote to this diminution, his steamboat voyage as a counterthrust which reconstitutes, or re-enchants, the world shrunk by the steamer. The conclusion of the novel signals the success of this project: looking down the Thames, the frame narrator now remarks that the river 'seemed to lead into the heart of an immense darkness' (p. 79).

By deleting the description of the steamer from the published version of *Heart of Darkness*, Conrad partially obscures this aspect of his fictional design. But some sense of what he is up to is conveyed by a fascinating passage early in the novel. Reminiscing about his childhood passion for maps, Marlow remembers that 'at that time there were many blank spaces on the earth'. Africa was one, 'a blank space of delightful mystery – a white patch for a boy to dream gloriously over' (p. 8). By the time he had grown up, Marlow continues, most such spaces had been filled in, but a sense of the unknown still hung over the upper Congo; it was still not quite charted: still a place of enchantment.

Marlow goes up the river, then, in part because he is dedicated to enchantment, drawn to a world radically different from the world of everyday, predictable familiarity. But this attraction, this need for mystery (which grew ever stronger in Europe as the domain of technological rationalisation expanded) impells Marlow to make something of the Africans that is quite inconsistent with Conrad's project of familiarisation. To preserve a domain of enchantment for himself and his European readers, Conrad has Marlow write 'zone of the demonic' across the 'blank space' of Africa, thus consigning the Africans to a familiar role as demonic others. He sacrifices their needs for adequate representation to his own need for mystery. That Marlow also writes 'zone of the human' across Africa is indisputable, but he does so in fainter script, and by the end of *Heart of Darkness* this script is all but illegible.

Heart of Darkness, then, offers a cruel corroboration of Conrad's warning that no European can be trusted to represent the colonised. Torn between his dedication to accurate and sympathetic representation and his need to affirm the existence of radical moral and epistemological darkness, Conrad makes his African characters bear the burden of that darkness and thus perpetuates identifications that justify European contempt and domination. It is a shame that his most widely read novel should contain his most pejorative representations of the colonised, but a consolation that it offers as well perhaps the most powerful indictment of imperial exploitation in English.

In their time, Kipling and Conrad were frequently compared, but from the distance of some eighty years the differences between their works are more apparent than the similarities. Conrad wrote about the raw edges of empire, Kipling about its great heart. Conrad's fiction is aesthetically ambitious, psychologically oriented, politically sceptical; Kipling's is more conventional, less interested in innerness, and basically affirmative in its treatment of imperial rule. It is not, in other words, a 'distintegrating' art: it sets out to celebrate and defend certain established positions, rather than to work corrosively on them. For the most part the certainties defended are those of imperial ideology. When Kipling criticises the crudest European representations of Indians, he does so on the basis of more sophisticated racist beliefs that still sustain white superiority and right to rule. But Kipling, like Conrad, is inconsistent. In *Kim*, his greatest Indian work, he celebrates a set of certainties that have nothing to do with race, certainties which in fact are directly antagonistic to all doctrines of racial superiority. The reversal becomes apparent when one approaches *Kim* by way of the two decades of stories that precede it.

In 'The Head of the District' (1890), a dying English official, ruler of a frontier district, addresses the Afghan tribesmen he has subdued:

> Men, I'm dying . . . but you must be good men when I am not here. . . . Tallantire Sahib will be with you, but I do not know who takes my place. I speak now true talk, for I am as it were already dead, my children – for though ye be strong men, ye are children.

'And thou art our father and our mother',[8] the Afghan chief replies, apparently satisfied with what Conrad's Babalatchi would have quickly dismissed as 'white man's talk'. But this consensus for dependency is threatened when a Bengali is sent to rule the district. The appointment is interpreted as an insult by the Afghans, who have consented to be ruled by the militarily superior English, but despise Bengalis as weaklings (here, as elsewhere in the stories, Kipling makes much of communal rivalries in India, and mocks the claims of western-educated Bengalis to be ready for posts of responsibility in the Indian Civil Service). 'Dogs you are', a fanatical blind Mullah declares to the Afghans, 'because you listened to Orde Sahib and called him father and behaved as his children' (p. 180). But the Mullah's rebellion, unlike that sponsored by Babalatchi in *An Outcast of the Islands*, fails miserably and is morally, as well as pragmatically, discredited. In the end, after the Mullah has been killed and the unmanly Bengali has fled, the same tribal chief is shown listening, and assenting, to the same paternalistic and racist rhetoric: 'Get hence to the hills – go and wait there, starving, till it shall please the Government to call thy people out for punishment – children and fools that ye be!' (p. 203). The ready hierarchy of imperial domination is thus reconfirmed; the challenge, which is Conrad's work would be authentic and would remain unanswered, is only a pretext for its dramatic re-affirmation.

Indian dependency is affirmed in a different manner in 'His chance in life' (1887), the story of Michele D'Cruze, a young telegraph operator 'with seven-eighths native blood'.[9] A riot breaks out in the town where D'Cruze is posted while the English administrator is away. (Kipling pauses at this point in the story for a cautionary admonition to his audience: 'Never forget that unless the outward and visible signs of Our Authority are always before a native he is as incapable as a child of understanding what authority means' (p. 88).) The Indian police inspector, 'afraid, but obeying the old race instinct which recognizes a drop of White blood as far as it can be diluted' (p. 89), defers to D'Cruze, who astonishes everyone, including himself, by taking charge and putting down the rioters. When an English administrator appears, however, D'Cruze feels 'himself slipping back more and more into the native . . . It was the White drop in Michele's veins dying out, though he did not know it' (p. 91). Once again, the contrast to Conrad is instructive: while Conrad uses characters of 'mixed blood' to challenge European claims to superiority, Kipling finds in one such character a pretext for parading racist notions of the distribution of the faculty of rule: responsibility.

A third story, 'The enlightenment of Pagett, M.P.' (1890), shows Kipling working again to make a case for English domination of India. The MP of the story's title is a liberal who has come out to study (and embrace) the National Congress movement, newly founded in 1885. Congress, the organisation that eventually brought independence to India, represented the newly emerging Indian community of western-educated and oriented professionals, men who believed, often correctly, that they were being denied positions in government because of their race. It was only one of a number of nationalist and reform-minded organisations that sprang up in India in the last quarter of the nineteenth century.

But in 'Pagett', Kipling writes as if Congress were an isolated and idiotic institution. Pagett, visiting an old school friend now in the Indian civil service, is 'enlightened' by a series of Indian, British and American witnesses who appear on business and testify enthusiastically against Congress. Some of their criticisms seem plausible, but by no means all of them. And the onesideness of the testimony ultimately betrays the partiality of the whole proceeding: Kipling's unwillingness to let the Congress position be heard at all. Significantly, the only witness to defend Congress, an organisation which numbered among its members numerous well-educated Indians and Englishmen, is a callow school boy, enthusiastic but ill-informed, who impresses even the sympathetic Pagett unfavourably.

The other witnesses testify not only against Congress but to the innumerable failings of the Indian people: their religious and racial hatreds, caste exclusiveness, political indifference, corruption, sexism and 'utter indifference to all human suffering'.[10] These disabilities, Kipling suggests, make any talk of equality or of elections mere madness. And they are ineradicable, a kind of racial fatality, 'eternal and inextinguishable' (p. 354).

The racist rhetoric of these three stories, with their stereotypic characterisations, their talk of 'blood', their designation of Indians as 'children', their rejection of all claims to equality, and their refusal to enter into serious dialogue, is typical of Kipling's short fiction in general, the scores of short stories he turned out in the eighties and early nineties. There are impressive Indian characters in a few of these stories, and occasional criticisms of the most brutally dismissive forms of racism. But the good Indians are all also good servants of the raj, and Kipling's own attitude substitutes paternal condescension for contempt. He represents the subject peoples from within the discourse of dependency, the paternalistic rhetoric of racist societies from the American South to the Gangetic Plain.[11]

Something of this tone of condescension lingers in *Kim*. Once again, the positively portrayed Indian characters are all loyal servants of the raj; Congress and the forces it represented seem to have disappeared altogether from the Indian scene. But in *Kim* there is none of the insistence on racial difference and English superiority that we find in so many of the stories. Indeed, in this single work Kipling presses as hard against racist modes of perception and representation as Conrad ever does.

Thus the Church of England chaplain who views the authentically holy lama 'with the triple ringed uninterest of the creed that lumps nine-tenths of the world under the title of "heathen"'[12] is depicted as a fool. And so, too, is the young English soldier who calls 'all natives "niggers"' (p. 108) and doesn't know a word of any Indian language. Kipling, who in his stories routinely casts Bengalis as cowardly weaklings, now presents a Bengali secret agent whose feats of courage and endurance 'would astonish folk who mock at his race' (p. 268).

The novel not only repudiates racist modes of characterisation, it dramatises this repudiation. Character after character – the Sahiba, Huree Babu Mokerjee, the Woman of Shamlegh – overcomes his or her racial prejudices. Even Mahbub Ali, the roguish Pathan horse trader and spy, grows more tolerant: he develops, as Mark Kinkead-Weekes has pointed out, 'away from the Pathan . . . whose opening words were always "God's curse on all unbelievers" . . . towards the Lama's tolerance, [learns] to stop himself with an effort from using his instinctive curse on the "other".'[13] If Kim, 'The Little Friend of All the World' (p. 23), is in one sense the catalyst of all this coming together, he also participates in it, shedding his own prejudices and sense of racial superiority. Throughout the novel, then, Kipling repudiates the hierarchical constructs of racist thinking. What is taken for granted in the earlier fiction is taken down in *Kim*.

Kipling is dreaming, of course, to imagine that the kind of interracial co-operation and comradeship he portrays in *Kim* could take root and grow under British imperial rule: this is E. M. Forster's point in *A Passage to India*. But by blinding himself in this one respect, Kipling is able to see beyond the horizon of his times and portray a world of yet to be realised interracial harmony. For this reason, *Kim* may well be a more effective antidote to racial antipathies than any of Conrad's works, which by their great gloominess tend to corrode at once any belief in racist modes of vision and any hope that they may be abolished.

Notes

1. Kenneth Burke: *Counter-Statement* (1931, reprinted Berkeley, California, 1968), p. 105.
2. B. V. Street: *The Savage in Literature* (London, 1975), p. 7.
3. Joseph Conrad: *Almayer's Folly* (1895; reprinted New York, 1923), pp. ix–x. Subsequent references to this edition will appear in the text.
4. Joseph Conrad: *An Outcast of the Islands* (1896; reprinted New York, 1926), pp. 109–10. Subsequent references to this edition will appear in the text.
5. Joseph Conrad: *Lord Jim* (1900: reprinted New York, 1968). Subsequent references to this edition will appear in the text.
6. Joseph Conrad: *Heart of Darkness* (1902; reprinted New York, 1963), p. 20. Subsequent references to this edition will appear in the text.
7. See Allon White: *The Uses of Obscurity* (London, 1981) and Jacques Darras: *Joseph Conrad and the West* (London, 1982).
8. Rudyard Kipling: 'The Head of the District', in *In Black and White* (1895;

reprinted New York, 1898), p. 172. Subsequent references to this edition will appear in the text.

9. Rudyard Kipling: 'His chance in life', in *Plain Tales From the Hills* (1888; reprinted New York, 1898), p. 86. Subsequent references to this edition will appear in the text.

10. Rudyard Kipling: 'The enlightenments of Pagett, M.P.', in *In Black and White*, p. 383. Subsequent references to this edition will appear in the text.

11. 'There is no originality in Kipling's rudeness to us', wrote Nirad C. Chaudhuri, 'but only a repetition, in the forthright Kiplingian manner, of what was being said in every mess and club.' Nirad C. Chaudhiri: 'The finest story about India – in English', in *Encounter*, VII (April 1957), p. 47.

12. Rudyard Kipling: *Kim* (1901; reprinted New York, 1959), p. 90. Subsequent references to this edition will appear in the text.

13. Mark Kinkead-Weekes: 'Vision in Kipling's novels', in *Kipling's Mind and Art*, ed. Andrew Rutherford (Stanford, California, 1964), p. 225. For further discussion of Kipling's change of attitude in *Kim*, see K. Bhaskara Rao: *Rudyard Kipling's India* (Norman, Oklahoma, 1967).

9 Manipulating Africa: the buccaneer as 'liberator' in contemporary fiction

ABENA P. A. BUSIA

It should be recognised at the outset that the 'Africa' being discussed here has very little to do with any Africa Africans themselves, from whatever part of the continent, might recognize as 'home'. This paper concerns itself with contemporary novels whose image of Africa is shaped by a long, continuing, literary tradition of a 'myth of Africa'; a tradition which owes its survival to its remarkable ability to adapt itself to the needs and tastes of changing British society.[1] Like those works of the nineteenth and early twentieth century which were primarily instrumental in delineating the parameters of this tradition in the novel, the works discussed here, written by British and American writers, and published since the mid-1960s, are all popular novels. They are stocked in vast numbers in bookstores, frequently read, widely distributed, and, in such places as airports, railways stations and bus depots, as readily available as fast foods.

There are two distinct literary traditions of novels of Africa which have combined to form the modern text.[2] These can be classified as the 'adventure' novels and the 'political-romance' novels. The adventure novels have their origins in the literature of conquest written for the amusement of Victorian boys. Produced at the height of imperial confidence, these stories emphasise all the true qualities of the English gentleman, especially his moral fortitude and courage.[3] The second tradition, more self-consciously political in outlook, uses Africa as the setting for a great psychological or spiritual drama of self-discovery. The idea seems to be that the trauma of the African experience would lead to the making of a psychically whole man.[4] The combination of these two traditions has produced the kind of novel we shall discuss here; novels which read predominantly like masculine adventure novels of conquest, but in which a deeply personal search for the self is bound up with an often messianic political mission.

These novels can be regarded as a type of 'wilderness' novel,[5] novels based on an ideological myth which opposes 'nature' to civilisation', which serve as a form of initiation ritual for the society which supports them. They share as a premise a belief in the necessity for violence in both private and social life, and they serve as vehicles for an expression of this violence in an Africa which is still regarded as being free from the dullness and deprivations of modern, western, suburban life. The heroes of these works undertake expeditions into a 'wilderness' – in this case Africa – as an attempt to transcend the circumscriptions of their middle-class lives, and in the end triumph over nature as well. Thus Africa can serve (regardless of whatever may be happening in this 'wilderness' itself), as a gladiatorial arena for the west both to exorcise the need to conquer, as well as to champion those once traditional values now apparently fighting a rearguard action for survival in the western world.

The one factor which makes such a use of Africa possible is the acceptance, in western literary fiction, of the 'otherness' of this continent. By the time we reach the works of the middle of this century it can be clearly demonstrated that the supposedly unbridgeable gulf between Africa and Europe has become so much a part of the language of popular thought that it has long since become the very factor upon which fictions are created. Thus, what the language of these texts reveals is not so much what is seen in Africa, but what is preconceived about her.[6] The idea of Africa, the 'dark continent', has changed but little in substance over the years and it is this stability which gives currency to the continuing myth.

This mythical idea of Africa is composed of a complex of elements which govern the presentation of the continent itself, and the portraits of her people. Throughout the literature, Europeans struggle for mastery over both the land, and her inhabitants. Yet were we to give credence to the image of the place for instance, the countries themselves are scarcely worth the efforts made to establish supremacy over them. Zangoro, in Fredrick Forsyth's *The Dogs of War* (1974),[7] is a fine literary specimen of a contemporary African country. There is hardly anything left of the economy – the women scratch a living through subsistence farming, the men hunt with scant success, and the children are a living mass of diseases and malnutrition. It is said absolutely nothing works, simply as a result of the white people having left. As a consequence, Zangoro has become 'a real banana republic', governed by one party and its vigilante youth organisation, who carry on a reign of terror which is corrupt, vicious and brutal. The place is a perfect target for 'liberation'.

If we consider the leaders to be overthrown, or their wretched people in need of liberation, as with much else in this tradition, their portraits have been updated, but many of the changes remain superficial. In contrast with novels of earlier decades, the stage-fronting of African characters is noticeable. Africans are no longer necessarily anonymous, and no longer necessarily minions, baggage and guns carriers or domestic servants. There is a preponderance of African presidents, freedom fighters, generals and the like, but all this means is that old stereotypes have been given new names. Underneath the trappings lurk all the old images; though fictional military coups have replaced tribal wars, venal generals bestial chiefs, and sycophantic polticians duplicitous witchdoctors, the stench of decay remains. It can come as no surprise, for instance, that the majority of literary rulers are dictatorial tyrants. Gawaka, Njala, Amin, Kimba[8] are all superstitious megalomaniacs who rule their countries through coteries of political 'yes-men' given a choice between compliance and death by torture. Like the rest of their brother African presidents, they must therefore be overthrown. However, the presidential door is a revolving one of coup, counter-coup. It ushers in new faces as it throws out the old. But fresh faces do not mean fresh blood, for the process repeats itself, and incoming presidents prove as self-seeking as the old, as they are truly simply the representatives of their people. The African populace in these texts are either as brutal as the rulers they throw up, or they have been so crushed into lassitude and compliance that Africa remains a place of violence, and rough justice remains the ruling ethic of the land.

Significantly for our purposes, where any form of benevolent and radical action needs to be taken, it is Europeans who organise it, and where any plan succeeds it is European inspired.[9] Africans labouring under the tyranny of dictatorship remain disorganised and incompetent until the European hero arrives to blaze the path to liberation. In a literature replete with mercenaries and freedom fighters the singular incompetence of the Africans is remarkable.

Were these novels to be taken at face value, one would have to believe that all Africans have proved incapable of adapting to any aspect of modern life whatsoever, without a helping hand from some interested westerner – what few attempts they make always end in failure.[10] As a small example, even supposedly seasoned veterans go into battle with their eyes either glazed or closed, their chests heaving, and using their guns like clubs;[11] so much for 'the natives'. In these novels the struggle for the liberation of Africa apparently has little or nothing to do with capable Africans, but is rather a political and moral question *for the European*.

The concerns of the novel of Africa have always been, and continue to be, grand. As in the nineteenth century Africa served in the literature as a forum for the dramatisation of British ideas and action, so today she still serves as a battleground for western ideological warfare, and all over Africa today the search for utopias continues to take place in these texts. Though there is still no real dialogue with the African people, these novels are still trying, somehow, to re-order the world of Africa in the name of justice, peace and sanity. The readers of this fiction are still reading a body of works in which the European authors continue to use 'Africa' as a vehicle for their peculiar private imaginations.

The peculiarity of these private imaginations however, lies in the fact that they are rendered public by one most persistent element of continuity. These novels, however different, have been demonstrably constructed within very clearly distinguishable and circumscribed limits. They have one basic plot, of which the first staple ingredient is one African country in political and, significantly, moral disarray. The moral aspect of the disarray is important for the evangelising mission and the ethnocentrism which are part and parcel of the baggage of the hero. Secondly, something in this country needs rescuing – either the country itself, or sometimes a group of expatriates, depending generally on the scope of the work in question. Some writers, such as Frederick Forsyth in *The Dogs of War* (1974), John Shannon in *Courage* (1975), or Leslie Watkins in *The Killing of Idi Amin* (1976), have the audacity of imagination to set out to save the very countries in which their novels are set. Others, such as Tasman Beattie in *Zambesi Break* (1977), David Beaty in *Excellency* (1977), or Cleary and Maher in *Sahara Strike* (1980), modestly confine themselves to rescuing a particular group of expatriates; nonetheless, we are never allowed to forget that these expatriates do somehow come to stand for good and a moral order which must be preserved from the threatening madness which is Africa. Though peace is sought, these novels are all essentially novels of violence in which peaceful transitions are no longer even entertained. In every case it is a group of expatriates who are introduced to effect the rescue and to save or liberate the land, and these expatriates are, above all, warriors.

It is these warriors, these bringers of liberation who are our 'buccaneers'. The word 'buccaneer' has been chosen because of the suggestion of male bravura and bravado it has acquired. To call them 'mercenaries' would have been the most obvious choice of word, as that is, generally, what they are. However, these men, and in particular their *leaders*, are not always hired and *paid* to kill or execute — and even when they are, they are often wonderfully convenient modern invention, a mercenary with a strong moral conscience. These men are by nature travellers, with the world at their fingertips. They are transient guests, free men, who volunteer themselves for a particular task and then depart, hence the word 'buccaneer' is more often more appropriate.

These texts reveal evidence of another patterning in the very descriptions of these buccaneers themselves. A typical team of such mercenaries generally includes the following stock figures, present in some guise or other; the man with a genuine potential for violence (for some reason, in both *The Dogs of War* and *Sahara Strike* he is Corsican) — this character may or may not be the same person as the obligatory vicious bully who indulges in gratuitous killing for the pleasure of seeing people die; the weak man who cannot endure the necessary rigours of mercenary life and is clearly out of his spiritual depth; the lost soul on a journey of redemption, as indicated by his presence in such novels as *The Dogs of War*, Peter Driscoll's *The Wilby Conspiracy* (1972), and Daniel Carney's *The Wild Geese* (1977); the white South African who learns brotherhood with a fellow black traveller is one new version of the man who is redeemed; the fun loving, beer drinking, womaniser with the heart of gold; and, leading them all, our amoral buccaneer hero who eventually experiences some kind of moral reawakening.

This buccaneer hero has a number of tasks to perform, and he succeeds because, like Tarzan, he is the supreme mediator.[12] He can endure all the challenging extremes of the natural environment, he can perceive and overcome the subtle genius of evil and subdue the vagaries of human behaviour, in fact he can manipulate whatever conditions the human or natural world may present him with, and survive. He has a series of moral lessons to learn on his journey onwards, and his world is one in which he will always become the master of these lessons, whether his adversary is Africa herself, her people, or other hostile Europeans. As readers, we see this hero being created in the course of journeys after grand heroisms, we watch him transcend the confines that Africa represents, and triumph.

In this paper we shall use Wilbur Smith's *The Dark of the Sun* (1968) as the specimen text from which to draw our detailed illustrations, although, as the novels are esentially variations on a common theme, any other text would have served as well. In *The Dark of the Sun* the main characters are four Europeans, the 'hero' Bruce Curry, the 'villain' Wally Hendry, and two others.

The portrait of Curry is that of the prototypical buccaneer leader whose appearance and character remain virtually unchanged in the novels of the last decade and a half. The buccaneer leader is always tough, handsome, intelligent, and private with a secret sorrow. He is a methodical, calm, restrained, if somewhat unbending man. A quiet, self-contained person, his authority is the first important trait to be established. Yet on top of all this he has a wonderful physique and is quite good looking. However, the buccaneer hero must be good looking without being pretty or vain, and must be meticulous without being fastidious. Curry finds this balance. His soft hair, which 'would be unruly and inclined to curl if it were longer', is of course kept close-cropped. He has a large slightly hooked nose which 'rescues his face from prettiness and gives him the air of a genteel pirate'. He has green eyes and a mouth as easily given to smiling as to sulking. That it is a long time since he felt any emotion is another key to the buccaneer hero; in fact he always has a great deal to control. Despite all his qualities as a commander, Curry is shown to be a man afraid of close communion with other men. He is suffering from what can be called the classic buccaneer dilemma: he has lost his woman. As is quite usual, he is a disaffected middle-class professional, in this case a successful lawyer who has lost everything, including his practice, in contesting his former wife for custody of their children. When he lost that battle he became a mercenary, as they all do.

173

In great contrast, Wally Henry is an extremely gross character. He also is of a type, but he does not always, as he must in this novel, carry the burden of that 'evil' which must be destroyed. In all he does he is utterly inhuman. Presented as cowardly and irredeemably coarse and cruel, in the course of the novel his actions compose a litany of sadistic behaviour. A merciless killer, Hendry travels through this novel as if the force of evil in some medieval morality play, with a modern setting. He recognises no need, as the others do, for redemption. He cannot learn from his experiences and he is given no reason, other than his generally bestial nature, of being in Africa at all. In this remarkably middle-class text where all true heroes are fundamentally still gentlemen, it is no accident that the villain is deprived working class; in the novel of Africa it is from this class that the two extreme types, the lovable buffoon or the unsophisticated villain, have customarily been drawn.

The desire and the ability to learn from the experience that is Africa, which Hendry so clearly lacks, is the quality which distinguishes the noble from the condemned. In this novel, this fact is emphasised by the stories of the other two Europeans on the mission. The youth André de Surrier has the simplest story. For him the heart of the story, the journey to Port Reprieve, is to be an initiation into the very traditional concept of 'manhood' which governs the entire novel. A homosexual in flight from scandal in his native Belgium, André ends up a mercenary in Elizabethville as part of the wreckage of the civil war in Katanga. In Port Reprieve he is captured by enemy troops and practically tortured to death, significantly for a homosexual, by having his testicles brutally crushed by their sadistic, hate-filled African general. Nonetheless, André does not scream but rather, before dying, finds the strength and courage to throw a grenade in the enemy headquarters where he is held prisoner, heroically destroying himself along with the enemy. This action is presented as an accolade and its significance need not be laboured; overcoming the literal, physical crushing of his testicles to throw the grenade, André liberates himself from his emasculation and is initiated into manhood and a noble brotherhood of fighters.

Mike Haig, the last of the Europeans, is one of a long line of characters who end up somewhere in Africa as a form of retreat.[13] A renowned Harley Street surgeon and member of the Royal College, he has ruined himself through alcoholism, and destroyed his practice by performing an operation whilst drunk and thereby killing his patient. By the time we meet him he has also killed his wife and unborn child by being too drunk to help her through a difficult labour. When he sobered up from this last failure, he signed up. In this text his transformation occurs when, drunk once again, he is burdened with the responsibility of delivering an African mother in the throes of a very difficult labour. His alternative is to live forever with the knowledge that he failed, yet again, to save the lives of a mother and child when it was in his power alone to do so. He performs the operation successfully, and is reborn as a doctor in this 'outpost of progress', a truly noble specimen of that valiant brotherhood of lightbearers to which they all belong.

It is in the nature of these liberators to be travelling to perform some official mission, and their journey appears to follow a particular route, with a specific sequence of gates and thresholds providing regular points of drama along the way. In following Bruce Curry and his fellow band of Europeans, we trace this supposed path to enlightenment, in this avowedly benighted continent. For in its structure this novel outlines the basic plan which we have found repeated with various forms of sophistication in all the novels we have so far considered.

The route followed by the heroes is schematic in its simplicity and its various sections can be counted.

1) Elizabethville → 2) UN Barrier → 3) Msapa Junction →

4) Cheke River Bridge → 5) Port Reprieve → 6) Cheke River Bridge →

7) Msapa Junction → 8) UN Barrier → 9) Elizabethville

Put simply, these are novels in which everybody begins at an origin, the metropolis or birth-place; in this case Elizabethville the capital city. This origin is guarded by a gate, a recognisable minor threshold, after which the mercenaries, and therefore the readers, recognise that those who go beyond set out on some kind of journey; in this text our heroes pass the UN Barrier. At the midway point there is a crucial central crossroads which represents the point of no return on the way in, and indicates the success of the venture on the way back; in this case the crossing at Msapa Junction. Then there is yet another gate, the threshold to the interior, which stands in relation to the 'heart of darkness', which is the object of the journey, as the first gate does to the origins; in this case we have the

Cheke River Bridge. Finally we reach the interior itself, the place which represents the end of the journey; in this case, Port Reprieve. It is in this interior that those who live are sifted from those who die, and the true heroes are those who manage to go to the interior and then to retrace their steps past all the gates to return to the outside world. This standard pattern, from the origin, over the crossroads, to a darkness from which few re-emerge, is retained whatever the ideological vision or quality of moral imagination of the writer concerned.

The Dark of the Sun is set in Katanga during the civil war, and the movement of the story follows our buccaneers on a mission from the capital city of Elizabethville to a beleaguered city called Port Reprieve. (Given the emphasis placed on the moral or spiritual dimensions of the journey, it can be no accident that the place to which our heroes are headed is called Port *Reprieve*.) Cut off from the rest of Katanga and surrounded by a hostile band of marauders, the noble citizens of Port Reprieve await the advent of our good band of heroes to set them free. Bruce Curry undertakes the journey because he believes his primary task is to liberate these stranded families, employees of a diamond mining company, and their fellow refugees in the christian mission hospital nearby. However, it is a not insignificant factor in the minds of those who send him, that it is a diamond mining station; there are pockets of people trapped all over the Katanga but not all of them are the guardians of four months' worth of unclaimed diamonds.

The mercenaries leave from Elizabethville and go past the barrier, through the junction, and over the bridge to Port Reprieve, the heart of darkness. The first part of the journey is the movement from Elizabethville to the UN barrier at the entrance to the city which marks the boundaries of – as it were – order and civilisation. Here hysteria overtakes the African troops and the mission is seriously jepoardised before it even gets underway. The train then goes from the UN Barrier to Msapa Junction and in that second stretch of the journey we have laid bare for us the foundations of the moral rebirths which are to take place. When they reach Msapa Junction, Wally Hendry executes his brutal murder of the two innocent black children in cold blood and gets himself placed under open arrest. This murder becomes one of the moral focal points of the journey and leads, in the third stage, to a conversation between Haig and Curry on the nature of evil, which places their spiritual journey in a specific context. The evil which Wally Hendry represents is confirmed by his reckless shooting of an enemy 'tribesman' at the Cheke River Bridge, the entrance to enemy territory. Beyond the bridge on the fourth part of the journey, there is the uneasy truce made between Hendry and the others as they must work in concert to get to Port Reprieve, and fulfil their official mission. At Port Reprieve there are the various dramas which make up the central battles, both moral and physical, of the journey.

The next stage is from Port Reprieve back to the Bridge. This being the return journey, those salvations which are going to take place have occurred, and the die is cast for the final battle between the representatives of good and evil. That is, the physical objective has been effected with a qualified success, and the moral journey has also been effected, but also with a certain amount of qualified success – Curry has his last lesson to learn and for this Hendry must remain alive. The truce that was necessary in order to effect the fourth and fifth stages of the journey – from the Bridge to Port Reprieve and back again – and complete the official mission, finally falls apart on the sixth movement, between the bridge and the return to Msapa Junction. This frees Wally Hendry to become himself again, and we reach the heart of the matter.

Bruce Curry has yet to learn the major lesson of the text, that of understanding the nature of evil. Though he had thought Hendry's murder of the two children 'a bad thing' to do, he had treated Hendry with indifferent tolerance. It takes him the rest of the journey to learn 'to stop playing dead', when he sees evil, to recognise and destroy it. It is for this reason that Hendry must stay alive even after Port Reprieve; he cannot die until Bruce Curry has learned why he must. (It cannot be overlooked, however, that the crime that Hendry commits which determines Curry he must be destroyed, is not the cold-blooded and vicious murder of two innocent, defenceless African children, but the later crime of the theft of the Port Reprieve diamonds, and the rape of Shermaine, Bruce Curry's woman, European of course, whom the well-intentioned but incapable African soldiers had failed to protect.) Bruce Curry stalks Wally Hendry and kills him before he reaches Msapa Junction a second time, thereby symbolically preventing 'evil' from returning to the outside world.

The important factor is to establish *Curry's* ability to pass beyond Msapa Junction once again, and this he does because he completes this *spiritual* battle. He kills Wally Hendry in single combat, in a battle which is made to carry the moral burden of the tale. When at the end we see Curry flying away, his mission completed, he is headed not simply to Elizabethville, but out of Africa altogether – to the outside world. In these novels this last 'flight' from the central crossroads is frequently literal. The last laps are left unwalked because the hero is triumphantly ready to go beyond the place of origin.

On this last flight, Curry is accompanied by the woman Shermaine. Success with women is also one of the classic attributes of the buccaneer, and finding out who ends up with the desirable woman as appendage is often a reliable way of sorting out which of the likely candidates is the true 'hero'. With many buccaneers this triumph represents a healing from the pains of the past, and Bruce Curry is no exception. He also has had to re-learn the meaning of true love in the course of this journey, and his remedy comes in the form of his love affair with Shermaine. Shermaine, one of the five women stranded at Port Reprieve, and the only person rescued, is the typical buccaneer's woman; she is European, beautiful, stranded in the middle of Africa, and in need of help, his help. She has been married to a man very much older than herself; the previous doctor at the mission station, who had died of fever within four months of their marriage. The marriage had been arranged, at long distance, by the nuns who had raised the orphaned Shermaine. Because the doctor had been a gentle, understanding, indeed saintly person, and because Shermaine herself, being only about eighteen, was inexperienced and timid, the doctor in these months had never 'claimed his rights' as a husband. Yet as unmarried women in the modern novel of Africa are generally, by definition, of questionable virtue,[14] Bruce has won the ultimate prize; in amazing fulfilment of male chauvinist fantasy, Shermaine is young, but old enough to be a consciously sexual woman; widowed, but still a virgin!

When faced with the necessity of killing Wally Hendry for raping Shermaine, Curry abandons the strictures of an impersonal, formal law whose jurisdiction he acknowledges and theoretically prefers, in favour of what are considered to be the more primal laws of natural and moral justice. He kills Hendry in single combat instead of waiting to hand him over to the correct legal authorities, as he had earlier planned. That act, of taking upon himself the power to advocate privately for a general good, honour and justice, is an increasingly common buccaneer act. Morality however seldom remains a private issue, for although the buccaneer undergoes a private spiritual re-birth, this private mission is frequently tied to a larger social mission, of which he is only a part. And yet where the private issue is often resolved, the public issue leaves us with a paradox. In these novels which deal, for the most part, with the problem of the governance of independent Africa states, for good or ill, we have a series of novels in which the meaning of the buccaneers' mission is not always identical with the final message of the text.

There are frequently two journeys undertaken, the official one, and a secret one. These novels give us a group of mercenaries, all of whom are recruited by a paymaster – the person (or persons) with an objective in mind who funds the journey. It is this paymaster who locates the buccaneer leader, and commissions him to recruit whoever else may be required to fulfil the mission. If not actually the representative of existing European powers, he can often be taken to be approved of by them. The stories concentrate on his aims, and it is these which are presented as the official object of the journey.

However, in several of these texts we have the introduction, towards the end, of a surprise – such as a diversion or a counter-coup within the confines of the action taking place. This exposes a pattern in which the novels then read as a record of conflicts and resolutions in battles concerning issues of European private and public morality, which are merely played out in an African context. This surprise is, by definition, always unexpected to the paymaster who thinks himself in control, and in this surprise action lies the distinction between the result of the action and the conclusion of the text, on which the moral burden of the tale rests.

It is not unusual, in the novel of Africa, for the representatives of the state or its bureaucracy, and the established institutions, to be placed in the role of adversaries against the central buccaneer hero. That there are divisions amongst the Europeans is not new. Yet there is a sense in which the role of 'evil' as played by Wally Hendry in *The Dark of the Sun* is now more frequently being taken over by the organs of the state, as personal roles take on overt political overtones. The real adversary in the single combat is now the European state, or those people the state respects. [As often as not, the state in question if not a 'puppet' African state, as in the case of Malawi in both Paul Theroux's *Jungle Lovers* (1971) and John Shannon's *Courage* (1975), is visibly a European government, as France in *Sahara Strike* (1980) or Britain in *The Dogs of War* (1974)]. It is these powers – often the victims of the 'surprise' ending in which the buccaneer, in spite of their money, takes affairs into his own hands – who are seen as fundamentally illegitimate. It is the imposition of their will on Africa which the buccaneer must resist. The kudos of the buccaneer hero lies in his ability to usurp action. He remains in control throughout, in spite of whoever may be paying the bills. In every case he seems to have the potential to set his world right, according to *his* lights, and to make the mission possible from his point of view. The moral victory is always his, and it is a peculiar truth that it remains his, even if, as is frequent, his 'revolution' fails.

The problem of power and authority has always been, and remains, the central question in these novels, however it is dealt with. The issue is still being debated: who is in power, who keeps him there, who really has the authority to make decisions – and in these texts it is certainly not the African.[15] As has been stated, the issues become a battle between competing European concerns, regardless of the passive Africans who continue, much to their surprise, to be acted upon. And in these battles between the European state and our moral hero, the state, technically, usually wins. That is to say, however various the solutions invented to bring this about, the basis of state or corporate power is rarely shaken, and the status quo remains intact.[16] However, as few novels sanction any form of corporate dictatorship (even when extra-governmental, extra-national and benevolent), when such powers recover from their surprise and win in the end, they have had all aura of legitimacy stripped from them. For our concerns, the crucial factor is that even when his adversary is a European state or its representative, the individual hero remains symbolically the bringer of enlightenment and liberation. Yet the sanctity of the moral hero in this context is itself an ill-considered sacred rite.

For example, the battle in *The Dogs of War* is presented as one between moral and amoral Europeans, regardless of the Africans. It is not enough that it requires a group of unsanctioned mercenaries to overthrow the government, but the prime movers are wealthy outsiders with the means to change the government for commercial gain. But more than this, the mercenaries then take it upon themselves to decide between rival Africans and choose a more suitable and just leader for President. The moral implications of staging a coup on behalf of a minority in one country to provide the basis for continuing a revolution for justice in another, are never even discused. The mercenary Cat Shannon's action is presented as triumph, but in substituting the benevolent protégé of mercenaries for a corrupt puppet of merchants, Forsyth simply substitutes one form of imperialism for another. The Africans remain passive and the Europeans achieve what *they* want. There remains the assumption in these texts that such actions would not only be beneficial, but would be acceptable as well, for the Europeans always know best.

Given this controlling factor of Europeans, those problems which are being battled in the African arena are naturally those which trouble the contemporary middle-class Europeans who are the heroes of these novels. Questions of uncertainty over the power of those who rule, both in Africa and through Africans, and the growing sense of the illegitimacy of that power, are reflected in the literature, and have become aspects of its paradigm. The erosion of trust in those who represent the supposedly legitimate European order, whether demonstrated, or implied, is indicated each time the buccaneer faces their representative as an adversary. Legitimacy seems to reside not with the state and larger institutions, but with the moral individual. The superior European comes to liberate, and whether he is liberating people or liberating a republic, the meaning of his act remains the same – for both liberations are done in the name of individual liberty, decency and democratic order. In the grip of the ever-strengthening tentacles of mechanistic, de-personalised, modern life, the novel of the 1970s asserts the possibility of individual creative action, against all the odds.

There is a sense in which Africa has become, like the rest of the Third World and outer space, one of the last battlefields where white men struggle for the future of mankind.[17] Those problems which perplex the European are fought out in an African arena still regarded as a perfect setting for trials of strength. She is the theatre for ideological battles, and the potential last holocaust. Yet it is important to bear in mind all the while, in the changing dynamics of European life as reflected in these works, the static position occupied by the African. The African still has little to do with the control of the major elements of the drama.

The notion of the black man as in need of control, and the white man as his best master pervades this literature.[18] The buccaneer abroad is still able to give himself the liberty of feeling that somewhere he can still choose to impose the right kind of order, and to safeguard those very good and wholesome aspects of life long treasured by English travellers on the African continent. Yet although the repressive aspects of the modern state are criticised within the pages of some of the texts, nonetheless, by sanctioning authoritarian behaviour, even on the part of their 'heroic' individuals, those works as a body act as an extension of that repression. The relationships of dominance and subservience survive, and the African remains a menace, always, like the contents of Pandora's box, threatening to jump out. It is the African who must be suppressed, and as this 'truth' too has become a constant factor within the literature, the texts themselves become elements of oppression. A re-composition of the relations of power in that respect has not yet been undertaken.

None of these novels exist in a vacuum, but arise out of a dynamic complex of prevailing social conditions.[19] The texts themselves as a body tell a story. Their paradigms indicate if not what stories *can* be told, then at least which *will* be told at any given moment. The stories which are told are very limited in their dramatic structure, and bounded by the literary conventions of the genre. Although these existing conventions are not of any individual artist's making, what he chooses to do with them however should be under his control. Each artist does in the end have the choice of conforming to, or exploiting, the paradigms which appear to limit his creative imagination.[20] Both in its language and its form, the novel on Africa reveals the need for a far more radical discourse.

There can in a sense be no answer to a myth. Africa is the object, not the subject, of discussion, and the dream, or the nightmare, she represents cannot be altered without destroying those now institutionalized structures of mind by which her images is evoked. The imagination is not infinite, but simply 'bounded in a nutshell' and merely considering itself king of infinite space. But the nutshell has a particularly thick skin, and this is the point. Each of the stories has worked within the imaginations of their authors, each of whom has their own particular biography. However, the nutshell boundaries of the patterns of experience are clearly visible. The infinite space of the private kingdoms of their imaginations is illusory. In re-presenting Africa to us, they give us back again those very structures which limit their own lives, and that representation has indeed come to stand for the object it is intended to mirror. The choice of the form and language of literature, the choice of its images, like all choice, finally reflects our personal and social values; we create and uphold that which we value and reject those things we will not support.

Notes

1. For a lucid analysis of this process see: Alta Jablow: *The Image of Africa in British Literature in the Nineteenth Century* (Unpublished PhD diss., Columbia Univ., 1963), and Dorothy B. Hammond: *The Image of Africa in British Literature of the Twentieth Century* (Unpublished PhD diss., Columbia Univ., 1963), or Dorothy Hammond and Alta Jablow: *The Africa that Never Was: Four Centuries of British Writing About Africa* (New York, 1970) which is a summary of both dissertations.

2. See for example, Hammond: *The Image of Africa*, p. 37; Jeffrey Meyers: *Fiction and the Colonial Experience* (Ipswich, 1973), p. vii.
   The contrast between the novels of the two traditions is best demonstrated by comparing Rider Haggard's *King Solomon's Mines* (1885), an imperial adventure novel, with Joseph Conrad's *The Heart of Darkness* (1897), perhaps the first, and certainly the most influential, of the psychological political romances.

3. See Hammond: *The Image of Africa*, pp. 146, 157; H. A. C. Cairns: *Prelude to Imperialism* (London, 1965), pp. 36–9.

4. See Hammond: *The Image of Africa*, chapter 5. One of the most interesting explorations of this thesis in a contemporary novel, in which the idea is considered from various contrasting points of view, is to be found in Philip Caputo's *Horn of Africa* (1980).

5. I owe this concept of the 'wilderness' novel to Fredric Jameson's 'The great American hunter, or ideological content in the novel', in *College English*, November 1972.

6. For a demonstration of this see Abena P. A. Busia: *Re-presenting Africa: Patterns of Experience in British Fiction 1948–1980* (Unpublished DPhil diss., Oxford Univ., 1983).

7. Fictional works will be referred to in the text by their title followed by the copyright date. Authors' names will always be given on first citation, but full publication details, giving the date of edition consulted, will only be given in the appended bibliography of novels, which is arranged in alphabetical order by *title*.

8. The presidents, respectively, of: David Beaty's *Excellency* (1977); Patrick Alexander's *Death of a Thin-Skinned Animal* (1976); Leslie Watkins' *The Killing of Idi Amin* (1976); Frederick Forsyth's *The Dogs of War* (1974).

9. There is always one exception which proves the rule, and Laurence Sanders' two Tangent novels *The Tangent Objective* (1977) and *The Tangent Factor* (1978) are the only two novels so far encountered in which the hero is an African who *inspires* the ideas and the action, and who is admired by the European eponymous hero. The European's sole function is to provide sufficient financial

support to bring to fruition the plans which have already originated in the mind of the African. As always these plans could not succeed without European participation, but Peter Tangent definitely plays a secondary role to Captain Obiri Anokye who remains the colossus of the text, and who holds the spiritual centre.

10. As for instance the attempted prison break and other such activities organised by the liberation group in *The Killing of Idi Amin* (1976), all of which end in disaster and needless death.

11. There are hosts of such incompetent soldiers, as in *The Dogs of War* (1974) and *The Dark of the Sun* (1968), to name but two.

12. For an exegesis on the hero as mediator see Erling B. Holtsmark: *Tarzan and Tradition: Classical Myth in Popular Literature* (London, 1981), chapter 4.

13. See for example Rider Haggard's *King Solomon's Mines* (1885); Graham Greene's *A Burnt Out Case* (1960); Ronald Hardy's *Rivers of Darkness* (1971); amongst many others.

14. Single women in Africa are invariably in flight from some kind of emotional turmoil involving a man, and more often than not in flight from some kind of secret or 'past' they wish to keep concealed. This pattern still persists, it is as true of the women in Ronald Hardy's *Rivers of Darkness* (1971), and Mona Newman's *Softly Shines the Moon* (1970), as it is of those in Harriet Tanner's *Early One Morning* (1964), Netta Muskett's *A Fettered Past* (1958) or William Loader's *No Joy of Africa* (1955).

15. This is a major theme of the novels, but not only as a result of their imperial legacy. At times of great upheaval, such as the decades of the 1950s and 1960s, the question of power determined the structure of the texts themselves, as well as the way in which they developed, with respect to one another, over those decades. See Busia: *Re-presenting Africa*, Part 2, for an examination of this question.

16. In fact, more often than not, those who really wish to threaten the status quo, like the hero of John Shannon's *Courage* (1975) are exterminated. Even when (as at the end of the film of *The Wild Geese*) the heroes survive to settle private scores against their paymasters, these are settled without upsetting any states or public institutions. Nonetheless, our sympathies are supposed to lie always with the morally victorious heroic individual, however harmless he may be rendered at the end, and whatever the public or political outcome of his journey.

17. For a discussion on the role of American Indians and the Third World in Hollywood film see: Tom Englehardt: 'Ambush at Kamikaze Pass', in *The Bulletin of Concerned Asian Scholars*, III, no. 1, winter/spring 1971.

18. The question of to what extent this notion affects or governs aspects of life other than the literature has always been, and remains, the subject of debate. P. Curtin in *The Image of Africa: British Ideas and Actions 1780–1850* (Madison, Wisconsin, 1964), H. Cairns in *Prelude to Imperialism*, and C. Lyons in *To Wash an Aethiop White: British Ideas on African Educability 1530–1960* (New York, 1975), among others, tackle some aspects of this problem for the imperial and colonial era. For the more recent decades covered by the subject of this paper, the collection *The Empire Strikes Back: Race and Racism in 70s Britain* (London, 1982), written and edited by the members of the Centre for Contemporary Cultural Studies in Birmingham, proves most valuable. The collection contains some persuasive arguments in support of the contention that these persistent popular notions continue to have influence even in the raging political and legal debates in Britain today over 'the race question'. In considering the extent to which literature mirrors society, two essays proved of particular interest: John Solomos, Bob Findlay and Simon Jones' 'The organic

crisis of British capitalism and race', and Errol Lawrence's 'Just plain common sense: the "roots" of racism'.

19. In accepting these works as a part of a tradition we must recognise two salient structuring features; first that the language of the imagination at one and the same time constructs and re-constructs reality, and second, that the forms of popular art, in common with mythic structures, satisfy the needs of the society which supports it.

For a detailed examination of the interaction between social and scientific discourse, and popular fiction, in the nineteenth and early twentieth century texts which consolidate this literary tradition, see B. V. Street: *The Savage in Literature, Representations of 'Primitive' Society in English Fiction 1858–1920* (London, 1975).

20. The point of course, is that although one could put the case for the merits of some of these individual texts, that is not what is at issue here. What *is* at issue, is that however meritorious any single text may be, because of the repeated, authoritative patterns of representation, they serve *en masse* as part of a subtle web of power and oppression within the popular culture, with respect to the dynamics of the relationship between the west and Africa.

Fiction bibliography:

The Barboza Credentials, Peter Driscoll (Philadelphia, 1976)
A Burnt Out Case (1960), Graham Greene (Harmondsworth, 1972)
Courage, John Shannon (New York, 1975)
The Dark of the Sun, Wilbur Smith (London, 1968)
Death of a Thin-Skinned Animal (1976), Patrick Alexander (New York, 1977)
The Dogs of War (1974), Frederick Forsyth (London, 1978)
Early One Morning, Harriet Tanner (London, 1964)
Excellencey (1977), David Beaty (New York, 1978)
A Fettered Past (1958), Netta Muskett (London, 1968)
The Heart of Darkness (1897), Joseph Conrad (New York, 1971)
Horn of Africa (1980), Philip Caputo (London, 1981)
Jungle Lovers, Paul Theroux (Boston, 1971)
The Killing of Idi Amin, Leslie Watkins (New York, 1976)
King Solomon's Mines (1885), Rider Haggard (New York, 1951)
No Joy of Africa, William Loader (London, 1955)
Rivers of Darkness (1971), Ronald Hardy (New York, 1974)
Sahara Strike, Dennis Cleary and Frank Maher (London, 1980)
Softly Shines the Moon, Mona Newman (London, 1970)
The Tangent Objective, Laurence Sanders (London, 1977)
The Tangent Factor, Laurence Sanders (New York, 1978)
The Wilby Conspiracy, Peter Driscoll (Philadelphia, 1972)
The Wild Geese, Daniel Carney (London, 1977)
The Zambesi Break, Tasman Beattie (London, 1977)

10 The revelation of Caliban: 'the black presence' in the classroom

KENNETH PARKER

If one were required to select the key words with which to characterise contemporary British society, and out of which its practices (including those in the classroom) stem, then those words might well be empiricism, pragmatism and common sense: 'empiricism' in its popular appropriation as derived wholly from the senses (*experiment* as well as *experience*, but contrasted with *theory*); 'pragmatism' as synonym for 'the art of the possible' at any given moment; 'common sense' as that which is perceived to be popularly held practical wisdom.

For those of us involved in teaching and learning, curriculum design would therefore appear to be a relatively straightforward procedure: to investigate what might be suitable for incorporation into the syllabus at various levels in the school curriculum, taking into account the needs of particular categories.

Such an approach implicitly assumes that some of the key co-ordinates – notably 'the text'; 'the black presence'; 'the classroom' – are somehow unproblematical, and that our chief (some would say our only) task is to proceed to action, that is to say to curriculum design and syllabus amendment: let us include a 'representative text' from each of (say) Wilson Harris or Lamming, Ngugi wa Thiong'o or Achebe, Narayan or Rao.

Now, central to my argument will be the proposition that the appeal to 'common sense' is manifestly inappropriate with regard to curriculum design, particularly when that is associated with the objective of incorporating a sense of 'the black presence' in the classroom. To illustrate: it is a 'common sense' view that a syllabus in literature should be designed around 'major writers'. Yet what the potential consequences for our theme of 'the black presence' if only 'major writers' are studied should itself be a subject for consideration; not simply because of the particular elements of our topic, but because such questions about the status of the author and about the status of the text are expressions of the recognition of a recent resurgence in this country of an interest in literary theory, where (for instance) questions about how we 'evaluate' (itself a word loaded with cultural assumptions) and about the validity of the category of 'literature' itself, are being re-investigated.[1] You will note one major absence in that debate: nowhere is there attention given to the topic of 'the black presence'. If one recognises the extent to which literatures in English have to do with England's past (conquest in the seventeenth century; slavery in the eighteenth century; imperialism in the nineteenth century; decolonisation in the twentieth century) one cannot help but interpret such an absence as a salutary indication of the extent to which 'the black presence' is treated – ignored, as if it did not exist.

The absence occurs in the least likely places. For instance, in the Centre for Contemporary Cultural Studies publication *Culture, Media, Language* (1980) in a lengthy section devoted to 'English Studies', no reference is made to literature about black people, or by black people. Similarly, in another book from the same Centre, *The Empire Strikes Back: Race and Racism in 70s Britain* (1982) and even in the chapter 'Schooling in Babylon', literature is not mentioned. Yet it is precisely at the intersection of these two components, namely literature and racism, that our theme has to be confronted.

Let me illustrate my point as follows: the study of Shakespeare has been (and quite properly continues to be) one of the dominant components of the school curriculum in English – if not in the study of the actual texts, then arguably because of the impact of Shakespeare scholarship upon the business of criticism. Now, how was this eminence achieved? When we speak of Shakespeare's 'greatness', when we seek to explicate his meanings, when we confidently concur with Ben Jonson that Shakespeare '. . . was not of an Age, but for all Time', do we not only take him out of the theatre, but also out of his own time? And when we do that, might it not be argued that we thereby lose precisely some of the contextual references that are critical to our understanding? Take *Othello* as an obvious example. James Walvin[2] records how, in the last decade of the sixteenth century, England was troubled by the twin forces of an expanding population and a shortage of food. 'As hunger swept the land, England was faced by a problem which taxed the resources of government to the limits'. Immigrants added to the problem, Walvin informs us, since no group was so immediately visible as the blacks who, by then, had begun to constitute an identifiable and sizeable minority in the cities. Queen Elizabeth was constrained to write to the Lord Mayors of some cities, complaining of the excessive number of blacks in the kingdom, and ordering their deportation. Now, bearing in mind that *Othello* was probably written around the period 1601–3, and first performed in 1604, to what extent did what Stuart Hall describes as a 'moral panic'[3] (in writing about a more recent series of events about 'race', orchestrated by the Rt. Hon. J. Enoch Powell, sometime member of parliament for a constituency in this city) enter Shakespeare's consciousness while he was writing the play, or colour the perceptions of the audiences during performances? While it is, of course, not possible to offer satisfactory answers to either of these questions, we do need to recognise their legitimacy as questions. *Othello* was not an isolated example of the portrayal of black persons in literature in Elizabethan and Restoration England: the researches of Eldred Jones, Ruth Cowhig and others reveal the extent to which black people were portrayed in the literature of the period in stereotypical and derogatory fashion.

Douglas A. Lorimer observes, in this regard:

> From the first trading contact with Africa in the mid-sixteenth century, Englishmen expressed ethnocentrically-based dislike of the African's physical appearance. This aversion also assumed the character of moral judgment, for English observers associated Africans with heathenism and natural bestiality. As the slave trade from West Africa and the institution of slavery in the New World became established, increasing references appeared to the elder Judaic and medieval Christian association beween the Negro and the Curse of Ham.[4]

Sarah L. Milbury-Steen has itemised the stereotypes as follows: Africans, *in general*, are portrayed:

> *physically*, as ugly, monkey-like, all look alike; bad-smelling; sensually acute.
> *mentally*, as deficient, incompetent, ignorant, unlettered, uncultured; unable to think abstractly; imitative (partially educated African is the worst).
> *morally*, as superstitious, heathen, primitive, savage; demonic, evil, cruel, unpitying, cannibalistic; large children, happy-go-lucky, undependable, lacking in sense of duty and foresight, cowardly, always

late, lazy; deceitful, covetous, liars and thieves; vain, ungrateful; oversexed, animalistic, copulate but do not make love; good (faithful) servants and soldiers.

emotionally, as unable to show emotion; impulsive, unstable, ruled by passions and moods; good dancers and singers.

African *men*, as unambitious, let women do all the work; endowed with large sexual organs; desirous of raping white women; disrespectful of black women because of polygamy; wife buying and selling.

African *women*, as drudges, beasts of burden; sex objects; unresponsive, poor lovers.

'Mulattoes', as impure, unnatural, undesirable; scorned, rejected by either race; cunning, crafty.[5]

It is important to notice the inexorable logic: from the empirical observation of external physical characteristics there is a 'natural' progression to deductions about mental, moral and emotional characteristics. It would be intriguing if teachers could conduct an experiment in which they asked their classes to itemise under each of the four headings above their perceptions of black people in general, or of Africans in particular, and to establish not only the extent to which the views stated above are still current, but where they originate, since Milbury-Steen's itemisation comes out of an analysis of contemporary literature – though, as I have indicated, the origins are not recent.

It is important to emphasise this continuous (and continuing) historical record of the portrayal of blacks as inferior, and to show that it dates from the time when England was undergoing its transformation from a pre-industrial and feudal system to a mercantilist capitalism in which the same ideas which seek to justify a society based upon property, authority and patriarchy at home also seek to justify ethnocentricism and slavery abroad.

The tradition to which I refer has an impeccable liberal ancestry. Our present-day empiricists and pragmatists may ponder the fact that it was the originator of the problem of induction, David Hume (1711–76), author of such classic texts as *A Treatise of Human Nature* and *An Inquiry concerning Human Understanding*, who asserted, firstly, that European culture was superior to all other cultures, and, consequently, that there was a causal link between race and culture, as follows:

There never was a civilised nation of any other complexion than white, nor even any individual eminent either in action or speculation. No ingenious manufactures amongst them no arts, no sciences . . . Such a uniform and constant difference could not happen, in so many countries and ages, if nature had not made an original distinction betwixt these breeds of men.[6]

It is during the Victorian period that these ideas become the common currency of the society, irrespective of class or nationality in Europe. Brian V. Street shows that

> The origin of the representation of alien peoples is to be found, in the nineteenth century, not only in popular literature, but also in contemporary science and in imperial politics, so that all three continually derive from and contribute to the changing image of 'primitive' man.[7]

Not only had publishing techniques been developed which enabled large quantities of very cheap fiction, especially in serial form, to become available, particularly aimed at the newly educated working classes, but the justifications for racism, and for the relationship between racism and the ideology of conquest and subjugation were now linked. Street's most significant conclusion is, however, that

> . . . many of the stereotypes had already hardened before the 'scramble for Africa', and imperialists tended to use theories already worked out by scientists and which lent themselves to political manipulation. Scientific theories of race provided a framework of thought with regard to primitive peoples which justified the actions of imperialists, but they arose, not out of an imperial situation, but in a pre-imperial world of science.

The impact upon literature of this combination of science and political ideology is nowhere illustrated better than with reference to books for boys. G. D. Killham has traced this phenomenon. He notes that the themes of the 'ethnographic novel' can be found in, for instance, G. A. Henty's books on the Ashanti campaigns. Novelists were

> . . . addressing themselves to a general public caught up in the enthusiasm of the overseas venture in Africa, they knew what their readers wished to read and to that taste they catered. Thus the generality of authors adhere strictly in their treatments of the African setting to an image of Africa which was in large part formed before they came to write their books.[8]

Kipling is the obvious example, later on, of the making of a popular racism – not only within the ranks of the working classes who became the ordinary soldiers, but also among the ranks of those whom George Orwell[9] calls the 'service classes' – the people who read *Blackwoods,* and who naturalised slogans such as: 'East is East and West is West'; 'The White Man's Burden'; 'The female of the species is more deadly than the male'; 'Somewhere East of Suez'; 'Palm and Pine'; 'The Road to Mandalay'.

Instead of doing the obvious by taking examples from Kipling in order to demonstrate these copybook maxims in action, let us look at an equally prominent writer on the subject of empire – and one who is generally higher regarded – Joseph Conrad. In *Almayer's Folly* (1895) the Dutchman Almayer marries a Malay girl who had been adopted by the Englishman Lingard, in order to gain the latter's good opinion and also to become his heir. A daughter is born, and Almayer endeavours to educate the girl, Nina, as if she were 'white' instead of 'half-caste', but she rejects her father because she considers him to be an adventurer, and elopes with one of the local men. Now, while there may be a critical argument as to what Conrad intended, the contemporary reviewers were in no doubt. Their comments reveal (betray?) the real ideology: the reviews emphasise, *inter alia*, the wife's hatred for her husband; the half-hearted love on the part of the daughter for her father; that Almayer is doomed because of the emasculating effect of the East; despite the fact that '. . . the European had hoped to educate his daughter and make a reasonable creature out of her: she was all he has to care for in the world, and she elopes with a Malay'.[10]

The elegantly expressed sentiments ineluctably combine the themes of patriarchy, property and purity (of race). Lingard, being English, adopts the Malay girl. That is proper, within bounds. Almayer, because he is not English, oversteps. And the penalty for 'going native' is as inevitable as in Greek tragedy – but only if one is willing to consider the loss of one's white identity as tragic.

Now, when we learn from J. I. M. Stewart that 'Conrad had voyaged among the islands but had no intimate knowledge of their inhabitants, whom he interprets in terms of the conventions of European fiction',[11] we have an important corroboration of Street's general thesis. Therefore, since Conrad is one of the keystones of 'The Great Tradition' of English literature, as well as a popularly read author, we have to locate his ideological position a little more carefully. There is no doubt that Conrad is fundamentally opposed to imperialism – if novels like *Nostromo* are not sufficient evidence, then the extensive statement of his political beliefs in *Autocracy and*

War (1905) cannot be denied. But one can be anti-imperialist and still be racist and colonialist. Jonah Raskin[12] has done an excellent job of showing how Conrad grew up as a native of a colonised country, how his earliest experiences were moulded by the experience of his parents' membership of a branch of the Polish nationalist movement that wanted independence from Tsarist Russia. But, as Avrom Fleishman[13] argues, this colonial heritage of allegiances and attitudes constituted the foundation for the development of a tradition of organic conservatism, which he identifies with the philosophy of Edmund Burke (1727–97). Unlike Burke, however, Conrad sees very little hope for the future of the organic community, since imperialism had gone too far to be reversed or arrested, and so '. . . Conrad finds himself a Burkean conservative in a Hobbesian world'.[14] The argument here is that there begins to be constituted a common body of expectations, a common mythology (demonology?) upon which both readers and writers draw, so that apart from individual and specific singularities of particular authors, there is also a shared set of features in (say) Conan Doyle's representation of Africa (or Germans, or the English working class), or A. E. W. Mason's India, or R. M. Ballantyne's South Seas. This is Conan Doyle:

> The door had flown open and a huge Negro had burst into the room. He would have been a comic figure if he had been terrific, for he was dressed in a very loud grey check suit with a flowing salmon-coloured tie. His broad face and flattened nose were thrust forward, as his sullen eyes, with a smouldering gleam of malice in them, turned one of us to the other.[15]

But place this vivid corroboration of the Milbury-Steen conclusions alongside an equally vividly captured moment from Conrad's *Heart of Darkness* (1902). The narrator, Marlow, informs us, approvingly:

> . . . I met a white man, in such an unexpected elegance of get-up that in the first moment I took him for a sort of vision. I saw a high starched collar, white cuffs, a light alpaca jacket, snowy trousers, a clean necktie, and varnished boots. No hat. Hair parted, brushed, oiled, under a green-lined parasol held in a big white hand. He was amazing, and had a penholder behind his ear . . . His appearance was certainly that of a hairdresser's dummy; but in the great demoralisation of the land he kept up his appearance. That's backbone. His starched collars and got-up shirt-fronts were achievements of character.

Conrad makes no attempt to recognise that this 'achievement of character' is dependent upon black service. But the moral point he makes is unambiguous: while Europeans are expected to maintain appearances, and thereby set an example and are measured by the extent to which they do so, blacks are different: they can be given the outer and visible signs, the trappings and the suits of civilisation, but these are dismissed as being skin deep.

What is important is to recognise how earlier, scriptural justifications for enslaving heathens become transformed and reinforced by scientific underpinning in terms of popular understanding of '. . . the survival of the fittest'. Leo Henkin[16] has shown how 'race' is used as a means of classification, with Europeans at the top of the evolutionary tree, and with 'primitive' peoples as representing earlier stages of European development, so that the simultaneous application of the discoveries of science, the impact of the interest in empire, and the products of literature combine to lead to Philip Curtin's classic conclusion:

> The view of Africa which began to emerge in the 1780s, drew some of its novelty from a new attitude on the part of the Europeans, but even more from the flood of new data that began to pour in – first from coastal travellers, then from explorers into the interior (and the early nineteenth century was the great age of African exploration), finally from the refinement and synthesis of these data in the hands of stay-at-home scholars and publicists. As the decades passed, British ideas about Africa became more and more detailed and better publicised. By the 1850s the image had hardened. It was found in children's books, in Sunday School tracts, in the popular press. Its major affirmations were the 'common knowledge' of the educated classes. Thereafter, when new generations of explorers or administrators went to Africa, they went with a prior impression of what they would find. Most often, they found it, and their writings in turn confirmed the older image – or at most altered it only slightly.[17]

Racism had a strong 'philosophical' underpinning. The views of David Hume in the eighteenth century, quoted earlier, find their echo in the nineteenth in that great Victorian sage, Thomas Carlyle (1795–1881). One example will suffice:

> One always rather likes the Nigger; evidently a poor blockhead with good dispositions, with affections, attachments, – with a turn for Nigger Melodies, and the like: – he is the only Savage of all the coloured races that doesn't die out on sight of the White Man; but can actually live beside him, and work and increase and be merry. The Almighty Maker has appointed him to be a Servant. Under penalty of Heaven's

curse, neither party to this pre-appointment shall neglect or misdo his
duties therein . . .[18]

Which brings us to 'the white man's burden', which as recently as
1929 could be justified by Sydney Haldane, Baron Olivier
(1859–1943) – a friend of the Webb's, a former secretary of the
Fabian Society, and Governor of Jamaica, as:

> . . . a doctrine . . . not essentially at all inhumane or ignoble, but liable
> to be accepted in somewhat crude interpretations by the colonising
> individuals whose activities and *enterprise* [my emphasis] created in
> practice the situation that was developing . . . a doctrine which might be
> briefly summarised thus: Tropical countries are not suited for settled
> habitation by whites. Europeans cannot work in that climate or rear
> their children there. The native can prosper and labour under good
> government, but is incapable of developing under his own country's
> resources. He is a barbarian, benighted, and unprogressive. One of the
> principal reasons for this arrested development is that his livelihood has
> been made so easy for him by natural conditions that he has not been
> obliged to work, or at any rate to work steadily and in a proper
> workmanlike manner. The European therefore must, in the interests of
> human progress, make arrangements to enable and to induce the black
> man to work productively under his direction and training. To him the
> economic profit, which the black cannot either create or wisely use; to
> the black man peace and protection, relief from disease and famine,
> moral and social improvement and elevation and the blessings of
> European culture in general.[19]

It is important to note that this characterisation of the black, the
savage and the primitive was constructed upon the base of a clear
conception of the idea of the nineteenth-century English gentleman.
This conception excluded (by definition) all women, all English
males who were not gentlemen, and all other Europeans were not
English. The English gentleman is seen as a rare amalgam of skills
and qualities which could be traced back to an Anglo-Saxon past,
out of which arose not only his achievements in the arts and
sciences, but also his social institutions and his ability to be placed,
rightfully, at the apex of the human pyramid. As Rider Haggard
asserts in *Allan Quatermain* (1887), heroes are gentlemen; and to
be an English gentleman is the highest rank to which a man can
aspire in this world. Similarly, in *King Solomon's Mines* (1885), Sir
Henry Curtis refuses to accept payment in return for his assistance
– since a gentleman does not sell himself for money!

The so-called innocuous 'boys' own' stories of Haggard, Henty,
Kipling and others consequently take on a rather different

colouration in the context of seeking to delineate the nature of the 'black presence'. Martin Greene is in no doubt. His assertion is that '. . . adventure tales that formed the light reading of Englishmen for two hundred years and more after *Robinson Crusoe* were, in fact, the energising myth of English imperialism'.[20] Examples of the rehearsal of that myth are numerous. Two (one about Africa, the other about India) will suffice. In John Buchan's *Prester John* (1905), the hero, Davie, observes what he understands the meaning of the white man's duty to be:

> He had to take all the risks . . . that is the difference between white and black, the gift of responsibility, the power of being in a little way a king, and so long as we know and then practise it, we will rule, not only in Africa alone, but wherever there are dark men who live for their bellies.

Nobody has popularised the myth – and made plain the inevitable implications – better than Rudyard Kipling. For instance, in 'His chance of life', he states: 'never forget that unless the outward and visible signs of our authority are always before a native he is incapable as a child of understanding what authority means, or where is the danger in disobeying it'.

Now, categorising those who are dispossessed as children enables those in authority to argue that (i) rebellion is proof of irrational behaviour; (ii) that force is therefore justified, just as parents are sometimes constrained to discipline their children. Such an argument places the dispossessed in a kind of double bind: (i) to obey is proof that they *wish* to be dominated; (ii) to rebel is proof that they *need* to be dominated. And this argument is not just accidental or odd; it is a deepseated and structured ideology: the man who would be king must convince his subjects that he is not merely temporarily, but fundamentally and permanently, superior. The defeat of the man who would be king is a direct consequence of breaking one of the central taboos – the man who would be king is overthrown because he forgets the first rule of domination: he takes a wife from among his subjects, and 'sinks' to their level.[21]

To what extent are beliefs of the kind noted above still extant today? I would suggest that the 'energising myth' lives on despite (because?) of the loss of empire, and because of the presence in the metropolitan society of the descendants of conquered peoples who daily give the lie to the myth. But the myth is pervasive, and particularly strong in educational circles. A question in a recent Oxford and Cambridge Examinations Board paper neatly illustrates the point, by asking: 'From your reading of *Mr Johnson*, do you think that the civilisation the white man was bringing to the bush was likely to make the natives happier?'. Strange how the pursuit of 'pure' literature, uncontaminated by non-literary criteria, is somehow absent, and how 'civilisation' and 'bush' and 'white' and 'native' are contrasted, with the former as donors and the latter as recipients. Another question, concerning the same text, asks the pupils to 'Write an imaginary dialogue between Joyce Cary and an African politician who wants to ban *Mr Johnson*'. Notice how Joyce Cary stands for civilised values, in conflict with sinister Africa.

Why, of all the texts which might have been chosen as an example of an engagement with the black presence, do Examination Boards appear to have this liking for *Mr Johnson*? The interest continues, one suspects, because the 'energising myth' is still strong. The introduction of texts by Achebe and Naipaul is an indication, not of the decline of the strength of the myth, but of its continuing capacity to incorporate and modify challenges.

To design a curriculum which might have a chance to combat the myth would require us to tackle the key components around which the myth has been constructed, namely imperialism (with regard to Africa, Asia and Latin America); nationalism (with regard to other Europeans, in particular, but also against Scots, Welsh and Irish); sexism and racism. To seek to combat racism, in isolation, will be neither sufficient nor successful.

To design a curriculum which foregrounds these elements is, by definition, to recognise that the more conventional strategy which seeks to amend the syllabus by the judicious incorporation of apposite texts will not do: will not do now not because of the earlier arguments around the nature and role of literature but because of the much more explicit ideological dimension in which this debate operates – as can be demonstrated from the report of the recent conference on the theme of 'Eng. Lit. or literatures in English: alternatives to the teaching and examining of English at 'A' Level', organised by the Association for the Teaching of Caribbean, African and Associated Literature. Three specific proposals emerged from that conference:

1. that the University of London Board must place its Afro-Caribbean option in literature on an equal footing with other 'A' level literature papers.

2. that a Working Party be set up to make relevant proposals for a new submission on 'A' level texts to another Examination Board.
3. that Local Education Authorities should provide more in-service training courses relevant to teachers and in teacher-educators wanting to teach Afro-Caribbean and other literatures in English.

Now, with regard to these proposals, the response of Professor Arthur Pollard (a founder member of the ATCAL, who was unable to be present at the conference, and who is also the Chief 'A' Level examiner for the University of London) is illuminating. At the conference, a speaker had argued that

> . . . any 'A' Level literature syllabus should lay its main emphasis not, as at present, 'on authoritative readings of the major authors', but on the *skills* required for an appreciation of literature; and that English should see itself as one of a number of disciplines each of which provide a different perspective for the understanding of the contemporary social and cultural life of the community.

The speaker had gone on to argue that

> . . . ethnic minorities, like the white working-class, are still very largely excluded from the official national culture and hence from the centres of power and institutional values. The examination system and the entry it offers to higher education may act as the channel into the official culture for the middle-classes, but at the moment it also acts as a block for any minority or working-class values finding their way into this official national culture – and it literally 'closes the door on access' to higher education for most people from these groups.[22]

This is quite clearly a serious intervention, which merits serious consideration. Professor Pollard's response was to dismiss it as '. . . part of that attack on established and traditional standards which is by now a familiar Marxist ploy'. I am not sure which of the Professor's comments are least attractive: the dismissal by associative 'smear', or the assumption that a phrase like 'established and traditional standards' has meaning, and indeed, has a meaning that we all recognise.

It is, however, Professor Pollard's next statement which is so magisterially instructive. He writes:

> The fact remains that, with the possible exception of Naipaul, there really is nothing in African and Caribbean literature to match in quality those works which are normally found within the substantive body of texts set at Advanced Level.[23]

No useful purpose will be served by seeking to match the names of those included in the Professor's 'substantive body of texts' against

197

those left out, since there would appear to be a fundamental and unbridgeable chasm between two radically opposed perceptions of what the business of education is about: the speaker at the ATCAL conference believes (and I share many of his principles) that education is about liberation from ignorance and prejudice, for preparation for living in and contributing to society; Professor Pollard appears to believe that it is about 'texts'. And even if we could agree about the status of the text, I would still want to insist that certain themes, styles and skills are sometimes best approached by selections from outside the 'substantive body'.

This brings us to the second of the conference proposals: this obsession with, not simply texts, but texts of a particular kind and towards a particular end – that of the jealous god of the 'A' Level syllabus. Why should there be this pressure to genuflect before the shrine of the commanding heights of the minority? What provision should our syllabus make for the majority who do not do 'A' Level, or indeed for the even greater majority who do not do even 'O' Level or CSE? Those who, for one reason or another, never encounter a 'major text', whether 'substantive' or not? While there is short-term merit in seeking to make relevant proposals for altering the balance of 'A' Level studies to incorporate some sense of 'the black presence', that is only the beginning of the project. A radical re-design of the curriculum will have to tackle not simply the disciplinary boundaries between (say) literature, history, theology and film, music, dance and anthropology, but also, for instance, the effects upon curriculum design of the proportions of children from different pasts in different regions – Wolverhampton compared with Wiltshire, Brent with Royal Berks. But, having started on this process of differentiation, how far do we go? Do we differentiate – and if so, how? – between the children whose parents come from different parts of Her Majesty's former empire? How specifically should we tailor our syllabus to the perceived needs of children whose parents were born black but British (or is it born British but black?), and those who hail from the Caribbean, from Asia, from Africa? And do we differentiate even further by taking into account perceived differences between (say) East and West Africa, particularly when one bears in mind that the nature of the colonial experience, as well as the process of decolonisation, was not the same? Or between Muslims from the Asian sub-continent and Muslims from Northern Nigeria? Or the whole question of gender, and the interaction between race and gender? What are the strategies by which a black girl can begin to seek an answer to that question? Which should she privilege – her gender, or her colour? Who is it can tell her who she is?

All these questions point us firmly in the direction of the third proposal of the ATCAL conference: that of the need for greater provision of relevant in-service teacher training. In the past decade or so, Local Education Authorities and higher education institutions have sought to meet this demand by providing what is commonly referred to as 'multi-cultural' education. The classic definition is American, and the philosophy is stated thus:

> Multi-cultural education is preparation for the social, political and economic realities that individuals experience in culturally diverse and complex human encounters. These realities have both national and international dimensions . . . multi-cultural education is viewed as an intervention and an on-going assessment to help institutions and individuals become more responsive to the human condition, individual cultural identity and cultural pluralism in society.[24]

At first sight the statement would appear to be one to which no 'right-minded' person could take exception. But, notice that the first sentence recognises that the society is racist, and that it will continue to remain so – indeed, will continue to remain unequal socially as well as economically. Next, the statement informs us that the objective of the educational process is 'preparation' for living in these 'realities'. In other words, the theoretical foundations of multi-cultural education are grounded in an acceptance of the nature of the society and of the place in it of individuals and of groups, and that the 'preparation' consists of seeking to devise strategies for making life somewhat less difficult for those who find themselves at the receiving end of prejudice in '. . . complex human encounters'. Conversely, for those who are the beneficiaries by virtue of being members of the dominant groups, multi-cultural education serves the purpose of making them recognise that they have to be sensitive to 'cultural identity' and to 'cultural pluralism'.

Now, I find this formulation particularly obnoxious, because behind the apparent façade of egalitarian principle lurks the reality of the modernisation of inequality, and of the attempt to seek the assistance of the dispossessed in this task. It is my experience, having been born in South Africa, and from living in Britain and in the United States, that the appeal to the recognition of 'cultural identity' and 'cultural pluralism' on the part of the dominant is an acknowledgement of difference. And from the recognition of difference there flow, inevitably, notions of superiority and inferiority, with the superior groups seeking to establish and then to maintain hegemony, and with the subordinate groups devising a whole range of (sometimes contradictory) strategies for survival. This is because even the theories on which they base their strategies flow out of the dominant society and are – indeed – often articulated on behalf of the subordinate by those who originate in, and have had the benefits of, the cultural habits and structures of feeling of the dominant society.

The 'official' British formulation of 'multi-cultural' education illustrates my point of how an apparently innocuous and well-intentioned principle can be rendered practically impossible to implement – not only because of the lack of competent practitioners, but mainly because again the foundations are suspect. The 1982 Schools Council leaflet states:

> in terms of educational practice [multi-cultural education] means that all school lessons need to employ curricula, curriculum materials and examinations which include examples drawn from a wide range of cultures and which avoid presenting solely anglo-centric views of the world.[25]

If one takes into account what actually happens in schools, it is difficult to see how 'all' (or even a large proportion of) lessons can be designed in order to enable the policy to be implemented – even if teachers are clear about what is required, how the objectives can be achieved, and work in an environment which encourages such innovation. Experience, as well as research, point rather to an opposite conclusion: of teachers as generally fairly conservative, and of secondary schools as sites of conventional and traditional practices geared to the demands of potential sixth form and higher education entrance pupils. In such an environment, even 'multi-cultural' education is seen as (at best) a distraction, and (at worst) not part of the tasks of the school. This particular argument is summarised as follows:

> The role of multi-cultural education falls within the scope of the compensatory education models which attempt to compensate educationally disadvantaged children through the development of special education projects – it takes schools and teachers away from their central concern which is basically teaching or instructing

children in the knowledge and skills essential to life in this society.[26]

One suspects that this rather narrow view of what education is, and what education is for, is probably still the reigning ideology in schools. By Stone's analysis, children who are disadvantaged because of their colour are relegated (with other children who are disadvantaged for other social or physical reasons) to the margins, and away from 'the central concerns' since children who are disadvantaged will clearly not be able to acquire, or expect to be enabled to acquire, the skills essential to life 'in this society'.

There is therefore a considerable degree of justification for the view that 'various multi-cultural education models developed and employed since the early sixties have attempted the cultural subordination and political neutralisation of blacks'.[27] Even if one concedes that this is an unintended effect, that effect nevertheless derives out of a failure to recognise that

> the important thing about multi-cultural education is that it should be a dynamic and political process, not merely a reselection of different cultural artifacts. It is about changing white attitudes more than adding this or that topic to the printed syllabus[28]

and that 'a conceptual framework for multi-cultural education can only become clearer if the issues of institutionalised racism and problems between dominant and subordinate groups are identified'.[29]

What I propose therefore, is a project which might enable teachers to begin to

(a) combat the stranglehold on the school curriculum of 'English', and with it, the dominant assumptions regarding 'substantive texts' and a 'great tradition', in order that affinities might be explored not only with colleagues in congruent disciplines (history, religious study, sociology) who are keen to break away from the restrictive demarcations of disciplines, but also with other forms (music, drama, film, art, etc);

(b) eschew tinkering with the outer fringes of the 'A' Level syllabus which seeks to include one or more token Third World writer, but which leaves the literary as well as the social context relatively unmodified by the inclusion;

(c) pay attention to the needs of all 11–16 year old children of all ranges of ability;

(d) foreground not only 'the black presence' but also other marginalised categories, notably women.

The justification for the general tenor of these proposals lies not in the attempt to assert a counter-ideology, but in that it provides scope in the first instance for alternative treatments and explorations of literature other than those of the dominant tradition. Only a substantial engagement with these alternatives will do, if the objective is to provide opportunities for an experiencing of different societies, or of different experiences of society. Only such an approach will make it essential to instigate a more pluralist educational practice to seek to ensure that educational discourses are broad enough to take cognisance of the social and individual worlds of the pupils.

The starting point might be in contemporary personal experience: what it is like to be black in Britain – for children, for their parents, their teachers, their schoolfriends whether black or non-black. An introduction via poetry seems obvious – poems by Linton Kwesi Johnson (*Dread Beat and Blood*; *Inglan is a Bitch*) or Grace Nicholls (*I Is a Long-Memoried Woman*) might be read in conjunction with anthologies of poetry from the Caribbean (Salkey: *Breaklight*; Dathorne: *Caribbean Verses*; Figueroa: *Caribbean Voices*; Ramchand & Grey: *West Indian Poetry*) or from Africa (Soyinka: *Poems of Black Africa*; Reed & Wake: *A New Book of African Verse*). A study of these poems might also be the starting point for pupils setting their own experience to verse.

Similar opportunities obviously exist when it comes to the study of drama, particularly if that study is allied to television, music, etc. One thinks here of (for instance) the work of Caryl Phillips: *Strange Fruit*, about the problems of a black family caught 'between two cultures', or *Where There is Darkness*, in which a West Indian takes stock prior to returning to the Caribbean after a decade in this country. Again, plays about contemporary experience in Britain can be linked to plays about Caribbean and African antecedents – Errol Hill: *A Time and a Season – West Indian Plays*; Derek Walcott: *Dream on Monkey Mountain*; James Gibbs: *Moralities for Modern Africa*.

The theme of contemporary experience is well-documented in fiction: Sam Selvon's *Moses Migrating* – in which Moses returns to the Caribbean after a decade in London, compared with (say) the same author's *The Lonely Londoners* or his earlier *Ways of Sunlight*, which is set in London as well as in Trinidad. This theme of the reality of England set in the context of the image which black people have of this island from the vantage point of the former colonies is dealt with by (for instance) Wilson Katiyo: *Going to Heaven* (about a Zimbabwean student in London) and Buchi Emecheta: *Second Class Citizen* (about a Nigerian girl in London, which combines the issues of racism and sexism).

Since one writer's theme of the 'loss of empire' is another writer's theme of the 'struggle for independence', this theme might be a fruitful one to contrast. With regard to the former, one can think of a variety of works by (for instance) Paul Scott and Doris Lessing – whose starting point seems to be the awareness of that loss, compared with (say) Evelyn Waugh and Graham Greene – whose starting point seems to be to resist that loss. One further approach might be to contrast (say) writers whose view of empire is based in their position as officials (Joyce Cary) and those whose involvement is one of intellectual liberalism (E. M. Forster).

The theme of the 'struggle for independence' is a particularly rich one. To name but one novel per region: Ngugi wa Thiong'o: *Weep Not Child* (East Africa); Chinua Achebe: *No Longer at Ease* (West Africa); Vic Reid: *New Day* (Caribbean); Sembene Ousmane: *God's Bits of Wood* (Francophone Africa).

Before and during this struggle for independence, how did people live under conditions of conquest? That might be a further theme. Two classic texts are Chinua Achebe: *Things Fall Apart*, and Ngugi wa Thiong'o: *A Grain of Wheat*, but one might also include (for instance) Can Themba: *The Will to Die*, Mbulelo Mzamane: *The Children of Soweto*, and Alex la Guma: *A Walk in the Night, and Other Stories* (South Africa); Orlando Patterson: *The Children of Sisyphus* and Roger Mais: *The Hills were Joyful Together* (Caribbean); Ferdinand Oyono: *Houseboy* (Francophone Africa).

Two particular themes might well find space under this aspect: firstly, that of the experience of childhood and adolescence, with works by (*inter alia*) Michael Anthony: *The Year in San Fernando*; H. G. de Lisser: *Jane's Career*; Merle Hodge: *Crick Crack Monkey*; and the celebrated *In the Castle of my Skin*, by George Lamming; secondly, the theme of keeping the past alive, under conditions of dispossession of not only land but culture: using materials from (*inter alia*) African creation myths in *The Origin of Life and Death*, ed. U. Beier; *Myths and Legends of the Swahili*, ed. Jan Knappert, and Mazisi Kunene's *Anthem of the Decades*.

The period of conquest for the dispossessed was, of course, the heyday of empire for the metropolitan society. For that theme the obvious material can be found in the adventure tales and romances: Robert Ballantyne: *The Coral Island*; John Buchan: *Prester John*; Joseph Conrad: *Almayer's Folly* or *An Outcast of the Islands*; Rider Haggard: *King Solomon's Mines* or *Allan Quatermain*; Kipling's poems and stories, and A. E. W. Mason: *The Broken Reed* can be contrasted with works depicting the experiences of the subordinated peoples: Thomas Mofolo: *Chaka*; Mazisi Kunene: *Emperor Shaka the Great*; Niane: *Sundiata: An Epic of Old Mali*; Sol. T. Plaatje: *Mhudi*; Achebe: *Arrow of God*; Equiano: *Equiano's Travels*; Oyono: *The Old Man and the Medal*; Kwakuri Azasu: *The Stool*.

More recently, writers have tackled a new theme: that of the responses to the 'failure' of independence, and texts such as Ngugi wa Thiong'o: *Petals of Blood* or *Devil on the Cross* and Wole Soyinka: *The Interpreters* might be useful in this regard.

It would also be fascinating to study how the dominant representation of blacks is incorporated into, and modified by, white writers whose perceptions are coloured by geographical proximity. I think here of (for instance) contrasting the metro-politan with the colonial (England versus the USA; England versus South Africa), but also about contrasting the colonial versions themselves – South Africa versus the USA. Texts might include Mark Twain: *Huckleberry Finn* and William Faulkner: *Light in August* with Sarah Gertrude Millin: *God's Stepchildren* or William Plomer: *Turbott Wolfe*. It might also be useful to look at the writings of black writers from these same habitats: Ralph Ellison: *The Invisible Man*; James Baldwin: *The Fire Next Time* and *Another Country*; Alex la Guma: *Time of the Butcherbird* and *And a Threefold Cord*.

Finally, it cannot be emphasised too strongly that while in *Othello* it is clearly the fact of the Moor's colour which energises the drama, Shakespeare also more generally introduces the theme of empire in other plays, of which *The Tempest* is, despite its complexity, perhaps the most rewarding to explore, particularly in the light of the critical work around it which refer to our theme of 'the black presence'. One thinks here of theoretical works by, for instance, Mannoni: *Prospero and Caliban – The Psychology of Colonisation*; Philip Mason: *Prospero's Magic – Some Thoughts on Class and Race*; and Leslie Fiedler: *The Stranger in Shakespeare*, but, in particular of George Lamming's seminal commentary in *The Pleasures of Exile* (1961) which brings us full circle, to the title for this paper. Lamming observes:

> ... Caliban is his [Prospero's] convert, colonised by language, and excluded by language. It is precisely this gift of language, this attempt at transformation which has brought about the pleasure and paradox of Caliban's exile. Exiled from his gods, exiled from his nature, exiled from his own name! Yet Prospero is afraid of Caliban. He is afraid because he knows that his encounter with Caliban is, largely, his encounter with himself ... Caliban is the very climate in which men encounter the nature of ambiguities, and in which, according to his choice, each man attempts a resolution by trying to slay the past. Caliban's history – for he has a most turbulent history – belongs entirely to the future ... In all his encounters with his neighbours – whether they be Kings or drunken clowns – Caliban is never allowed the power *to see*. He is always the measure of the condition which his physical experience has already defined. Caliban is the excluded, that which is eternally below possibility, and always beyond reach. He is seen as an occasion, a state of existence which can be appropriated and explored for the purposes of another's own development.

The liberation of Caliban, and his revelation of himself, is therefore not simply a matter of ensuring that 'the black presence' is expressed in the classroom, but more fundamentally, it is a contribution to the project of destroying racism in contemporary Britain.

Notes

1. C. Belsey: *Critical Practice* (London, 1980), ch. I, 'Criticism and commonsense', and Tony Davies: 'Common sense and critical practice: teaching literature', in P. Widdowson (ed.): *Re-reading English* (London, 1982).
2. *Black and White: A Study of the Negro and English Society 1555–1945* (London, 1973).
3. 'Race and moral panics', British Sociological Association Public Lecture, 1978, reprinted in *Five Views of Multi-Racial Britain* (Commission for Racial Equality, London, 1978).
4. *Colour, Class and the Victorians: English Attitudes to the Negro in the Nineteenth Century* (Leicester, 1978), p. 21.
5. *European and African Stereotypes in Twentieth Century Fiction* (London, 1980), pp. 35–6.
6. Quoted in P. Curtin: *The Image of Africa – British Ideas and Actions 1780–1850* (Madison, Wisconsin, 1964), p. 41.
7. Brian V. Street: *The Savage in Literature – Representations of 'Primitive' Society in English Fiction 1858–1920* (London, 1975), pp. 2–5.
8. *Africa in English Fiction 1874–1939* (Ibadan, 1968), p. 6.
9. 'Rudyard Kipling', in *The Collected Essays, Journalism and Letters of George*

Orwell, Vol. 2 (Harmondsworth, 1968).

10. Conrad: The Critical Heritage, ed. Norman Sherry (London, 1973), pp. 47–61.
11. Eight Modern Writers (Oxford, 1963), p. 189.
12. The Mythology of Imperialism (New York, 1971).
13. Conrad's Politics (Baltimore, 1967).
14. J. A. MacClure: Kipling and Conrad – the Colonial Fiction (Cambridge, Mass., 1981), p. 96.
15. 'The Adventure of the Three Gables', in The Case-Book of Sherlock Holmes (Harmondsworth, 1951).
16. Darwinism in the English Novel 1860–1910 (New York, 1940).
17. Curtin, The Image of Africa.
18. 'Shooting Niagara – and After' (1867), quoted in V. G. Kiernan: 'High imperial noon', in Theo Barker (ed.): The Long March of Everyman (Harmondsworth, 1975). Kiernan notes that 'About this time Carlyle, along with Kingsley, Ruskin, Tennyson and others, was active in defending Governor Eyre of Jamaica, charged with excessively brutal repression there in 1865.' Edward John Eyre, 1815–1901, had been a colonial official in Australia, New Zealand, St Vincent, and had become governor of Jamaica in 1864. An uprising by the local people was suppressed by the military, and Eyre was accused of brutality and illegality, especially in the execution of George Gordon, a black member of the Jamaican legislature. Eyre was recalled to London in 1866, and several attempts, prompted by (among others), John Stuart Mill and Herbert Spencer, were made to have him tried for murder. These attempts were forestalled by a committee of admirers, including those mentioned above.
19. White Capital and Coloured Labour (London, 1906; rev. 1929).
20. Martin Green: Dreams of Adventure, Deeds of Empire (London, 1980), p. 3.
21. R. Kipling: Phantom 'Rickshaw (Allahabad, 1888).
22. ATCAL Bulletin 7, August 1982, p. 2.
23. ATCAL Bulletin 8, December 1982, pp. 2–3.
24. National Council for the Accreditation of Teacher Education; Washington DC: Standards for the Accreditation of Teacher Education (Washington, 1978; rev. 1982).
25. A. Craft: Multi-Cultural Education (Schools Council, 1982).
26. M. Stone: The Education of the Black Child in Britain (London, 1981).
27. C. Mullard: 'Multi-racial education in Britain', in J. Tierney (ed.): Race, Migration and Schooling (New York, 1982).
28. A. Green: 'In Defence of Anti-Racist Teaching', in Multi-Cultural Education, 10, No. 2.
29. J. Gundara: 'Approaches to Multi-Cultural Education', in Tierney, Race, Migration and Schooling.

Selected bibliography

Achebe, C.: 'An image of Africa', in *Research in African Literatures*, IX, no. I, 1978.

Adewumi, M. F.: *Racial Attitudes in the European Literature of Africa from H. Rider Haggard to Joyce Carey* (unpublished PhD diss., Arizona State Univ., 1977).

Baldensperger, F.: 'Was Othello an Ethiopian?', in *Harvard Studies*, XX, 1938.

Ballhatchet, K.: *Race, Sex and Class under the Raj* (London, 1980).

Banton, M.: *Race Relations* (London, 1967).

Barker, M.: *The New Racism* (London, 1981).

Barzun, J.: *Race – A Study in Superstition* (New York, 1965).

Baudet, H.: *Paradise on Earth: Some Thoughts on European Images of non-European Man* (New Haven Conn., 1965).

Bissell, B.: *The American Indian in English Literature of the Eighteenth Century* (New Haven, Conn., 1925).

Blassingame, J. W. (ed.): *Slave Testimony: Two Centuries of Letters, Speeches, Interviews and Autobiographies* (Baton Rouge, Louisiana, 1977).

Botsford, J.: *English Society in the Eighteenth Century as Influenced from Overseas* (New York, 1924).

Braithwaite, R H. E.: *The Negro in English Literature 1765–1841* (unpublished MA thesis, London Univ., 1957).

Browne, P. L.: *Men and Women, Africa and Civilisation: A Study of the African Stories of Hemingway and the African Novels of Haggard, Greene and Bellow* (unpublished PhD diss., Rutgers Univ., 1979).

Buchan, W.: *John Buchan: A Memoir* (London, 1982).

Butcher, P.: 'Othello's racial identity', in *Shakespeare Quarterly*, III, 1952.

Cairns, H.: *Prelude to Imperialism* (London, 1965).

Carlson, J. A.: *A Comparison of the Treatment of the Negro in Children's Literature in the Periods 1929–1938 and 1959–1968* (unpublished PhD diss., Univ. of Connecticut, 1969).

Carrington, C.: *The Life of Rudyard Kipling* (New York, 1955).

Centre for Contemporary Cultural Studies: *The Empire Strikes Back: Race and Racism in 70s Britain* (London, 1982).

Collins, H. R.: *His Image in Ebony: the African in British Fiction during the Age of Imperialism* (unpublished PhD diss., Columbia Univ., 1951).

Cornell, L.: *Kipling in India* (London, 1966).

Cowhig, R.: *Haply for I am Black; A Study of Othello's Race, of Changing Racial Attitudes, and of the Implications of such Changes for the Production and Interpretation of the Play* (unpublished PhD diss., Manchester Univ., 1974).

Craton, M.: *Testing the Chains: Resistance to Slavery in the British West Indies* (Ithaca and London, 1982).

Curtin, P. D.: *The Image of Africa – British Ideas and Action 1780–1850* (Madison, Wisconsin, 1964).

Selected bibliography

Curtis, L. P.: *Anglo-Saxons and Celts* (New York, 1968).

Dabydeen, D.: *Some Aspects of William Hogarth's Representation of the Materialism of his Age* (unpublished PhD diss., London Univ., 1982).

Daniell, D.: *The Interpreter's House: a Critical Assessment of the Work of John Buchan* (London, 1975).

Darras, J.: *Joseph Conrad and the West: Signs of Empire* (London, 1982).

Davis, C. T. and Gates, H. (eds.): *The Slave's Narrative: Texts and Contexts* (New York, 1985).

Davis, D. B.: *The Problem of Slavery in Western Culture* (Ithaca, NY, 1966).

Dykes, E. B.: *The Negro in English Romantic Thought* (Washington, 1942).

Echeruo, M. J.: *Joyce Carey and the Novel of Africa* (London, 1973).

Echeruo, M. J.: *The Conditioned Imagination from Shakespeare to Conrad* (New York, 1978).

Edwards, P. and Walvin, J.: *Black Personalities in the Era of the Slave Trade* (London, 1983).

Egoff, S. A.: *Children's Periodicals in the Nineteenth Century*, Library Assoc. Pamphlet no. 8 (London, 1951).

Eldridge, C. C.: *Victorian Imperialism* (London, 1978).

Erdman, D.: *Blake – Prophet against Empire* (Princeton, 1969).

Fairchild, H.: *The Noble Savage: A Study in Romantic Naturalism* (New York, 1928).

Fanon, F.: *Black Skins, White Masks* (New York, 1976).

Faure', F.: 'Pourquoi Othello est noir', in *Annales de la Faculté des Lettres d'aix*, XLI, 1966.

Fleishman, A.: *Conrad's Politics* (Baltimore, 1967).

Fryer, P.: *Staying Power: The History of Black People in Britain* (London, 1984).

Fyfe, C.: *Africanus Horton: West African Scientist and Patriot* (Oxford, 1972).

Granqvist, H.: *Stereotypes in Western Fiction on Africa: A Study of Joseph Conrad, Joyce Carey, Ernest Hemingway, Karen Blixen, Graham Greene and Alan Paton* Umea Papers in English, no. 7 (Umea, Sweden, 1984).

Green, M.: *Dreams of Adventure, Deeds of Empire* (London, 1980).

Greenberger, A. J.: *The British Image of India* (Oxford, 1969).

Hall, S. *et al.*: *Culture, Media, Language* (London, 1980).

Hammond, D. and Jablow, A.: *The Africa that Never Was: Four Centuries of British Writing about Africa* (New York, 1970).

Harper, M. S. and Stepto, R. B. (eds.): *Chant of Saints: A Gathering of Afro-American Literature, Art and Scholarship* (Champaign, Illinois Press, 1979).

Harris, W.: 'The frontier on which *Heart of Darkness* stands', in *Research in African Literatures*, XII, no, I, 1981.

Heffernan, W. A.: *English Travellers to Africa 1700–1800* (unpublished PhD diss., Fordham Univ., 1970).

Henkin, L. J.: *Darwinism in the English Novel 1860–1910* (New York, 1940).

Holmes, M.: *Shakespeare's Public* (London, 1960).

Holtsmark, E. B.: *Tarzan and Tradition: Classical Myth in Popular Literature* (London, 1981).

Hopson, J. O.: *Attitudes towards the Negro as an Expression of English Romanticism* (unpublished PhD diss., Univ. of Pittsburg, 1948).

Howarth, P.: *Play Up and Play the Game: the Heroes of Popular Fiction* (London, 1973).

Howe, S.: *Novels of Empire* (New York, 1949).

Hunter, G. K.: 'Othello and colour prejudice', in *Proceedings of the British Academy*, LIII, 1967.

Irvine, W.: *Apes, Angels and Victorians* (London, 1955).

Selected bibliography

James, W. L.: *The Black Man in English Romantic Literature 1772–1833* (unpublished PhD diss., Univ. of California, 1977).

Johnson, L. A.: *The Devil, the Gargoyle and the Buffoon: the Negro as Metaphor in Western Literature* (New York, 1971).

Jones, E.: *Othello's Countrymen: the African in English Renaissance Drama* (Oxford, 1965).

July, R. W.: *The Origins of Modern African Thought* (London, 1968).

Kain, R. M.: *Primitivism, the Theory of Equality and the Idea of Progress in English Anti-Slavery Literature 1772–1808* (unpublished PhD diss., Univ. of Chicago, 1934).

Kaplan, R. P.: *Daniel Defoe's Views on Slavery and Racial Prejudice* (unpublished PhD diss., New York Univ., 1970).

Kiernan, V. J.: *The Lords of Human Kind* (London, 1969).

Killam, G. D.: *Africa in English Fiction 1874–1939* (Ibadan, 1968).

King, B.: *The New English Literatures: Cultural Nationalism in a Changing World* (London, 1981).

Lamming, G.: *The Pleasures of Exile* (London, 1960).

Little, K.: *Negroes in Britain* (London, 1948).

Livingstone, J. H.: *The Impact of Africa upon Major British Literary Figures 1787–1902* (unpublished PhD diss., Univ. of Wisconsin-Madison, 1977).

Lorimer, D.: *Colour, Class and the Victorians* (London, 1978).

Lynch, H. R.: *Edward Wilmot Blyden: Pan-Negro Patriot 1832–1912* (Oxford, 1967).

Lyons, C.: *To Wash an Aethiop White: British Ideas on African Educability 1530–1960* (New York, 1975).

McClough, N. V.: *The Negro in English Literature* (Ilfracombe, 1962).

MacClure, J. A.: *Kipling and Conrad – the Colonial Fiction* (Cambridge, Mass., 1981).

McDonald, H. T.: *Africa as a Fictive World: Seven Modern Responses from Joseph Conrad to Graham Greene* (unpublished PhD diss., Univ. of SouthWestern Louisiana, 1975).

Mahood, M.: *The Colonial Encounter* (London, 1977).

Mason, P.: *Kipling* (London, 1975).

Meyers, J.: *Fiction and the Colonial Experience* (Ipswich, 1973).

Milbury-Steen, S. L.: *European and African Stereotypes in Twentieth Century Fiction* (London, 1980).

Miles R. and Phizacklea, A.: *Labour and Racism* (London, 1980).

Miles, R. and Phizacklea, A.: *Racism and Political Action in Britain* (London, 1979).

Moore-Gilbert, B. (ed.): *Literature and Imperialism* (London, 1983).

Mphahlele, E.: *The African Image* (London, 1974).

Mtubani, V.: *Slavery and the Slave Trader in English Poetry to 1833* (unpublished PhD diss., Exeter Univ., 1980).

Majder, Z.: *Joseph Conrad* (New Brunswick, NJ, 1983).

Opoku, S. K.: *The Image of Africa 1660–1730* (unpublished PhD diss., Princeton Univ., 1967).

Orwell, G.: *Inside the Whale and other Essays* (London, 1940).

Parker, K. (ed.): *The South African Novel in English: Essays in Criticism and Society* (London, 1978).

Paul-Emile, B. T.: *Slavery and the English Romantic Poets. Coleridge, Wordsworth and Southey* (unpublished PhD diss., Case Western Reserve Univ., 1971).

Price, L.: *The Inkle and Yarico Album* (Berkeley, Calif., 1937).

Rao, K. B.: *Rudyard Kipling's India* (Norman, Oklahoma, 1967).

Raskin, J.: *The Mythology of Imperialism* (New York, 1971).

Selected bibliography

Rodney, W.: *A History of the Upper Guinea Coast 1545–1800* (Oxford, 1970).

Rutherford, A. (ed.): *Kipling's Mind and Art* (Stanford, Calif., 1964).

Sandison, A.: *The Wheel of Empire* (London, 1967).

Sherry, W. (ed.): *Conrad: The Critical Heritage* (London, 1973).

Shyllon, f.: *Black Slaves in Britain*, (London, 1974).

Shyllon, F.: *Black People in Britain 1555–1833* (Oxford, 1977).

Smith, J. A.: *John Buchan: A Biography* (London, 1965).

Soyinka, W.: *Myth, Literature and the African* (Cambridge, 1976).

Stewart, J. I. M.: *Eight Modern Writers* (Oxford, 1963).

Stocking, G.: *Race, Culture and Evolution* (New York, 1968).

Street, B. V.: *The Savage in Literature – Representations of 'Primitive' Society in English Fiction 1858–1920* (London, 1975).

Sypher, W.: *Guinea's Captive Kings* (Chapel Hill, 1944).

Troesch, H. de: *The Negro in English Dramatic Literature and on the Stage* (unpublished PhD diss., Case Western Reserve Univ., 1940).

Tucker, M.: *Africa in Modern Literature: a Survey* (New York, 1967).

Wait, I.: *Conrad in the Nineteenth Century* (Berkeley, Calif., 1979).

Wali, O.: *The Negro in English Literature with Special Reference to the Eighteenth and Early Nineteenth Centuries* (unpublished PhD diss., Northwestern Univ., 1967).

Walvin, J.: *The Black Presence: A Documentary History of the Negro in England, 1555–1860* (London, 1971).

Walvin, J.: *Black and White: A Study of the Negro and English Society 1555–1945* (London, 1973).

Watson, C.: *Snobbery with Violence* (London, 1971).

Weston, P.: *The Noble Primitive in English Fiction 1674–1796* (unpublished PhD diss., Exeter Univ., 1977).

Whitney, L.: *Primitivism and the Idea of Progress* (Baltimore, 1934).

Williams, E.: *Capitalism and Slavery* (Chapel Hill, 1944).

Williams, P. A. R.: *Poets of Freedom: The English Romantics and early Nineteenth Century Black Poets* (unpublished PhD diss., Univ. of Illinois at Urbana-Champaign, 1974).

Withington, R.: *'Shakespeare and race prejudice'*, in *Elizabethan Studies in Honour of G. F. Reynolds* (Boulder, 1945).

Yellin, J. F.: *The Intricate Knot: Black Figures in American Literature 1776–1863* (New York, 1972).

Index

Index

Index